SWINDOLL
LEADERSHIP
LIBRARY

SCRIPTURE

Its Power, Authority, and Relevance

ROBERT SAUCY

Charles R. Swindoll, *General Editor*
Roy B. Zuck, *Managing Editor*

WORD PUBLISHING
NASHVILLE
www.wordpublishing.com
A Thomas Nelson Company

SCRIPTURE
Swindoll Leadership Library

Published in association with Dallas Theological Seminary (DTS):

General Editor: Charles R. Swindoll
Managing Editor: Roy B. Zuck

The theological opinions expressed by the author are not necessarily the official position of Dallas Theological Seminary.

Library of Congress Cataloging-in-Publication Data

Saucy, Robert L.
Scripture: its authority, power, and relevance / by Robert Saucy
p. cm.—(Swindoll leadership library)
Includes bibliographical references and indexes.

ISBN 0-8499-1367-5

1. Bible—Evidences, authority, etc. I. Title II. Series.

BS480 .S324 2001
220.1–dc21

2001026268
CIP

Printed in the United States of America

01 02 03 04 05 06 BVG 9 8 7 6 5 4 3 2 1

To my colleagues, the administration, faculty, and staff at
Talbot School of Theology,
whose words and walk
have enriched my life
and made my ministry
there a true delight in the Lord.

Contents

Foreword

MY GREATEST PASSION IN LIFE remains explaining the Scriptures in the clearest terms possible and then watching God's Word take hold in people's lives. In fact I have dedicated my life to that singular focus. I spend the majority of my time poring over the ancient text, mining it for the gold that lies within. The Bible is not man's book about God; it is God's book about man.

In every age people have aimed their flaming arrows of criticism at the sacred Scriptures, and never more so than today. Our own generation's battle for the Bible has raged on and off with varying degrees of casualties. And believe me, it is a battle. The inerrancy of Scripture is not a doctrine to be trifled with. For me, it is a bedrock issue, one of a few fundamentals of the faith.

The Word of God is the source, the revelation of all we know about life, death, and the hereafter. It is the guidebook for living this life successfully, the owner's manual for how to have a relationship with the Savior. Without this unique revelation from above each of us would remain lost in a sea of relativism.

I believe that this book, *Scripture,* by Robert Saucy, will become a recognized work in classrooms, churches, and studies around the world. He is no newcomer to theological studies undertaken at the highest levels of scholarship. He earned the Master of Theology degree in 1958 and the

Doctor of Theology degree in 1961, both from Dallas Seminary. For many years he has served at Talbot School of Theology, defending the Bible against its critics. He has witnessed firsthand the rise in attacks from the front lines of the academic battlefield. Dr. Saucy knows all too well that once Scripture is relegated to anything less than the very Word of God, all manner of doctrinal error is certain to follow.

Special agents of the Federal Bureau of Investigation in Quantico, Virginia, are trained in spotting counterfeit currency. They are not asked to study the fake bills; in fact they spend weeks poring over the authentically minted money. The "legal tender" becomes their daylong study as they learn every detail of our country's treasury notes. The minted plates are the authority, the final word, on what is considered legal and useful. Without that authority, that standard, various subtle errors could creep into our nation's currency.

And so it is with the Bible. Without the Word of God as our standard, the church is open to every wind and wave of doctrine. Scripture is our watermark, our official, authorized Word from God Himself. I cannot emphasize enough how grateful I am to Dr. Saucy for pouring his time and energy into this work. And I am equally grateful for you, and for your interest in understanding, in a deeper way, the vital truth of *sola Scriptura,* "Scripture only."

—Charles R. Swindoll
General Editor

Acknowledgments

I AM GRATEFUL to Dr. Charles Swindoll for the invitation to write this book. His presidency of Dallas Theological Seminary made me aware again of how much I am indebted to the faithful faculty of that school. When I was a student there, the faculty not only expounded the Bible but by their teaching and life truly proclaimed the Word of God, which must always be central in our ministries and lives.

A special thanks is also due to Dr. Roy B. Zuck for his gracious but firm prodding as his helpful comments kept me going in the midst of a busy time. His careful editorial work has made this a much more useful book. My thanks also to the editors and staff at Word Publishing for their part in bringing this work to life.

I am also indebted to the administration, faculty, and secretarial staff at Talbot School of Theology. Their encouragement and help in so many ways, and the example of their own love of the Word of God provided a delightful motivational environment for this work.

My grateful thanks also to my wife, Nancy, who faithfully and patiently (and not a few times sacrificially) supported me in so many ways during the writing of this work and in our life together for forty-five years.

Above all, I praise the Lord for His infinite love and grace to me. Because of His revelation of Himself in His Book, the study for this book was a joy and a personal blessing. Despite regularly reading and teaching from the Bible for many years, to step back and look again at what the Bible is has caused me to recognize as never before the amazing treasure that God has given us in the Scriptures. Sometimes it is easy to forget what we have in the Bible. Like Jesus, whose appearance in His first coming was like an ordinary man, the Bible appears in the humble garb of human words and sentences. But also like Jesus, the Bible is divine, the very Word of God.

I hope that this book will help readers see the absolute uniqueness of the Bible among all the other books in the world. There is something about the Bible that makes it completely different from all other books ever written. It is the very speech of God through which He addresses us as His creatures so that we might enjoy that fellowship of life for which we were created.

My setting forth the nature of the Bible in this work and defending it against its critics, therefore, has one simple goal: that through it you will come to see again (or for the first time) the inestimable value of the Bible and to treasure it above all books. I hope you will revere it as the authoritative Word of God and let it rule your beliefs and conduct. And above all I hope that you will regularly spend time in it, mining, contemplating, and ingesting into your heart its truths as divine nourishment for your soul.

Introduction

A glory gilds the sacred page,
Majesty like the sun;
It gives light to every age,
It gives, but borrows none.

—William Cowper

The existence of the Bible as a book for the people is the greatest benefit which the human race has ever experienced.[1]

—Immanuel Kant, philosopher (1724–1804)

Introduction

THE BIBLE is the most important book in the world. This is the conviction of Christian believers, but also of thoughtful political statesmen, royalty, and renowned intellectuals. King George V of England declared, "The English Bible . . . in a secular aspect, is the first of national treasures, and is, in its spiritual significance, the most valuable thing that this world affords."[2] At the coronation of Queen Elizabeth II, as she held the Bible in her hands as an expression of faith and allegiance, the archbishop of Canterbury declared, "Here is Wisdom; this is the Royal Law; these are the Lively Oracles of God."[3]

Patrick Henry, the colonial American patriot famous for his immortal words, "Give me liberty or give me death," said of the Bible, "This is a book worth more than all the others that were ever printed."[4] Sounding a similar note, the Russian novelist Fyodor Dostoevsky, after recommending the reading of the entire Bible in the Russian translation, declared, "One gains, for one thing, the conviction that humanity possesses, and can possess, no other book of equal significance."[5]

In more recent times Billy Graham said of the Scriptures, "No other book can touch its profound wisdom, its poetic beauty, or the accuracy of its history and prophecy. . . . The Bible embodies all the knowledge man needs to fill the longing of his soul and solve all his problems. . . . I want to be saturated with the Bible. I want to know it by heart before I die."[6] No wonder he constantly says in his messages, "The Bible says. . . "

The inestimable value of the Word of God for believers is evident in their willingness to sacrifice their lives for possessing it. In the great persecution of the church in A.D. 303, the Roman emperor Diocletian was determined to destroy the Scriptures. Any copy of the Bible that was found was burned. Thousands of believers and their families were martyred for possessing portions of the Word of God. This killing and destruction of the Scriptures went on for two years, after which a victory column was erected over the ashes of a Bible with words that indicated that the Bible is "extinct." But only twenty years later the emperor Constantine proclaimed the Bible the infallible judge of truth. Enemies of God have made similar attempts to destroy the Bible in a variety of ways. But God has preserved it—sometimes at great cost on the part of His people, a cost which for them was nothing in comparison with the treasure of Scripture.

This eminent status that Christians have accorded the Bible has earned them the epithet "People of the Book." This name was apparently first coined by Muhammad, who applied it primarily to Jews but also to Christians because of the importance they both placed on a written revelation. Muslims have also come to be included in this terminology because of the significant place that all three of these religions place on their sacred scriptures in comparison to the place of writings in other religions.

To the Jews their sacred writings were the full revelation of God to His people. But for Christians, that place belongs to Christ, who is God, who came to this earth to reveal Himself personally (Heb. 1:2). As such, Christ is the living Lord and final authority over the church. But this does not reduce the Scriptures to some kind of secondary authority, as is sometimes suggested. For how do we know Christ, except through the Bible? And how does He exercise His authority except through His Word, even as He did while here on earth? As we will see later, there is an intrinsic connection between the Word of God revealed in the person of Jesus Christ and the Word of God revealed in the Bible.

The Bible is essential in Christianity because it is the record of God's saving intervention in human history. Yet even more than simply the history of God's saving activity, the Bible itself is part of that activity. His Word tells us what His actions mean, and it reveals how we can receive His salvation.

The absolute necessity of the Bible for Christianity has been illustrated by comparing it with the sacred writings of Hinduism. If all the writings of Hinduism were destroyed and no Hindu remained alive, so that Hinduism was totally absent from all human minds on earth, it is still conceivable that Hinduism could arise again, because it is basically a way of life. If people thought this way once, there is no reason why they could not do so again. On the other hand, if all copies of the Scriptures were obliterated and all remnants of Christianity were completely gone from the face of the earth, including all historical references to its existence, it would be impossible for Christianity to rise again. Why? Because it is more than a way of life. It is a historical religion founded on the actions of God in history, and the Bible records that salvation history.

The Bible is different from all other books because it is *God's* Word. Other books, no matter how profound, are only human words. The number of people who view the Bible as an infallible authority is probably increasing in the world as liberal churches are declining and Christianity is growing significantly in many parts of the world.

But there is also a disturbing dichotomy between this high esteem for Scripture and the actual function that it plays in people's lives. Especially in the Western world, a growing religious pluralism and a corresponding tolerance of all views, coupled with a continuing destructive rationalistic criticism of the Scriptures, are undermining conviction in its final authority, even in many good churches. Diverse views on how to interpret the Bible also leave many people in doubt as to what it actually teaches. Together these forces are gnawing away at the Scriptures as the pillar of truth that supports the believer's life.

Most significantly, lack of trust in the effectiveness of Scripture plagues many believers today. We honor the Bible as God's holy Word, but we don't read it. When perplexed with life's problems, we are more likely to turn to other sources than to the Scriptures for help and comfort. The reasons for this lack of confidence are many and complex. First, we are embedded in a cultural climate of antiauthoritarianism. We don't want anyone, whether human or divine, to tell us what to do. Closely allied with this is the failure of many believers to obey the Scriptures, to receive them into their hearts in obedient trust in such a way that their lives are transformed. Therefore many people conclude that the Scriptures are not very effective.

The Bible, of course, claims to occupy the central place in God's relationship to His human creatures. Only by the Scriptures can we come to the knowledge of God, which, Jesus said, is eternal life (John 17:3). The Scriptures sustain and nourish that life so that we may grow in our experience of God. Thus the prominence of Scripture as "the Book" of human history accords with reality, and failure to give it that place in our lives results in loss.

But what is this book that we call the Bible? How did we get it? What makes it authoritative? Is it really inerrant? Why are sixty-six books included and others excluded? How are its teachings related to the teachings of the church or human reason? How can we understand its teachings? What do we need to do to experience the transforming power of the Bible? These and other questions are the subject of this study, with the goal that the Scriptures will fulfill their promised dynamic in our lives.

One

The Scripture is a tree, or rather a whole paradise of trees of life, which bring forth fruits every month, and the fruit therof is for meat, and the leaves for medicine. It is . . . as it were a shower of heavenly bread sufficient for a whole host, be it never so great, and as it were a whole cellarful of oil vessels; whereby all our necessities may be provided for, and our debts discharged. In a word it is a pantry of wholesome food against mouldy traditions; a pharmacist's shop (Saint Basil calleth it) of preservatives against poisoned heresies; a code of profitable laws against rebellious spirit; a treasure of most costly jewels against beggarly rudiments. Finally, a fountain of most pure water springing up into everlasting life.

—From the "Address to the Reader," prefixed to the Authorized [King James] Version of the Bible of 1611 by its translators

One

Why Is the Bible Called the Book of Life?

THE BIBLE is unique among all the world's books because its words are charged with the life and power of God. Not that God is linked to ink and paper or ancient scrolls. But His presence is communicated through the truth of His Word. The unique power of His Word has been experienced by believers and unbelievers alike. J. B. Phillips, who gave us one of the first paraphrases of the New Testament, testifies to his own experience in carefully studying the Scriptures. In the preface of his work he wrote, "The present translator . . . is continually struck by the living quality of the material on which he is working. Some will, no doubt, consider it merely superstitious reverence of 'Holy Writ,' yet again and again the writer felt rather like an electrician rewiring an ancient house without being able to 'turn the mains off.' "[1]

Similarly, the French savant, Jean-Jacques Rousseau (1712–1778), whose philosophical views paved the way for humanistic liberalism, was also struck by the unique dynamic of the Bible. "I must confess to you," he wrote, "that the majesty of the Scriptures astonishes me; the holiness of the Evangelists speaks to my heart and has such striking characters of truth, and is, moreover, so perfectly inimitable, that if it had been the invention of men, the inventors would be greater than the greatest heroes."[2] One does not hear many words like these today from leading philosophers, but that is due, no doubt, not so much to the fact that the

Bible no longer impacts the human heart but to the fact that it is less likely to be read.

THE POWER OF GOD'S WORDS

We have all heard the saying "Sticks and stones can break my bones, but words can never hurt me." But experience tells us all that this is not really true. Words do hurt us, but they also heal. Even of human words, the Bible says, "Death and life are in the power of the tongue" (Prov. 18:21). "A soothing tongue is a tree of life; but perversion in it crushes the spirit" (15:4). The power of the human tongue is like a rudder that controls a ship or a small fire that ignites a whole forest (James 3:4–6; see also Prov. 25:15).

If human words are that powerful, how much more are God's words! Human words, of course, are limited by the creaturely limitations of individuals. But there is no such limitation to the power of the words of the infinite God. Jesus said to His disciples, "The words that I have spoken to you are spirit and are life" (John 6:63), that is, they have the power of the Holy Spirit and are life-creating. On this occasion many who were following Jesus turned away to walk with Him no more. But the disciples, having received His words, experienced their power. When asked if they too would leave, Peter, who undoubtedly spoke for all of them, responded, "Lord, to whom shall we go? You have words of eternal life" (6:68).

The writer to the Hebrews declared, "The word of God is living and active and sharper than any two-edged sword, and piercing as far as the division of soul and spirit, . . . and able to judge the thoughts and intentions of the heart" (Heb. 4:12). Interestingly the word "living" is applied by the same author to God Himself (3:12; 9:14; 10:31; 12:22). The living God sends His Word forth with His life. And because the Word is "living," it is also "active."

In a stinging indictment of the false prophets who spoke their own words with not "the slightest benefit" to the people, God proclaimed the power of His true word: "Is not My word like fire . . . and like a hammer which shatters a rock?" (Jer. 23:29, 32). To the prophet Jeremiah, God declared, "Behold, I am making My words in your mouth fire and this people wood, and it will consume them" (5:14). When the prophet refused for a time to speak the word that God gave him, he felt something of this same effect in his own "heart" and in his "bones," as the word became "like a burning fire" (20:9).

Throughout Scripture God effects His will by His powerful word. All the vastness of the universe came into existence by His word. Eight times in Genesis 1 we read the words, "And God said. . . ." As the Scripture writer says, "The worlds were prepared by the word of God" (Heb. 11:3). And the psalmist affirmed, "By the word of the LORD the heavens were made" (Ps. 33:6). And all things continue to exist, for they are sustained "by the word of His power" (Heb. 1:3).

God's words are like powerful messengers that run throughout the earth to accomplish His will. "He sends forth His command to the earth; His word runs very swiftly" (Ps. 147:15). The apostle Paul prayed "that the word of the Lord may spread rapidly [literally, 'run'] and be glorified" (2 Thess. 3:1). When God's ancient people cried out in their sickness (which was due to sin), the psalmist said, "He sent His word and healed them" (Ps. 107:19–20). And when God's word "runs," it runs powerfully and effectively. "My word . . . which goes forth from My mouth . . . shall not return to Me empty, without accomplishing what I desire, and without succeeding in the matter for which I sent it" (Isa. 55:11).

The early church faced much persecution. Starting out as a small group of common people with few "great men" by human standards, they nevertheless prevailed over all adversaries. The impact of their preaching of the gospel, the "word" of God, was felt across the then-known world. "The word of God kept on spreading" (Acts 6:7); "the word of the Lord continued to grow and to be multiplied" (12:24); "the word of the Lord was growing mightily and prevailing" (19:20). The apostle Paul was imprisoned for his witness for Christ, which has been the experience of many believers throughout church history, but "the word of God," he wrote, "is not imprisoned" (2 Tim. 2:9). Imprisonment may halt the movements of human messengers, but it cannot stop the power of God's message. In fact, imprisonment may actually turn out, as in Paul's case, "for the greater progress of the gospel" (Phil. 1:12).

Jesus Christ is God's personal Word to man. "In the beginning was the Word, and the Word was with God, and the Word was God. . . . And the

Word became flesh, and dwelt among us" (John 1:1, 14). As God's powerful presence is in His Son, the incarnate Word, so the same powerful presence is in the word that proceeds out of His mouth. At the end of this age, heaven will open and the triumphant warrior, the King of kings and Lord of lords, whose name is "The Word of God," will come riding on a white horse to destroy the nations by the sharp sword that comes from His mouth (Rev. 19:11–16). The picture is nothing less than the personal Word of God exercising His power by the authoritative word from His mouth. The words that proceed from the mouth of God share the power of the incarnate Word.

LIFE THROUGH THE WORD

The God of the Bible is the "living God." He alone has life in Himself, and all other life is dependent on Him. As the psalmist said, "For with Thee is the fountain of life" (36:9). Every living creature came into existence and is sustained by Him. Turning away from God therefore leads only to death. This is exactly what many have done—turned away from God. Instead of gratefully acknowledging Him and the goodness of His bestowed life, the first humans disobeyed God. Then, cut off from the source of life, the state of their existence came to be what the Scriptures call "death."

One cannot look at the condition of human existence in the world today without recognizing this fact. Strife and suffering seem to be on the increase. And where these are not personally experienced, there is still an inner unrest of heart, a discontent that constantly pursues more and more pleasure, power, and some kind of spiritual experience. The greatest need of people is life, the life that God intended. He offers this to anyone who will receive it, and He does this through His Word.

In the ancient Near East, people sought the forces of life, which were thought to be connected to gods, by magical incantations and rites. In contrast, God's people find life in a right relationship to God through His Word. Moses set before the people of Israel two paths, the path of life and prosperity and the path of death and adversity. The outcome would be determined by following or rejecting the Word of God (Deut. 30:15–20). The word that Moses brought from God was "not an idle word for you; indeed it is your life" (32:47). The prophets too stated that life depends on walking faithfully according to God's statues and ordinances (for example, Ezek. 18:9; 20:11). Amos foresaw a day when the judgment of God will bring famine, not "a famine for bread or a thirst for water, but rather for hearing the words of the LORD." As a result the people will "stagger from sea to sea," as the foundation of their life was removed (Amos 8:11–12).

People today experience similar results when they turn from God's words in favor of their own words. The fundamental truth throughout Scripture remains true: As creatures of God we do not have life in ourselves. It is available only because of the grace of God. Even Jesus, who was human as well as divine, applied the words of Moses to his own life: "Man does not live by bread alone, but man lives by everything that proceeds out of the mouth of the LORD" (Deut. 8:3; see Matt. 4:4).

Life is found in God and is given through His Son. Jesus said, "I am the resurrection and the life," and "I am . . . the life" (John 11:25; 14:6). So the earlier disciples believed and found it to be true, confessing that "in Him was life, and the life was the light of men" (1:4). To them Jesus was the "Prince [or 'author' or 'pioneer'] of life" (Acts 3:15).

But the life-giving Lord gives Himself through His living Word. The apostle John wrote, "That which was from the beginning, which we have heard, which we have see with our eyes, which we have looked at and our hands have touched—this we proclaim concerning the Word of life" (1 John 1:1, NIV). The "Word of life" was the living incarnate Word whom they had seen and touched. But it was also something that they had "heard" (1:3). It was a message of life that they heard in words that were proclaimed. Early believers were encouraged to hold fast "the word of life" (Phil. 2:16; see also Acts 5:20). The word conveyed in human words is "the word of life" in that it proclaims the message of true life found in Christ. Even more, through its proclamation it creates life in everyone who receives it.

The "new birth," the miraculous transformation of a person who is spiritually dead, comes about by the power of the Word. In the parable of the sower Jesus likened the Word of God to seed (Luke 8:11). A grain of wheat or kernel of corn may look lifeless, but when planted in the ground it produces a living plant. Similarly, the Bible, God's written Word, may seem like any other book, but when it is planted in the soil of the human heart, it has amazing power to produce spiritual life. Following this same seed image, Peter wrote, "For you have been born again not of seed which is perishable but imperishable, that is, through the living and abiding word of God" (1 Pet. 1:23). The same truth is expressed in a variety of ways: "He chose to give us birth through the word of truth" (James 1:18, NIV). "God has chosen you from the beginning for salvation through sanctification by the Spirit and faith in the truth" (2 Thess. 2:13). God continually appeals to people to receive His Word as the means to life and salvation: "Listen carefully to Me, and eat what is good. . . . Incline your ear and come to Me. Listen, that you may live" (Isa. 55:2–3).

The apostle Paul taught and experienced in his own ministry the power of the Word in bringing people to new life and salvation. "The word of the cross," he said, "is the power of God" (1 Cor. 1:18, 21). "For I am not ashamed of the gospel, for it is the power of God for salvation to everyone who believes" (Rom. 1:16).

Life is found only through union with Christ, and that union with Christ is attained solely through faith produced by the powerful Word. As Paul wrote, "Faith comes from hearing the message, and the message is heard through the word of Christ" (Rom. 10:17, NIV). In other words, the message is the power that incites faith.

The great church father Augustine (354–430) spoke of the power of the life-giving Word in his own experience. After describing his turmoil and agony of soul as he struggled between the pull of his sinful desires and the tug of God, he then wrote what happened.

> Weeping in the bitter agony of my heart, suddenly I heard a voice from the nearby house chanting as it might be a boy or a girl (I do not know which), saying and repeating over and over again, "Pick up and read, pick up and read." . . . I checked the flood of tears and stood up. I interpreted it solely as a divine command to me to open the book and read the first chapter I might find. . . . I seized it [the book of the apostle], opened it and in silence read the first passage on which my eyes lit: "Not in riots and drunken parties, not in eroticism and indecencies, not in strife and rivalry, but put on the Lord Jesus Christ and make no provision for the flesh in its lust" (Rom.

> 13:13–14). . . . At once, with the last word of this sentence, it was as if a light of relief from anxiety flooded into my heart. All the shadows of doubt were dispelled.[3]

The power of the truth written in Scripture also brought new life to Martin Luther. He had done everything that a "good monk" in the Roman Catholic Church of his time could possibly do to assuage the unrest of his heart. Then he was appointed professor of Bible at Wittenberg University. As part of his new duties, he studied and taught the Book of Romans. In the process of this engagement with the Scriptures, his heart was gripped by the concept of the "righteousness of God," which, Paul declared, was revealed in the gospel (Rom. 1:16–17). "I had greatly longed to understand Paul's letter to the Romans, and nothing stood in the way but that one expression 'the righteousness of God,' because I took it to mean that righteousness whereby God is righteous and acts righteously in punishing the unrighteousness. . . . Night and day I pondered until . . . I grasped the truth that the righteousness of God is that righteousness whereby, through grace and sheer mercy, he justifies us by faith. Thereupon I felt myself to be reborn and to have gone through open doors into paradise. . . . This passage of Paul became to me a gateway into heaven."[4]

This belief in its life-giving nature made the proclamation of the Word of God the all-important task of the early church. Repeatedly Paul prayed for enablement to speak the Word of God with boldness (Eph. 6:19–20; Col. 4:3). His great desire was that "the word of the Lord may spread rapidly and be glorified" in his ministry (2 Thess. 3:1). The proclamation of the Word of God and the demonstration of its life-giving nature before the world enabled the church to prevail and grow in a world dominated by spiritual darkness. The same is true today.

An evangelist who used the Bible almost exclusively in his personal witnessing was once asked by his friends, "What do you do when an unsaved person does not accept the Bible as having any authority?" The evangelist responded, "Well, if I had a fine Damascus sword with a keen double-edged blade, I would not sheathe it in a fight just because the other man said he did not believe it would cut."

This is not to suggest that studying evidence for the reliability of the

Bible has no value. Reasons for believing the Bible can often help someone hear the truth of Scripture. But we must always remember that "the sword of the Spirit" is not our words or even our arguments. It is, rather, the Word of God. Jesus said that the Holy Spirit would convict the world "concerning sin, and righteousness, and judgment" (John 16:8). The fact of sin, the fact that God's righteousness is found in Jesus, and the fact of coming judgment are truths people need to acknowledge if they are to receive eternal life. They are also truths that strike a chord in the honest human heart. As one African believer put it, "The Bible tells me my heart." They are also the truths that have the power of the Spirit in them.

A brilliant physician discovered this in an encounter with D. L. Moody. He admitted that he went to hear Mr. Moody only for laughs. "I knew he was not a scholar, and I felt sure I could find many flaws in his argument. But I found that I could not get at the man. He just fired one Bible text after another at me till they went home to my heart straight as bullets from a rifle. I tell you, Moody's power is in the way he has his Bible at the tip of his tongue."[5]

The effectiveness of the Word of God in producing salvation explains why many enemies of the gospel have failed in their attempts to eliminate the Bible. In the last great persecution of Christians before Christianity became a legal religion in the Roman Empire, Roman authorities were considering ways to crush Christianity once and for all. When an apostate Christian in the emperor's council heard them speak of burning all the Christians, he responded, "It is no use to burn the Christians, for if you burn every Christian alive today, and leave a single copy of the Scriptures remaining, the Christian church will spring up again tomorrow." So the emperor issued a decree ordering the destruction of all copies of the Bible.

GROWTH THROUGH GOD'S WORD

The Word is active in bringing about salvation, but it is also the nourishment and medicine needed for spiritual growth. The testimony of an old Scottish Christian finds an echo in every believer's heart: "I have a most depraved and sinful nature, and do what I will, I find I cannot make myself holy. My friends cannot do it for me, nor do I think an angel in heaven could. One thing alone does it—reading and believing what I read in that blessed Book; that does it."

Jesus' words, previously noted, point to this truth: "Man shall not live on bread alone, but on every word that proceeds out of the mouth of God" (Matt. 4:4). Many in our affluent world are beginning to realize that material things alone ("bread") cannot really satisfy. We need bread, but we need more than bread. The church father Jerome (around A.D. 340–420) was right when he said, "Therefore if anyone is not feeding on the Word of God, that person is not living." Real life comes with union with the living God, who is constantly speaking (the form of the Greek word for "proceeds" in Matt. 4:4 signifies a continuing action) His Word for those willing to listen and receive it.

Jesus said of believers, "They are not of the world, even as I am not of it. Sanctify them by the truth; your word is truth" (John 17:16–17, NIV). The impact of these words is vividly captured in the paraphrase by Eugene Peterson in *The Message*: "They are no more defined by the world, than I am defined by the world. Make them holy—consecrated—with the truth; Your word is consecrating truth."

Christ's prayer for His followers is that they would not follow the death-dealing false loves and values of this world, but would be holy. What produces this supernatural transformation in the believer's life is God's truth conveyed through His Word. As the New Living Translation expresses it, "Make them pure and holy by teaching them your words of truth."

Peter said that the nourishing value of Scripture is like milk for babies. After declaring that we are born again through the Word (1 Pet. 1:23), he added, "Like newborn babes, long for the pure milk of the word, that by it you may grow in respect to salvation" (2:2). Paul told young Timothy that believers are "constantly nourished on the words of the faith" (1 Tim. 4:6). He also challenged believers to "put on the new self [lit., 'man'], which in the likeness of God has been created in righteousness and holiness of the truth" (Eph. 4:24). The "newness" that we are to put on is the holiness and righteousness which "come from the truth."[6] The process of renewal thus takes place because "the new person is ultimately related to the truth of the gospel and of the apostolic tradition, a moral truth able to give rise to the virtues of righteousness and holiness in those who receive it."[7]

Everything required for our personal Christian growth is found in the inspired Word of God. It is "profitable for teaching, for reproof, for correction, for training in righteousness; that the man of God may be adequate, equipped for every good work" (2 Tim. 3:16).

The Word of God is like food to help us grow. The implications of this truth are tremendous, both for individuals and the church. Because of its nourishing life-giving power, Paul exhorted believers to "let the word of Christ richly dwell within you" (Col. 3:16). Then this richly indwelling Word brings about certain results (3:17–4:1), which are essentially the same as those produced by the filling or control of the Spirit (Eph. 5:18–6:9). This suggests a vital connection between the indwelling Spirit and the indwelling Word. The Holy Spirit fills or controls us as the truth of the Word of Christ is richly dwelling in us. In other words being "filled with the Spirit" comes about by our letting Him implant the Word of God deeply in our hearts.

The only weapon the believer has in offense against the forces of evil is the "sword of the Spirit, which is the word of God" (6:17). By calling God's Word "the sword of the Spirit" the apostle declared that the Scriptures are the instrument through which the Spirit exerts His power. As we take up the sword of the Word, we are enabled by the power of the Holy Spirit to triumph over external enemies as well as our own inward lusts that war against us. When Paul left his fellow believers at Ephesus and wanted to commit them to the highest possible good for their lives, he committed them "to God and to the word of His grace, which is able to build you up and to give you the inheritance among all those who are sanctified" (Acts 20:32).

After declaring the revelation of God in the wonders of nature in Psalm 19:1–6, David extolled the wonders of the revealed Word of God (19:7–11). The connection between these two forms of God's revelation is the concluding reference to the domination of the sun in nature, especially its searching heat: "It rejoices as a strong man to run his course. Its rising is from one end of the heavens, and its circuit to the other end of them; and there is nothing hidden from its heat" (19:5–6). Peter Craigie notes, "Just as the sun dominates the daytime sky so too does the Torah dominate human life. As the sun can be both welcome, in giving warmth, and terrifying in its unrelenting heat [the psalmist living in the Near East would know this more than most people], so too the Torah can be both life-imparting, but also scorching, testing, and purifying. . . . There could be no life on this planet without the sun; there can be no true human life without the revealed word of God in the Torah."[8]

In verses 7–9 the psalmist spoke of the values of the revealed Word, values that he no doubt had experienced in his own life. "The law of the Lord is perfect, *restoring [reviving, refreshing] the soul*; the testimony of the Lord is sure, *making wise the simple*. The precepts of the Lord are right, *rejoicing the heart*; the commandment of the Lord is pure, *enlightening [brightening] the eyes*. The fear of the Lord is clean, *enduring forever*; the judgments of the Lord are true; *they are righteous altogether*" (italics added).

The four statements in verses 7–8 focus on the factors that contribute to a meaningful existence: vigor and vitality, wisdom to live successfully and avoid the heartaches of foolishness, and the joy of the Lord which gives us strength. Then the two statements in verse 9 affirm that these are possible because the Word is everlasting and righteous.

The "delight [of the righteous one] . . . in the law of the Lord" (Ps. 1:2) reaches its "full flowering" in Psalm 119, which has been called "The Rich and Precious Jewel of the Word."[9] Derek Kidner summarizes the rich blessings of the Word for believers as liberation, light, life, and stability.[10] No more appropriate and needed benefits could be imagined when we remember that the believer's life on this earth is constantly described in Scripture as "walking." Enoch "walked with God . . . God took him" to Himself (Gen. 5:24). God instructed Abraham, as he does all His people, to "walk before Me" (17:1). To "walk" with God, we need these four provisions—liberation, light, life, and stability—which are given by the Word.

If people are honest, they must acknowledge that they are unable to live as they know they should. They are bound by what Scripture calls the bondage of sin. *Freedom* comes through submitting to the Word of God—not release from it, as many today believe. The psalmist declared, "And I will walk at liberty, for I seek Thy precepts" (Ps. 119:45). "At liberty" signifies being freed from a confining space and set in a broad or open place. The restrictions of sin are broken, and the believer is set free to live the fullness of life intended by his Creator. Moffatt's paraphrase of the verse captures the thought: "I will obey thee eagerly, as thou dost open up my life." The psalmist's exuberance for living in the freedom of God's Word is evident when he wrote, "I shall run the way of Thy commandments, for Thou wilt enlarge my heart" (119:32). The Hebrew word for "enlarge" is the same word used of "placing in a broad place." The oppression of sin brought bondage and restriction of cares and anxiety, but God's Word gave him hope.

To walk without faltering, a person must also have *light.* If you have had the experience of being in absolute darkness, such as deep in the Carlsbad Caverns of New Mexico, you realize this truth. Thus Scripture calls us to "walk in the light" because God Himself is "light" (1 John 1:5, 7; see also John 12:46). The light of God shines on us through His Son, "the light of the world" (8:12; see also 1:4–5), and through the Scriptures, which reveal Him. Thus the psalmist wrote, "Thy word is a lamp to my feet, and a light to my path" (Ps. 119:105). "The unfolding of Thy words gives light; it gives understanding to the simple" (119:130; see also 19:8). The writer of Proverbs likewise asserted, "For the commandment is a lamp, and the teaching is light" (Prov. 6:23).

The light of the Word is so powerful that it transforms those who receive it, giving them *life.* Jesus said, "Believe in the light, in order that you may become sons of light," that is, those characterized by light (John 12:36). Paul wrote, "You were formerly darkness, but now you are light in the Lord; walk as children of light" (Eph. 5:8). As light, believers shine "as lights in the world." Like a bright star in the heavens, believers hold out the light of the Word for others (Phil. 2:15). Paul called the Scriptures "the word of life" (2:16) because they give spiritual life and cause that life to grow. David declared, "For you have delivered me from death and my feet from stumbling, that I may walk before God in the light of life" (Ps. 56:13, NIV). Over and over the life-quickening power of the Word for the believer is seen in Psalm 119. "I will never forget your precepts, for by them you have preserved my life" (119:93, NIV). "My soul cleaves to the dust; revive me according to Thy word" (119:25). "This is my comfort in my affliction, that Thy word has revived me" (119:50). "Sustain me according to Thy word, that I may live" (119:116).

Walking also requires *stability* or sureness of foot. No life is free from the battering of outward adversaries and inward turmoil of doubt and insecurities. But through the Word believers find solid ground and steadiness. "If Thy law had not been my delight, then I would have perished in my affliction. . . . The wicked wait for me to destroy me; I shall diligently consider Thy testimonies" (119:92, 95). "Those who love Thy law have great peace, and nothing causes them to stumble" (119:165).

Two great themes in the Bible summarize its life-giving truth: the revelation of our sin and the revelation of the Savior.

The Word Reveals Sins

In revealing sin the Word discloses the righteous standards of God and our failure to live by them. "How can a young man keep his way pure? By keeping it according to Thy word" (Ps. 119:9). James likened the Word to a mirror in which we can see ourselves just as we are. Etched on this mirror is God's standard, "the perfect law" to show us our defects (James 1:23–25).

While the metaphor of the mirror suggests an inactive reflector, the writer of Hebrews declares that the Word *actively* exposes us. It leaves nothing hidden. Describing the Word as "living and active and sharper than any two-edged sword," he declared that the living Word "penetrates even to dividing soul and spirit, joints and marrow; it judges the thoughts and attitudes of the heart" (Heb. 4:12, NIV). Taken together, the soul and spirit speak of our immaterial being, and the joints and marrow relate to our physical nature. The joints unite bones, and marrow is within the bones. So God's Word penetrates our whole person.

There is nothing that the Word cannot penetrate. Everything about us is "open and laid bare [by the Word] to the eyes of Him with whom we have to do" (4:13). The Greek word rendered "laid bare" comes from a word for throat and pictures an animal about to be sacrificed with its neck bent back and its throat exposed. So the penetrating Word of God exposes all that we are and leaves us totally and absolutely vulnerable before God. A Chinese man, after hearing the Bible for the first time, said to the missionary, "I know this is God's Word because it tells me all that I am."

We see the exposing effect of the Word on the believer in the experience of Peter. On the night of Jesus' arrest, immediately after Peter denied his Lord three times, "the Lord turned and looked at Peter. And Peter remembered the word of the Lord . . . and . . . went out and wept bitterly" (Luke 22:61–62). In this case the "word" refers to Jesus' specific word in which He predicted Peter's denial, but the principle applies to the written Word, the Bible. The Scriptures show believers their sins and encourage them to turn from them.

The Word Reveals the Savior

It is one thing to see God's holy standard in the Scriptures and be convicted of our failure to match it, but it is quite another matter to be able to do something about it. One evening at the dinner table, one of my daughters pointed out to me that my nose was not straight. This was not exactly a new revelation. The mirror has shown me that consistently. The problem is that there is not too much I can do about it. Our problem with sin is much the same. The Bible reveals that all people are sinners and fall short of God's pattern for life. But as beneficial as that revelation of ourselves may be, it does no good unless we find some means of change.

The Bible, however, is more than a revelation of God's standard and a mirror of our failure. It reveals the message of God's great work of redemption through Christ. By the gospel we begin the Christian life and by the same gospel we grow. When Paul wanted to stimulate believers to sanctification and spiritual growth, he asked them to remember what happened to them the moment they believed in Christ. They had died with Christ and were resurrected to newness of life in him (Rom. 6:1–11). Their sins were forgiven and they became new creations. The key to spiritual growth, according to the apostle, is to consider the great facts of the gospel and to live according to them.

The Old Testament ordinance of the red heifer (Num. 19) provides a striking illustration of the cleansing and renewing power of the Word. According to the Mosaic Law anyone who had been defiled or become unclean had to be purified before he could again resume his place in society. For the purpose of cleansing, a red heifer was taken outside the camp of Israel and slain. Some of its blood was then sprinkled in front of the tent of meeting seven times as a sacrifice to the Lord. After this, the animal was burned totally to ashes, which were then gathered up and mixed with water, which was called the "water to remove impurity" (19:9). Anytime one of God's people were defiled (in this instance by contact with death), this water was applied to them and they were ceremonially cleansed.

The effectiveness of the water lay in the fact that it contained the ashes of a sacrificial death. Every time it was applied, the benefits of that death were evident. This same principle—the death of Christ—makes the Word of God effective for cleansing (Eph. 5:26). Jesus' blood sprinkled once for all at Calvary gives the believer new life. But as we walk in this life we become defiled. We need the repeated application of the truth of Christ's triumph over sin and our newness of life in Him. This message is brought to us in the Word. As we read and meditate on it, the Spirit of God uses it to purify our lives.

Besides revealing the Savior as the One who cleanses our lives, the Bible also manifests the matchless perfection of His person. He is our Head and Pattern, and we are to be conformed to His image (Rom. 8:29). The process of our conformation to Christ is outlined in 2 Corinthians 3:18: "But we all, with unveiled face beholding as in a mirror the glory of the Lord, are being transformed into the same image from glory to glory, just as from the Lord, the Spirit." In this process the Scriptures reveal the glory of Christ. By His own testimony, He is the theme of all Scripture (John 5:39). As the Spirit illumines the Scriptures, He shines the spotlight of Christ and glorifies Him before us (16:14). When we behold Him, we are gradually "transformed into the same image."

When we spend extended periods of time with a person whom we respect and admire, we begin to take on certain traits of that person. This process is all the more effective when we spend time with Christ through meditation on the Scriptures. The power of the living Word by the Spirit of God works in us to conform us to our perfect Lord.

CONCLUSION

God is present among us through His Word. He sent His personal Word, Jesus Christ, to live in human history in order to make Himself known to the world. He continues to reveal Himself through His written Word. So the power to change us and make us agents of change in this world is the

Word of God. The power of the church in the world lies not in human wisdom or ingenuity or strategies of ministry, but in the Word of God proclaimed in word and life.

In his ministry the apostle Paul depended on the power of the Word. He said, "I did not come with superiority of speech or of wisdom . . . my message and my preaching were not in persuasive words of wisdom, but in demonstration of the Spirit and of power, that your faith should not rest on the wisdom of men, but on the power of God" (1 Cor. 2:1, 4–5). Paul was not disdaining communication skills that can improve the clarity and power of the truth being proclaimed. Rather he was determined that his audience not be drawn to his oratorical skills, cleverness of mind, profound vocabulary, quick wit, or storytelling abilities, but rather to the message itself, the message of the Word of God. He preached the "word of the cross," which he knew was foolishness to the world (1:21, 23, 25), but which has the power of God to save (1:24). No matter our human abilities, we are only "earthen vessels" or "clay pots" (2 Cor. 4:7), who have the privilege of proclaiming the message of the gospel, which is the power of God to bring the lost to life in Christ and which can nourish that life in the believer.

Two

It is not easy to know [duties], except men were taught them by God himself, or by some person who has received them from God, or obtained the knowledge of them through some divine means.

—Pythagoras, sixth-century B.C. Greek philosopher

Two

What Is Divine Revelation?

THE NEED FOR A REVELATION FROM GOD

HUMAN BEINGS are religious creatures. Consciously or unconsciously we live by beliefs that we cannot ultimately prove through empirical research or human reason. A bumper sticker brought this home to me. Apparently designed as a swipe at Christians it read, "You keep on believing; I will keep on evolving." Whoever put this on his or her car apparently wanted to distinguish religious faith from science. But the truth of the matter is that evolution cannot be proven by scientific evidence any more than can the existence of God.

German philosopher Immanuel Kant (1724–1804) pointed out that the human mind inevitably asks questions about life that are religious questions, and that the answers cannot be proved by human means. He testified that "all the interests of my reason, speculative as well as practical, combine in the three following questions: (1) What can I know? (2) What ought I to do? (3) What may I hope?"[1] "Human reason," he wrote elsewhere, "unceasingly progresses, urged on by its own feeling of need, towards such questions as cannot be answered by any empirical application of reason, or principles derived therefrom; and so there has ever existed in every man some system of metaphysics."[2] By a "system of metaphysics" he meant the attempt to find answers to the ultimate human questions that cannot be found through any scientific study of the universe itself.

Why is it that apart from an authoritative revelation to us, we can never know the answers to the questions that inevitably arise in the human heart? Two answers can be given to that question. First, our perspective is highly limited. No one today was around when the world came into existence or when the first human beings arose. We can't grasp the whole of human history. Each of us fills only an infinitesimal spot in the stream of time. We are like marchers in a long parade. We may be able to view and understand something of the participants around us, but unless someone gives us the pattern of the entire parade, we have no idea of what the whole show looks like or its final destination.

Second, human understanding is hindered by sin. Unbelievers are "darkened in their understanding" (Eph. 4:18) and "futile in their speculations" (Rom. 1:21). This does not mean they have lost the ability to reason. Instead, the content of reason or what one believes as true leads to erroneous conclusions. While many people do not accept the biblical concept of sin, thinkers of all ages have recognized a disturbance in human reason. As someone observed, there are few things reason can discover with so much certainty and ease as it own insufficiency.

We are all rationalizing creatures. That is, we all have a tendency to justify what we do in our behavior, to rationalize our actions. If we don't want to live according to truth, we try to find reasons that will support our behavior. So our reasoning is not a neutral capacity that we use to search for objective truth. It is a means by which people try to support the desires of their hearts.

One of the most interesting and yet perplexing questions that demonstrates this need of revelation is that of our own identity as humans. The question "What is man?" has dogged thinkers of all ages. This question stems from the ability of the human spirit to transcend or stand above or apart from other things or persons, even the world, and make them conscious objects of observation and study. Now if we stand outside of these things, looking at them in our minds, so to speak, it is obvious that we cannot derive the full meaning of our own existence from them. For as observers we are not included in what we are considering.

We cannot even gain the meaning of our existence by studying ourselves. For in doing so, there is always a part of us that is not "object," since there must at the same time be a part of us that is the "subject" doing the observation. To put it another way, in self-consciousness there is always an "I" that is doing the observing as well as an "I" that is observed. We can consider ourselves and then in our imagination step back and see ourselves looking at ourselves, and if we desire to carry this on, we can see the self that is looking at the self that in turn is looking at the self, ad infinitum, until we cannot hold it all together anymore. The point is that no matter how far we carry on the process, there is always an "observing I" that we cannot observe. Thus there is a dimension of us that can never be the object of our observation. There is always a dimension of our self that stands outside all of our thought, namely, the subject doing the thinking. Who is this subject? Unless someone tells us who we are, we can never know.

In Psalm 8:4 the psalmist asked, "What is man, that Thou dost take thought of him? And the son of man, that Thou dost care for him?" He was wondering about the place of human beings, each one an infinitesimal speck, in comparison to the magnitude and splendor of the starry heavens above. He found his answer not in studying nature or philosophy, but only in God, who has revealed that He takes thought of him and cares for him, and has given him rulership over creation. Without this relationship to God, the psalmist would never have known of his place in the universe.

Many people have lost confidence in human reason to supply answers to these ultimate human questions. For people who reject God in our "postmodern" times there simply are no answers, no absolute truth. They say we must each decide truth for ourselves. For them, human beings cannot answer the ultimate questions of life with any objective absolute truth. According to Plato, man's duty is "either to be taught or to find out where the truth is, or if he cannot, at least to take the best possible human doctrine and the hardest to disprove, and to ride on this like a raft over the waters of life and take the risk; unless he could have a more seaworthy vessel to carry him more safely and with less danger, some divine doctrine to bring him through."[3] How true! What we need is "some divine doctrine" or, as another person put it, "some word of God."

But is it reasonable to believe that there is such a word? Yes. Both the nature of humankind and the nature of God lead us to expect such a revelation.

The enduring questions of the human mind concerning the supernatural argue that a transcendent realm exists. One would surely not expect that the Creator would make us so that we have these questions about our existence and then provide no answer. Even naturalistic evolution argues that there is something in the environment that sustains a particular being or else it dies and ceases to exist. The fact that people have these questions and continue to have them argues even on evolutionary grounds that there is something in our environment that provides answers to these questions for which we cannot find answers either in ourselves or in the created world about us.

When we think also of the nature of God, it is reasonable to expect Him to disclose Himself to us. Every intelligent being we know desires to communicate with others and make himself or herself known. It is reasonable, therefore, to presume that a personal God, especially a God of love, would desire to communicate with others. This is all the more plausible when we consider the biblical teaching that people are made in the image of God and that they desire fellowship with Him. Surely a God of love would respond to the need of His creatures, especially a need that He planted within them. If we grant, then, that a revelation from God is what we would expect from Him—given the nature of humanity and of God—is such a revelation possible? Can an infinite God communicate with people who are finite creatures?

Some have argued that we can only know a being who corresponds to our nature, and therefore we cannot know God who is so completely different. True, the God of the Bible is presented as the incomparable One. God declared, "To whom then will you liken Me that I should be his equal?" (Isa. 40:25). But in all of His infinite difference, He made man in His image and likeness (Gen. 1:26), and included in this divine likeness is the capacity for personal communication. Surely this gift would find its first use in communicating with the Creator. To exalt the greatness of God and then limit His ability to make a creature with whom He can communicate is quite absurd. The One who gave us eyes to see, ears to hear, and a mind to understand can certainly use these same faculties to communicate with us.

We need a word from God, and God has met that need. This is the claim of Christianity. It is a "revealed" religion, that is, a religion based on a word from God. Clearly all philosophies of life built on atheism or agnosticism are devised by human thought. To try to discover God by human reason, or by some mystical experience that seeks to transcends reason, yields either a god that is simply a name for some aspect of our own nature or a mere passive god whom we study and investigate like any other "object" in the universe. The result in either case is still human knowledge, rather than the thoughts of the transcendent God.

THE CONTEMPORARY PROBLEM OF REVELATION

What is revelation? Is all human knowledge revelation in the sense that humans discover reality? Is divine revelation simply the human discovery and experience of God or is it something more? Is there any evidence that God has revealed truth to humans in a supernatural way?

The Fact of Revelation

The idea of God making Himself known to humanity through acts or words of revelation pervades the Bible. As the following verses illustrate, the people of the Bible claimed to know God and His truth because He revealed it to them.

- The secret things belong to the LORD our God, but the things revealed belong to us and to our sons forever. (Deut. 29:29)
- Surely the LORD God does nothing unless He reveals His secret counsel to His servants the prophets. (Amos 3:7)
- For to us God revealed them through the Spirit. (1 Cor. 2:10)
- God, after He spoke long ago to the fathers in the prophets in many portions and in many ways, in these last days has spoken to us in His Son. (Heb. 1:1–2)

The English word "revelation" derives from the Latin *revelatio* ("uncovering" or "laying bare"), which was used by Jerome in the Latin Vulgate, the version of the Bible prepared in the fourth and fifth centuries. The key biblical terms denoting revelation are *apokalyptō* (Greek) in the New

Testament and *gālâ* (Hebrew) in the Old Testament. Both verbs have the basic meaning "to uncover, to reveal," and are used in Scripture for the unveiling of divine truths that were previously hidden. Other terms, too, convey the idea of divine revelation. The Hebrew *ra'â* means "to see," and is often used when God appeared to show something to someone. Words related to that verb speak of the person who received revelation as a "seer" and what was seen as "a vision." The ordinary word meaning "to know" (*yāda'*) was also commonly used.

Other Greek terms are "make manifest" (*phaneroō*), an "appearing" (*epiphaneia*), and "to point out or make known" (*deiknymi*). In addition to these words that suggest revealing something or making something known, other terms such as "the word of the Lord" and God's "law" or "instruction" point to the results of divine revelation. Taken together these several words show that the idea of divine revelation pervades the Bible.

The Modern Problem of Revelation

The human need for revelation from God and the fact of its provision by a loving God are clearly taught in Scripture. But what exactly is revelation, and how does it take place?

The early Christian understanding of revelation. From the earliest days of the church, Christians, like Old Testament believers, understood that revelation means God's making Himself, His power, and His truth known to people. This took place in a number of ways. But the goal was to bring individuals to a personal saving relationship with God, which included a cognitive communication of truth. Many of those activities in history through which He revealed Himself to His people and called them into a saving relationship with Him were written down and became known as sacred writings, the Scriptures.

The Bible then was not only a record of revelatory activity; it is itself revelation, God's Word. The early believers, of course, always recognized that we can't know all there is to know about God. Yet they believed that He has revealed some information about Himself, His creation, and His will and purposes—especially the plan of salvation. There was some disagreement in the early centuries over which writings should be included in the category of "Scripture," and also how to interpret certain parts of it. But there was no disagreement over the nature of Scripture as the Word—the revelation—of God.

In the Middle Ages the church began to consider the authoritative *interpretation* of Scripture as revelation along with the Scriptures themselves. The Roman Catholic Church said that only the church could authoritatively interpret the Bible. So the church's teachings became viewed as revelatory *along with* the Scriptures. This, however, did not change the traditional understanding of the Scriptures as God's revelatory Word. The Reformers rejected the idea of additional revelation, but their understanding of the nature of the Bible was also the historic position—it is the revealed Word of God.

The modern view of revelation. Today many people no longer hold this historic view of revelation. They say it is impossible to believe that God has revealed Himself with absolute truth in a book. This change of perspective resulted from the broad change of thinking in the Western world that began in the seventeenth century with the so-called Age of Reason and blossomed in the "Enlightenment" in eighteenth-century Germany.

Immanuel Kant said that the "Enlightenment is man's leaving his self-caused immaturity. Immaturity is the incapacity to use one's intelligence without the guidance of another. . . . Having the courage to make use of your own intelligence is therefore the motto of the Enlightenment."[4]

This movement was characterized by three concepts. First, the Enlightenment leaders rejected external authority, whether the Bible, the church, or the state—because people, they said, should not be bound by ancient customs and creeds. Second, human destiny lies in progress, based on the belief that nature and humanity is basically good. Third, the knowledge of God and religious truth is ultimately attainable through human reason, a view that essentially rendered supernatural revelation unnecessary.

This led to the idea that people by reasoning cannot know absolute truth. All humans in their search for truth are only "on the way" to truth. Why? Because they are finite and they are conditioned by their limited historical perspective. Therefore people can arrive at only relative truth, not final absolute truth. Despite this limitation, however, reason remained the ultimate avenue to truth and its final criterion. There could be no truth that was not universally reasonable. This optimistic confidence in human reason is the defining characteristic of the modern age, which began with the Enlightenment.

The postmodernism of today is marked by a loss of confidence in human reason to bring the utopia promised by science. Central to the radical leaders of this movement is the total rejection of any objective truth. Despite seeing all human truth as culturally conditioned and historically relative, modernism still held to an objective reality and ultimate truth, which could be pursued and increasingly realized for the good of humankind. Postmodernism, on the other hand, denies the reality of an ultimate truth and therefore rejects its pursuit. There is no universal truth out there to seek; each person creates truth for himself or herself.

Even though it rejects modernism's rationalism, postmodernism is still the child of the Enlightenment's exaltation of human reason as the final authority. It is the logical end of a rationalism that still retains the fundamental plank of the Enlightenment, namely, human reason as the final arbiter of truth, even if that truth is only personal and self-created. In a sense postmodernism is the logical conclusion of a sinful rationalism that rejects all external authority.

Enlightenment's approach to reason impacted a number of Christian thinkers. They felt that pre-Enlightenment theology was no longer tenable. If Christianity was to be relevant and have meaning for people today, it somehow had to accommodate the new emphasis on the validity of rationalism for attaining truth. As a result, many Christian theologians came up with new ways to explain the concept of revelation and the nature of the Bible.

Some said revelation came *through human subjective experience*. Optimism about the ability of human reason to uncover all truth essentially led some to deny all special revelation. They said God reveals Himself through the natural processes of universal reason. The Bible is therefore nothing but the confirmation of the religion of reason, often stated in fictitious stories. When people accepted the idea that the knowledge from reason could be derived only from the experiences of the senses, then knowledge of God was sought in the realm of human subjectivism. This led Friedrich Schleiermacher (1768–1834) to believe that revelation takes place in our religious experiences. He said we experience revelation through what he called our "God-consciousness" or our "feeling of dependence." The Bible, then, is not the objective revelation of divine truth; it is not the Word of God. Rather the teachings of the Bible are only the experiences of the Christian community expressed in words. The idea of revelation in the religious experience became popular in the theology of liberalism, of which Schleiermacher is called the father.

Others teach that revelation comes *through events in which God personally encounters individuals*. For many theologians, equating subjective religious experience with divine revelation brought God too close to human beings. History, especially during the first half of the twentieth century, demonstrated that people are sinful. And so they need an objective message from God, the One who is transcendent and who can encounter individuals in their sinfulness. Revelation and its expression in human words was more than human insight into spiritual and moral things.

This view was initiated by the Swiss theologian Karl Barth (1886–1968) and is part of what is called neoorthodoxy. According to Barth and others, revelation occurs in events through which God reveals Himself. These events include the saving acts of God in history such as the call of Abraham, the Exodus, and the person and work of Christ. These events became revelatory experiences for the first witnesses, as God encountered them in His saving presence. This revelation, however, did not consist of words or truths about God; what was revealed was God Himself. The Scriptures are the authoritative *witness* to this revelatory encounter in God's once-for-all saving acts, but they are not the revelation *itself*. God continues throughout history to use this original witness of the Scriptures to confront people in similar revelatory occasions in which He encounters individuals to reveal Himself.

This "encounter" is referred to as God "speaking," and its content is "the Word of God." But this Word is never equated with human words, such as those in the Bible. Rather the "Word" is personal, that is, God Himself in His revelation, and particularly Jesus Christ, the Word of God. This revealed Word encounters us not as information, but as God's saving presence, and this calls for obedience, not assent to certain truths. As noted, the Scriptures in this view of revelation are the unique witness to God's original revelatory saving acts. They are written by fallible humans and are therefore marred by errors. Nevertheless the authors were led by the Holy Spirit to give a sufficiently reliable record of the events and their saving significance in the Scriptures so that they become the avenue through which God continues to reveal Himself to individuals in personal revelatory encounters. In this view revelation does not occur unless someone is actually encountered by God. Thus to say that the Bible is the revelation of God, whether one recognizes it as such or not, in this view, is invalid.

Still others teach that revelation comes *through universal history*. According to German theologian Wolfhart Pannenberg (1928–), revelation is God's demonstrating His deity in the process of history. To him, revelation is not found in subjective religious experiences or through supernatural encounters, as in the two previous views. Rather, God is conveyed, he says, in all of reality but especially in human history and particularly in His actions with His people, as witnessed in the Scriptures. Because human experiences are continuing, this revelation is not complete. The resurrection of Christ proves that the God of Israel is the true God.

In this view God's revelation through His historical actions does not need the support of any supernatural revelatory Word. Rather the manifestation of God in history is open to anyone. When we thoroughly investigate our world and our own human nature, using the best critical tools of modern scholarship, we recognize the reality of God by the light that His presence sheds on our experiences. The resurrection of Christ obviously has significance for human life, and Pannenberg argues strongly for its historicity.

In these three previous views the Bible is not seen as the revealed Word of God. Instead it is the historical record of God's people who recognized His activities in their history. It also contains the record of some people who through nonverbal prophetic experiences were given glimpses of that revelation that will be manifest in the future. As a fallible human record, all the teachings and data of Scripture are subject to examination by critical reason and investigation to determine whether they are factual and truthful.

These views of revelation since the Enlightenment have several elements in common. First, they all accept human reason as the final criterion of truth. Even those who desire to have a Word that addresses humanity from outside still accept the conclusions of rationalistic scientific historical criticism in saying that the Bible has errors in it and is not the objective truth of God. Second, revelation is conveyed only indirectly through human religious subjectivism. Revelation may come through the exalted insight of human reason, through emotional religious experience, or through an encounter with God. But revelation is never the direct communication of divine truth, coming to individuals as objective propositional teachings. Third, because revelation is mediated indirectly through human experience and never objectively, it never communicates absolute truth. Its truth is always conditional in some way by its limited historical environment and therefore is always relative.

CONCLUSION

Clearly the issue of divine revelation is one of the most fundamental theological questions. For only with a revelation from God can we find authoritative answers to any theological question. The devastating effects of the modern denial of an objective revelation from God are evident in the confusion of beliefs and relativistic morals of many people today. Only by accepting the biblical teaching that our loving Creator has clearly revealed Himself and His will to us in a revelation that is distinct from our own experience can we find satisfying answers to our human questions.

Three

What though nor real voice nor sound
Amidst their radiant orbs be found?
In reason's ear they all rejoice,
And utter forth a glorious voice;
For ever singing, as they shine,
"The hand that made us is divine."[1]

—Joseph Addison

Three

What Is General Revelation?

IN A SENSE the theme of Scripture is the reality of divine revelation. God has made Himself known so that we as His intelligent creatures might know Him and have personal communion with Him. Because God is the Creator and Sustainer of the universe, it is only natural that creation witnesses to that fact. Thus the Bible depicts the revelation of God through many avenues—means that may be classified as general revelation and special revelation. General revelation is revelation that is addressed to and therefore available to all people at all times. Special revelation, on the other hand, is revelation that God has given at special times to certain people. These categories are sometimes labeled "natural" and "supernatural" revelation, respectively, suggesting that general revelation is communicated through natural phenomena while special revelation is conveyed through supernatural intervention. Both forms of revelation are mentioned in Psalm 19. David began that psalm by writing that the heavens and other phenomena of nature tell of the glory of God and reveal truth about Him (19:1–4), and then he discussed the values of "the law of the Lord" (19:7–11).

THE FORMS AND CONTENT OF GENERAL REVELATION

Scripture teaches that God reveals Himself to all people through the marvels of His created handiwork and especially through the wonder of our own human nature.

Consciousness of the world about us and the vast heavens that extend beyond our knowledge inevitably evoke the question, "Where did all of this come from?" Until modern times, thinkers who have contemplated that question have always answered that they came about by God. The very existence of the universe calls for a final "cause"—a Creator. And its order and design points to an intelligent Designer.

The rise of naturalism and materialism, both of which deny the supernatural, has influenced some people to deny the existence of God. But the evidence from creation still forces us to acknowledge His existence. The popular Big Bang theory of the origin of the universe points to a beginning and therefore to a Creator. The intricate and complex designs in nature increasingly give evidence of an intelligent Designer.

All this shows that Henry Wadsworth Longfellow was correct when he wrote, "Nature is a revelation of God; art a revelation of man."[2] Even as the works of individuals reveal their abilities and powers, so the universe displays the characteristics of God. "The heavens are telling of the glory of God; and their expanse is declaring the work of His hands" (Ps. 19:1). The "glory of God" refers to the very nature of God made manifest. It is the display of His attributes or characteristics.

Paul wrote that nature reveals several characteristics of God. Speaking of people who have not received any special revelation, he said, "That which is known about God is evident within them; for God made it evident to them. For since the creation of the world His invisible attributes, His eternal power and divine nature, have been clearly seen, being understood through what has been made, so that they are without excuse. For even though they knew God, they did not honor Him as God, or give thanks" (Rom. 1:19–21).

God's creation reveals His "eternal power" and "divine nature"—qualities that show Him to be God and worthy of worship. Though He is not part of nature, as some religions affirm, and though He is invisible, God is nevertheless disclosed in His handiwork. It bears His marks so clearly that no one can escape the fact of His existence. Richard Wurmbrand, well known for his suffering as a Christian under the former communist authorities of his homeland Romania, tells the story of a Russian couple who were sculptors but who had been taught all their lives that there was no God.

> Once, we worked on a statue of Stalin. During the work, my wife asked me: "Husband, how about the thumb? If we could not oppose the thumb to the other fingers—if the fingers of the hands were like toes—we could not hold a hammer, a mallet, any tool, a book, a piece of bread. Human life would be impossible without this little thumb. Now, who has made the thumb? We both learned Marxism in school and know that heaven and earth exist by themselves. They are not created by God. So I have learned and so I believe. But if God did not create heaven and earth, if He created only the thumb, He would be praiseworthy for this little thing.
>
> "We praise Edison and Bell and Stephenson, who have invented the electric bulb, the telephone and the railway and other things. But why should we not praise the one who has invented the thumb? If Edison had not had a thumb, he would have invented nothing. It is only right to worship God who has made the thumb."
>
> The husband became very angry. . . . "Don't speak stupidities! You have learned that there is no God. And you can never know if the house is not bugged and if we will not fall into trouble. Get into your mind *once and for all* that there is no God. In heaven there is *nobody*!"
>
> She replied: "This is an even greater wonder. If in heaven there were the Almighty God in whom in stupidity our forefathers believed, it would be only natural that we should have thumbs. An Almighty God can do everything, so He can make a thumb, too. But if in heaven there is nobody, I, from my side, am decided to worship from all my heart the 'Nobody' who has made the thumb."[3]

Even the ongoing processes of nature that sustain life and activity give evidence of God's presence. The Lord "did not leave Himself without witness, in that He did good and gave you rains from heaven and fruitful seasons, satisfying your hearts with food and gladness" (Acts 14:17; see also 17:24–27). We commonly refer to catastrophes as "acts of God," but the apostle declared that the normal beneficial workings of nature we so often take for granted are evidence of the reality of God. Jesus, for example, said that God feeds the birds of the air and makes flowers and grass more splendid than King Solomon's glory (Matt. 6:26–30). The phenomena of nature reveal God's existence and something of His nature to all people "in as inescapable fashion as the sun during its course across the heavens sheds its light and heat upon man everywhere on the earth (Psalm 19:6)."[4]

Beyond the complexity of the body, as seen in the Russians' conversation about the human thumb, our human nature reveals God's personality. Speaking to the Athenians, with their numerous altars, including one to "the unknown God," Paul argued against the worship of all human-crafted altars by pointing to our own nature. "In Him we live and move and exist, as even some of your poets have said, 'For we also are His offspring.' Being then the offspring of God, we ought not to think that the Divine Nature is like gold or silver or stone, an image formed by the art and thought of man" (Acts 17:28–29). If we are the creatures of God, Paul said, He is at least as great as we are, and that means that He is a living person.

Centuries earlier, the prophet Isaiah used the same reasoning against people who thought they were getting away with their evil deeds. They asked, "Who sees us?" or "Who knows us?" But Isaiah responded, "You turn things around! Shall the potter be considered as equal with the clay . . . ? Or what is formed say to him who formed it, 'He has no understanding'?" (Isa. 29:15–16). Similarly the psalmist chided the "senseless" and "stupid" among the people: "He who planted the ear, does He not hear? He who formed the eye, does He not see?" (Ps. 94:9). In essence God says, "Look at yourselves. Your nature and abilities as humans point to Me, your Creator, who is greater than you are."

Another way in which general revelation affirms God's existence is the course of human history, which He controls. As the Lord of history, He reveals Himself in the affairs of humankind. Addressing the Athenians on Mars Hill, Paul declared that God has "made from one, every nation of mankind to live on the face of the earth, having determined their appointed times, and the boundaries of their habitation, that they should seek God, if perhaps they might grope for Him and find Him, though He is not far from each one of us; for in Him we live and move and exist" (Acts 17:26–28). The arrogant king of ancient Babylon had to learn the hard way that "the Most High is ruler over the realm of mankind, and bestows it on whomever He wishes" (Dan. 4:32; see also 4:34–37). The truth of Proverbs 14:34 is evident to all thoughtful students of history: "Righteousness exalts a nation, but sin is a disgrace to any people."

The law that God has written innately in all human hearts is another affirmation of general revelation. The powerful Creator is also the moral Lawgiver and Judge. Everyone has at least some sense of right and wrong. "For when Gentiles who do not have the Law [written] do instinctively the things of the Law, these, not having the Law, are a law to themselves, in that they show the work of the Law written in their hearts, their conscience bearing witness, and their thoughts alternately accusing or else defending themselves" (Rom. 2:14–15).

The apostle also wrote that we use this knowledge of right and wrong to judge others, but that unfortunately it does not have the power to make us perform what is right. He concluded, "Therefore you are without excuse, every man of you who passes judgment, for in that you judge another, you condemn yourself; for you who judge practice the same things" (2:1). Immanuel Kant concluded that two things fill the human heart with awe: "the starry heavens above and the moral law within." Although he rejected the authority of the Bible, this sense of "oughtness" made him believe in the reality of God. C. S. Lewis testified that this fact of moral law led him away from atheism.

Some social scientists object that the moral laws by which we seek to operate through our consciences are only the product of our society. They are placed there, they say, by our educational environment. True, we may have learned some of the rules of acceptable behavior from our parents or others, but this does not prove that the reality of these rules is the product of our teachers any more than the reality of the multiplication tables, which we also learned in school, is the product of our teachers.

Furthermore, while there are considerable differences in moral codes between societies, there are amazing similarities at fundamental levels. We have often heard that in some cultures thieves or treacherous persons are highly regarded, whereas in others they are considered outcasts. Today many people believe that moral standards are purely personal. They say there is no universal code of right and wrong that is binding on all people. But the real test of our moral sense as humans is not in what we prize in actions toward others or even in what we ourselves think is moral or immoral. The true revelation of our rule of right and wrong comes in what we prize in relation to ourselves. A thief may be highly honored among his people when he steals from others, but he does not approve of stealing when it is against himself! Likewise, it may be honorable among some people to kill others, but is there anyone who feels that it is a good thing to have his closest friend killed or for himself to be killed? When evaluated in this manner, it quickly becomes apparent that although our moral criteria have been somewhat twisted because of sin, deep standards of right and wrong are still common to all people.

This sense of right and wrong, and the uneasy feeling that comes when we have violated some standard, is witness to everyone of a moral God. "The sense within me that I owe a debt," Robert Browning wrote, "assures me—somewhere must be Somebody, ready to take his due. All comes to this: where due is, there acceptance follows. Find Him who accepts the due."

If we alone are the constructors of our moral nature, then guilt would be no problem—just change the standard, and the sense of moral oughtness will be gone, along with the guilt for not acting accordingly. But only sociopaths—whom we acknowledge as abnormal—are capable of living without moral conscience. Every normal person has a sense of moral "responsibility," which by definition is that he is "responding" to someone outside of himself—Someone who has written a standard of righteousness within the hearts of everyone.

THE EFFECT OF GENERAL REVELATION

Because of general revelation, everyone does in fact have some knowledge not simply of a god, but of *the* true God of the Bible. As Paul told the Athenians, God makes Himself known as Creator, Sustainer, and Ruler of history (Acts 17:24–26) so that they and all people "should seek God . . . though He is not far from each one of us" (17:27).

Paul's words about the revelation of God to those who reject Him are even more explicit about their knowledge of God: "What may be known about God is plain to them, because God has made it plain to them. For since the creation of the world God's invisible qualities . . . have been clearly seen, being understood from what has been made, so that men are without excuse. For . . . they knew God" (Rom. 1:19–21, NIV). That this is a knowledge of the true God is seen from what the apostle says these people did with it. They knew God but did not honor Him as God (1:21). They "suppress the truth in unrighteousness" (1:18). The false gods they worshiped were the result of deliberately denying the knowledge of the true God and substituting their own philosophies and self-focused thoughts and choosing to worship other gods. "Professing to be wise, they became fools . . . they exchanged the truth of God for a lie, and worshiped and served the creature rather than the Creator" (1:22, 25).

The purpose of general revelation to cause people to seek God is thus thwarted by sin. The problem is not fundamentally one of the intellect, but of the will. Ever since the entrance of sin into the world through the temptation to be like God (Gen. 3:5), people have refused to surrender to the only true God. They choose to live an ego-centered rather than a God-centered life. From this improper and perverted base, they seek to construct a satisfying philosophy of life. They give their own meaning to the data of general revelation rather than acknowledging God and seeking to understand things from His perspective.

General revelation, however, still serves God's purposes. Because the knowledge of the true God is given through creation to every person, it leaves them "without excuse" before God (Rom. 1:20). The moral knowledge that all people have from God will one day be the standard by which they are judged (2:14–16). The inexcusable position of everyone is made plain by the fact that they all tend to judge others by their own innate sense of right and wrong. If the statements they use to accuse others were turned toward themselves, they would clearly indict themselves for their failure to live according to what they know is right (2:1–3). While general revelation tells us nothing about God's salvation from this problem of sin, it does strongly point out its need.

General revelation also contributes to the preservation of human society and culture. The ideas of truth and falsehood, justice and injustice, which help to maintain order among peoples, have their source in this revelation. In short, general revelation helps to check the tendency of sin to create chaos and degeneration. Left alone, human nature would soon bring civilization to an end.

Also the fact that all people are aware of God through general revelation serves the task of evangelism. The apostle Paul found Athens "full of idols," including one with the inscription "to an unknown God." So he used this awareness of God through general revelation as a point of contact to tell the Athenians about the true God found in Jesus Christ (Acts 17:16–31). Despite the fact that many in more recent times do not give the same overt evidence of a religious nature like the Athenians with their idols, the biblical teaching on general revelation says that they do have an awareness of the existence of God, and that can serve as a point of contact in our witness to them.

Four

God's friendship with men begins and grows through speech: His to us in revelation, and ours to Him in prayer and praise. Though I cannot see God, He and I can yet be personal friends, because in revelation He talks to me.[1]

—J. I. Packer

Four

What Is Special Revelation?

THE NEED FOR SPECIAL REVELATION

WHILE THE UNIVERSE and human nature reveal something of God, they were never designed to supply all that God wants us to know about Himself and His will for us. God made us for Himself. He created us for fellowship with Him, our Maker. Surrounded by the beauty of the Garden of Eden, Adam and Eve knew the handiwork of God, but to know God personally they needed direct communication. From the beginning, therefore, God revealed Himself not only through His creation but also directly through words.

Gazing at creation and reflecting on their own nature could never help Adam and Eve come to know that God's will for their lives and His purpose for them was to rule the earth (Gen. 1:26–28) and tend the garden (2:15). God had to communicate this to them in words. We don't know the full extent of God's personal communication with the first human beings. However, the form of the word "walking" in the phrase that God was "walking in the garden in the cool of the day" (3:8) intimates that it was a regular occurrence. The same word was used later in relation to God's presence in the tabernacle. So one commentator concludes that the Garden, like the tabernacle, was the place of God's presence, and that "maybe a daily chat between the Almighty and his creatures was customary."[2] Thus from the very beginning general revelation through nature provided the background for personal verbal communication.

The entrance of sin into the world heightened the need for personal communication. Through nature and conscience, history reveals that people have come to realize that there is a God and that He has established the world on the principles of moral law. People are also conscious that no one is able to live up to this law consistently. But nowhere in nature or in people themselves do we find a way out of this dilemma.

The history of religions reveals that when people do not receive the special revelation of God, they find no true release from guilt. Religions are established in search of answers, but apart from special revelation, religious people remain trapped within the knowledge they have through general revelation. They know they ought to live up to certain standards, but they don't. Consequently they establish ways to compensate for their failure.

Inevitably religions founded on general revelation are religions of works. Without the special revelation of God's forgiveness through Christ, they give no rest from the burden of guilt. As the psalmist wrote, "The heavens are telling of the glory of God" (Ps. 19:1), but it is "the law of the Lord [that] is perfect, restoring the soul" (19:7).

Special revelation adds certain truths lacking in the revelation of God in creation, and it also gives people the ability to see the truths in general revelation correctly. Until a person is brought back to God through a personal relationship with Jesus Christ, he or she cannot view the world from God's perspective. Only the illuminating work of God can open eyes blinded by sin. The one who spoke of God's glory in the heavens was a godly person (19:1). But an atheistic astronomer views the heavens and comes to a different conclusion. John Calvin, the great French Reformer, aptly illustrated the necessity of special revelation for one to read the "book of nature" correctly. "Just as old or bleary-eyed men and those with weak vision, if you thrust before them a most beautiful volume, even if they recognize it to be some sort of writing, yet can scarcely construe two words, but with the aid of spectacles will begin to read distinctly; so Scripture, gathering up the otherwise confused knowledge of God in our minds, having dispersed our dullness, clearly shows us the true God."[3]

Special revelation, through which God communicates directly in a personal way, is thus vital for human life. From the beginning we were created for a personal relationship with God. When sin entered the human race, it disrupted that fellowship and brought alienation between God and humanity. But God's loving plan to restore that broken relationship requires all the more that He speak His word of grace to us through special revelation.

THE FORMS OF SPECIAL REVELATION

How does God communicate with us? Some scholars say that God has revealed Himself in His mighty acts throughout history, but not in words. Others point to the personal revelation of God in Christ. Since He is called the Word of God (John 1:1), they argue that the words of the Bible cannot be the Word of God. Such conflicting teachings demand that we look carefully at what the Bible says about God's special revelation.

The writer of Hebrews declared, "God after He spoke long ago to the fathers in the prophets in many portions and in many ways, in these last days has spoken to us in His Son" (Heb. 1:1–2). As this statement suggests, special revelation has included a variety of methods, climaxing in the coming of the Son of God. The following is an overview of the principal methods of God's special revelation.

Theophanies

A prominent way in which God revealed Himself during the early portions of human history recorded in Scripture was through theophanies. The word *theophany* comes from two Greek words, *theos* ("God") and *phainō* ("to make visible" or "to appear"). A theophany is therefore an appearance of God.

In some instances the form of this appearance is not revealed. For example, Scripture simply records, "And the LORD appeared to Abram" (Gen. 12:7). In other instances the record indicates that God took different forms in making Himself visible. On one occasion, Abraham welcomed three men into his tent to show them hospitality. Two of them were angels, but the third was the Lord Himself (18:1–2, 22; 19:1). The mysterious "man" who wrestled with Jacob at Peniel was also an appearance of God, for Jacob said, "I have seen God face to face, yet my life has been preserved" (32:24, 30).

Several times God's appearing is said to be as "the Angel of the Lord." The Angel of the Lord appeared to Moses as flames of fire from within a bush that was not being consumed (Exod. 3:2–4). But this angel also appeared in a personal form, and scriptural statements make clear he was no ordinary angel. Something about the appearance of the angel or his prophetic message made Hagar, fleeing in the wilderness, declare, "Thou art a God who sees . . . Have I even remained alive here after seeing Him?" (Gen. 16:9–13). From His "awesome" appearance, His prophetic speech, and the way He "ascended in the flame of the altar," the parents of Samson knew that the angel who spoke with them was the Angel of the Lord, whom they recognized as God (Judg. 13:3–23; see also the Angel's appearance to Gideon; 6:11–24).

Although not literal "theophanies," the Angel appeared in dreams (Gen. 31:11–13) and spoke to individuals without any visible appearance (for example, 22:11–12). Many Bible students believe that the Angel of the Lord was none other than the Son Himself temporarily manifesting Himself before He took on human nature at His birth in Bethlehem. While this may not be conclusive, the fact that He can pardon sins and the fact that He bears the name of God clearly indicate that He is a revelation of God. In one sense the coming of Christ in human flesh was also a theophany, but it differed from all the rest. In the other instances God simply assumed a form; in the birth of Jesus, God the Son took on Himself a genuine human nature.

Dreams and Visions

Although dreams did not play a major role in revelation, on a number of significant occasions, especially in the Books of Genesis and Daniel, God communicated to His servants in dreams. Well-known instances include Jacob's dream of a ladder extending from earth to heaven (Gen. 28:12–16) and the dreams of Joseph concerning his being exalted above his brothers (37:5–7, 9). Solomon (1 Kings 3:5) and Joseph, the husband of Mary (Matt. 1:20; 2:13, 19), also received divine revelation in dreams.

Nor were dreams limited to God's people. The pharaoh of Egypt and King Nebuchadnezzar of Babylon were given dreams about God's future plans (Gen. 41:1–7; Dan. 2:3, 31–35). In both cases, however, the interpretations were conveyed through those who belonged to God's people. Most of these revelatory dreams included speech from God although some, as with Joseph's dream about himself and his brothers, did not.

Visions were much more common as a means of revelation, especially to the prophets. In some instances what was seen was described in a pictorial scene. Ezekiel clearly saw the temple in Jerusalem in a vision (Ezek. 8:3). However, with Amos "what he saw concerning Israel" (Amos 1:1) also involved the hearing or perceiving of words. Visions were commonly associated with prophets so much so that they were sometimes called "seers" (for example, 2 Sam. 24:11; 1 Chron. 9:22; 2 Chron. 16:7; 29:30).

Direct Communication

Frequently God spoke directly to people. Expressions such as "God said," "the word of the Lord came unto me," and "thus said the Lord" occur repeatedly in the Bible. In some instances there seems to have been an audible sound, as with Paul's hearing the voice from heaven (Acts 9:4) and young Samuel's hearing God speak (1 Sam. 3:4, 6, 8, 10–14). At other times it must have been some type of inward speech, such as we may use in silent prayer to God. When an angel commanded Philip to "join" the chariot of the Ethiopian official (Acts 8:29), or the Holy Spirit told Peter that three men were looking for him (10:19) or told the church to send out Barnabas and Saul (13:2), it was probably this type of speaking. This kind of disclosure may have been what Paul received from Christ in the Arabian desert (Gal. 1:11–17).

A unique direct communication was given to Moses. Exodus 33:11 states, "Thus the LORD used to speak to Moses face to face, just as a man speaks to a friend." When Miriam and Aaron questioned the authority of Moses, God said that He spoke with them through visions and dreams, but with Moses, "I speak mouth to mouth," meaning with a direct intimacy (Num. 12:6–8).

Angels

Occasionally God used angels to communicate His revelation. They appeared in this role especially at the beginning of a new work of God. For example, the Law was given to Moses through the mediation of angels (Acts 7:53; Gal. 3:19). An angel also announced the good news of the birth of the Savior (Luke 2:10, 13). One of the most interesting examples of revelation through an angel occurred with Daniel. On two occasions God answered his prayer for Israel by sending messages through angels, one of whom was Gabriel (Dan. 9:20–21; 10:10–21). While angels are superior to people in many ways, it is clear that they are only messengers of God's Word and not its originators. Their limitation in knowledge is evident in Peter's statement that even angels "long to look" into the good news of the gospel (1 Pet. 1:12).

Miracles

When God communicated His word directly to man, He often gave evidence of His presence by performing miracles. By a miracle, we are referring to an act that is different from ordinary events. Normally God operates His universe according to what we call "natural laws," which He has established as part of creation. A miracle occurs when God chooses to act in an extraordinary way for the purpose of revealing Himself.

The biblical language for miracles shows their revelatory function. Speaking of the miracles of Jesus, Peter described them as "miracles and wonders and signs" (Acts 2:22). This is not a reference to three different kinds of acts, but the same act seen from three viewpoints. The term "miracle" looks at the deed as a display of power. From the perspective of their striking character and the amazement evoked, they were "wonders." And the word "signs" points directly to their purpose as revelatory events. Signs in Scripture are like pointers that direct our attention to something.

According to Old Testament prophecies, the Messiah would come and work miracles as signs that point to His messiahship. For this reason the Jews continually asked Jesus, "What sign do You show to us?" (John 2:18; see also Matt. 12:38; 16:1). The miracle of the healing of the paralytic (Mark 2) illustrates these three dimensions of a miracle. Clearly, God's dynamic power was displayed when the paralytic man lying on the pallet got up and walked (2:12). The effect of wonder is seen in the statement that "they were all amazed and were glorifying God, saying, 'We have never seen anything like this' " (2:12). But the ultimate point of the miracle was stated by Jesus: "that you may know that the Son of Man has authority on earth to forgive sins" (2:10). This authority belongs only to God; thus the miracle was a revelation of the deity of Jesus Christ.

Miracles are involved in revelation in two important ways. First, they point to the fact that revelation is happening. They make us sit up and take notice that God is at work. Second, they reveal something of the nature of God's power and the purpose for which He exerted it. Although in some cases it may be difficult to see anything more than the evidence of God's power over nature, as in Jesus turning water into wine (John 2), most miracles in Jesus' ministry revealed God's power to overcome sin and its effects. The healing of the sick and lame and the restoration of sight to the blind all point to the triumph of God over the misery of sin. The raising of Lazarus and others who had died announced the fact that sin's ultimate power is broken, and death, the last enemy of humanity, can be vanquished by God's power. The resurrection of Christ is portrayed as the ultimate demonstration of the supernatural miraculous power of God (Eph. 2:19–20).

While miracles are a form of revelation, their full significance is known only through the Scriptures. Miracles are thus seen as signs pointing to messengers of the Word. As Peter wrote, miracles "attested" or "accredited" the person of Christ to the people. They validated His person and therefore also His words, which declared God's will and purpose. The apostle Paul wrote that the miraculous works that God performed through him were "signs of a true apostle" (2 Cor. 12:12). These "signs and wonders and miracles" validated Paul as an apostle of Christ and therefore affirmed that his teaching was from God.

The Person of Christ

The writer to the Hebrews declared that "in these last days God has spoken to us in His Son" (Heb. 1:2). In this Word the revelation of God reaches its climax. The "many portions" of God's speech that had previously been revealed through "many ways" were only fragments pointing to the coming of Him "in whom are hidden all the treasures of wisdom and knowledge" (Col. 2:3).

In the Incarnation we gain additional knowledge of God as He revealed Himself in a different way. For Christ did not so much *make* a revelation of God as He *is* the revelation. He is God incarnate, that is, God in human flesh. It is one thing to receive knowledge about a person, but this never compares with meeting the person himself.

In Jesus Christ the world was confronted by God Himself. John declared that "no man has seen God at any time; the only begotten God . . . He has explained Him" (John 1:18). This must not be interpreted to mean that Jesus was simply a greater teacher of divine truth than all previous teachers. He "explained" God in the sense that to view Him was to see God, even as he told Philip, "He who has seen Me has seen the Father" (14:9). He could say this because "in Him all the fulness of Deity" was resident; God in all His fullness dwelt in Christ in bodily form (Col. 2:9).

The revelation of God in Christ was given through His teachings. He was recognized as *the* Teacher sent from God (John 3:2), speaking the words of God as none had done before. But in addition to words, God spoke through Jesus' person and work, which were climaxed in the Cross and the Resurrection. In Jesus' sacrifice for sin, God revealed His infinite love and also His infinite holiness and righteousness. Jesus is not simply the climax of revelation; He is the theme of all revelation. Scripture testifies to Him (John 5:39), for the prophets before Him and the apostles after Him were inspired by the Holy Spirit, who is also the Spirit of Christ (1 Pet. 1:11; Rev. 19:10).

The Scriptures

One final form of revelation is the written Word. Much of the Bible is the written record of revelation, which was given in many of the forms we have already noted. Dreams and visions were recorded, and direct communication of God's words to the prophets was written down. When God spoke directly to people, they were conscious of His controlling influence. When dreams and visions occurred, the individuals were basically passive recipients of the message of God. Most certainly, when God wrote the Ten Commandments with His finger on the tablets of stone, Moses could do nothing but bring them to the people.

On the other hand, in contrast to those who were conscious of the overpowering influence of God in giving His revelation to them, a number of the human writers of Scripture wrote the Word without such conscious influence. The Spirit of God worked within and through their own personalities to reveal His truth. Their minds and emotions were totally involved as they recorded God's truth. Yet the Spirit of God controlled them so that what they wrote was exactly what God wanted to communicate. We might say that in this form of revelation God and man were joined more closely than in any way except in the person of Christ. It is only natural that such revelation would occur primarily in New Testament times when God by His Spirit began to take up residence in believers' hearts.

All these forms of revelation show that there was a fundamental progression in the types of revelation used throughout history. All these methods, other than that of the unique person of Christ, may be summed up in three forms—appearance of God, or theophanies; some type of direct communication or prophecy; and inspiration. They advance from the visible and external to the internal, from what stands apart to what is intimately near. This clearly follows the progression of God's entire relationship with human beings. In the Garden of Eden, Adam and Eve were separated from God because of sin. But through redemption in Christ, God brings believers near Him and by His Spirit He resides in the human heart in ultimate fellowship. Despite these differences in the forms and relationships, however, the Bible never makes any distinction as to the revelatory value of each form. All equally revealed God.

Several facts about special revelation may be noted. First, special revelation is act and word. Contrary to many scholars who see God's special revelation only in the "mighty acts" of God, the various forms God used to communicate with His people demonstrate that He used both actions and words. All the forms mentioned could be categorized under one or both of these headings. Without God's interpretation of His actions, they would not have been fully understood. Many witnessed the Exodus out of Egypt, the Babylonian captivity of Israel, the death of Christ, or the empty tomb. But all did not see the same meaning in these acts. Only God's revelation can tell us, for example, that the crucifixion of Christ was "for our sins." Unless God reveals the meaning of His actions, we can never be sure of their full significance.

A revelation through words is also necessary for a personal relationship. While perhaps most people would choose deafness over blindness, in reality the blind suffer less emotional disturbance than do the deaf. The reason has to do with the importance of words for personal relationship. As Bernard Ramm explained, "The warm personal relationships of life are carried on by means of conversation, and the deaf man is largely severed from those relationships. The soundless world is far more frustrating than the sightless world. Radio drama is entertaining but a television drama robbed of the sound track is drained of all meaning. *In life as in drama it is the word which carries the meaning; it is the word which is the element of cohesion; and it is the word which is the necessary presupposition for warm personal friendships.*"[4] God's special revelation is designed for personal fellowship. And this requires words so that we might understand God's actions and respond to them.

Second, special revelation is personal and verbal. The fact that the Bible is the Word of God is the subject of the following chapter. But it is necessary here simply to note that our review of the forms of special revelation demonstrates that there is no dichotomy between Christ as the personal Word of God and God's verbal Word. It is, of course, possible to focus on the words of Scripture without fellowshipping with the living Word of whom it speaks. Some of the Jews in Jesus' day studied the Scriptures intently, believing them to give the way of life. But Jesus told them, "It is these [Scriptures] that bear witness of Me; and you are unwilling to come to Me, that you may have life" (John 5:39–40). Unfortunately some "Bible-believing" people know all about the Bible, but they do not have a living relationship with Christ.

According to the Scriptures, there can be no real separation between the written words and the personal Word. In our own communication with another person, his or her words are the way we get to know that person's thoughts and feelings. In a real sense a person's words are an extension of that individual as he or she seeks to bridge the distance between himself or herself and another. So the living God who came to earth in the person of His Son, Jesus Christ, reveals His heart and mind to humanity through the medium of language, the verbal Word of God.

Third, special revelation is intelligible only in the context of general revelation. God reveals Himself in His handiwork *and* in personal communication. The artist and the architect, in fact all of us, tell something about ourselves in what we do. Whether a person's desk is neat or messy reveals something about that individual. An artist also communicates in words to his family and friends, and those words go beyond simply letting his work speak for him. So God reveals Himself in the splendor and awesomeness of the work of His creation and also in direct and personal communication with His personal creatures.

This was Adam and Eve's situation in Eden. As Warfield explains, "The impression is strong that what is meant to be conveyed to us is that man dwelt with God in Eden, and enjoyed with Him immediate and not merely mediate communion. . . . Had man not fallen . . . every man would have enjoyed direct vision of God and immediate speech with Him."[5]

The entrance of sin brought spiritual and personal alienation from God and with it a disastrous loss of personal communication. Like Adam, sinners feel uncomfortable in the presence of God. His awesome holiness made the people of Israel ask for Moses to talk to God for them. But in love God has sought out sinful people, communicating His grace in actions and word in order to bring them back into that fellowship for which life was designed. Biblical history reveals that this communication has grown and will grow until believers will one day be at home in His presence.

The revelation of God in nature and His personal communication in special revelation belong together. The Lord speaks His word and acts within history to restore our relationship with Him. But without the knowledge of God as the Almighty Creator and Ruler of all things, the One who is righteous and good, these special interventions through acts and words to bring us back to Him would not be intelligible or credible. It would be difficult to accept Him as Redeemer if we did not know Him also as Creator.

CONCLUSION

Many people live as if there were no God, and some hold views of reality, such as naturalism, that logically exclude God. But modern surveys as well as human history demonstrate the truth of Scripture that human beings recognize the existence of God (though they don't always acknowledge it). He created us to know Him, and therefore He makes Himself known. His revelation fully satisfies our questions about the meaning of human existence. Through the world about us He reveals His eternal existence and almighty power. Through His special action and words He communicates His personal character as a God of love and gracious redemption. Through it all He reveals Himself so that we might know Him, whom to know is eternal life.

Five

The best book to be read by him who is inquiring into the evidence of the Bible is the Bible itself. . . . Search the Scriptures honestly and diligently, and you will find out whether they are from God, or whether they speak of themselves.[1]

—Robert L. Dabney

Five

Are the Bible's Teachings Unique?

THE BIBLE claims to be the special revelation from God, the very Word of God. But other religious groups also claim that their sacred texts were revealed by God. Muslims, for example, believe that their holy book, the Koran, is divinely inspired; they say the archangel Gabriel revealed it to Muhammad. Mormons believe that Joseph Smith received a direct revelation from God engraved on golden plates, which he translated and published as The Book of Mormon. Other religions also have their sacred writings. Their adherents view these writings as "sacred" texts that convey truths about ultimate things.

Since these various writings have differing messages, they cannot all be from God, who cannot lie. How then can we know which "scripture" is in reality the voice of God? We cannot, of course, appeal to some higher authority to tell us, "This is the voice of God" or "This isn't." If anyone were to make that determination, he would have to be an authority above God Himself. But this is logically impossible, if we accept the common definition of God as the Supreme Being.

The voice of God to us must be self-authenticating. That is, when God addresses us as His creatures, we must be able to recognize His words as the voice of God. They must stand out from other words. When we compare the Bible with the other claimants, that is exactly what we find. The Bible bears the marks of a supernatural book. This chapter discusses the unique teachings of the Bible and chapter 6 considers some other facts about the Bible that point to its supernatural character.

When we consider the central teachings of the Bible, we find that their scope and grandeur transcend all other human writings. All the true words of human teachers together simply do not compare with those of Scripture. As F. W. Farrar wrote, "What problems do these books leave unexamined? What depths unfathomed? What height unscaled? What consolation unadministered? What conscience unreproved? What heart untouched?"[2]

> We search the world for truth; we cull
> The good, the pure, the beautiful
> From graven stone and written scroll,
> From all old flower-fields of the soul;
> And, weary seekers of the best,
> We come back laden from our quest,
> To find that all the sages said
> Is in the Book our mothers read.[3]

Besides transcending human writings in the vastness of its message, the Bible's essential truth is actually contrary to natural human thought. The entire message of the Bible aptly illustrates God's statement through the prophet Isaiah: "For My thoughts are not your thoughts, neither are your ways My ways . . . for as the heavens are higher than the earth, so are My ways higher than your ways, and My thoughts than your thoughts" (Isa. 55:8–9).

THE CONCEPT OF GOD

From beginning to end, the Bible focuses on God. This perspective appears in David's words in 1 Chronicles 29:11. "Thine, O Lord, is the greatness and the power and the glory and the victory and the majesty, indeed everything that is in the heavens and the earth; Thine is the dominion, O Lord, and Thou dost exalt Thyself as head over all." He is the sovereign God, who rules the universe, directing all things to their end for His glory.

Also God is absolutely holy, and His holiness elevates Him far above humans with their sin. After envisioning God in His awesome holiness, Isaiah responded, "Woe is me, for I am ruined!" (Isa. 6:5). With sin, we cannot exist in the presence of God. Yet along with His holiness He possesses infinite goodness, love, and mercy. "The LORD is good to all," David declared, "and His mercies are over all His works" (Ps. 145:9). Within His sovereign holiness and justice, God in His infinite love worked out a plan of salvation for sinful people.

The God of the Bible, especially in His holiness, is naturally contrary to sinful human beings; therefore He is not a human invention, as many have asserted. As Christian apologist Colin Chapman says, "The uncomfortable thing about the God of the Bible is that he so often cuts across our personal desires and wishes. He does not allow us to be selfish, and always confronts us with an uncompromisingly high standard. This is *not* the kind of God man creates when he sets out to make a god in his own image."[4]

The very nature of God is a mystery that no human can fully comprehend. Throughout history people have believed in many gods (polytheism) or a single Unitarian god. The Bible alone presents the unique God who is both one God and three persons—Father, Son, and Spirit. This Trinitarian concept of God is not a contradiction to human reason, as some charge. The Trinity does not mean there are three Gods. God is one divine Being who exists eternally in three personal manifestations. While not an irrational contradiction to human minds, such a concept of God is not a human invention; it is a revelation from God.

Moreover, being triune in nature, the God of the Bible answers our human quest for knowledge of God and a relationship with Him more profoundly than any other religion. The belief in one supreme God is found in many religions, even some that have multiple lesser gods. But that God in those belief systems is so transcendent and distant that he cannot be known. Like one of the deities of the citizens of Athens in the apostle Paul's day, he is "an unknown god" (Acts 17:23). Hindus, in describing the nature of God, use expressions like "Divine Darkness" or "That of which nothing can be said."[5] For Buddhists, whatever reality there is cannot be defined or described. They say we can only maintain a "noble silence" in the face of the unknowable.[6] Primitive African religions similarly speak only of "the Unknown."[7] Islam's emphasis on the transcendent sovereignty of their God, Allah, also renders him like the God of deism, essentially beyond human knowledge with little personal communion with human beings and without the attribute of love.[8]

Judaism's understanding of God, based on the Old Testament, has much in common with the Christian God. But Judaism's rejection of the Trinitarian nature of God also results in a distant God, when compared to the God of Christianity, who is Father, Son, and Holy Spirit. Moses was allowed to glimpse only the trailing edge of God's glory, but in Jesus God came personally into human history. As Philip said, "Show us the Father and that will be enough for us" (John 14:8, NIV; see also 1:14, 18). Only if the Holy Spirit is God and not a creature can we have intimate fellowship with God Himself. "Religion cannot afford to be satisfied with anything less than God. In Christ God himself comes to us, and in the Holy Spirit he imparts himself to us."[9]

The unique God of the Bible satisfies our need not only for revelation but also for salvation. The great Reformer Martin Luther rightly said, "By no other means than that of an eternal person could we be rescued from our terrible fall into sin and eternal death; such a person alone could have power over sin and death, to expiate our sin and to give us instead righteousness and eternal life; no angel or creature could do this, but it must be done by God himself." Only the God of the Bible provides a redemption that is by God Himself.

The God of the Bible, who is Father, Son, and Spirit, is also the only explanation of an eternal God of love. A Unitarian God can exercise no love in a personal relationship without creating an object for His love. Only if there are personal relationships within God Himself can He be a God who "is love" by nature from all eternity. Only if God is relational in His being can He provide the model for our relational unity (see John 17:21–22).

Also the God of the Bible satisfies the need for One who is both transcendent—standing over creation and history as its sovereign Lord—and One who is also present with us in history. Humans have always tended to lose God in one of two heresies. On the one hand He may be lost in an abstract transcendence so that He is virtually unknowable, as is true in many human religions. One the other hand He may be thought of as so immanent within creation that He is essentially dissolved into the processes of nature and history itself, as in pantheism and process theology. Only the Trinitarian God has entered history to reveal Himself, while at the same time remaining outside of history as its transcendent Lord.[10]

Because the God of the Bible is beyond human reason, He therefore could not be the product of human invention. As one person warned years ago, "As he that denies this fundamental article of the Christian religion [the Trinity] may lose his soul, so he that much strives to understand it may lose his wits."[11] As believers we gladly worship God, who is greater than we are and whose nature we cannot master with our finite minds. For it is in His triune nature that He satisfies our heart's deepest desire for a relationship with Him as the one God who is *above* us, *for* us, and *in* us.

THE CONCEPT OF CHRIST

In all the sacred writings of other religions there is no person like Jesus Christ. Born of a virgin in humble surroundings, He was the eternal Son of God. He was Creator of all, yet He went to the cross to die at the hands of His creatures. J. N. D. Anderson summarizes the unique place of Christ among all religions. "Other religions may, indeed, include the belief that God, or one of the gods, manifested himself once, or many times, in human form, or that some 'divine light-substance' has passed from one individual to a succession of others. But Christianity alone has dared to claim that 'the one, omnipresent, omniscient Ground of all existence' has uniquely intervened in his creation, not by assuming the mere form or appearance of a man, but by actually becoming incarnate; not by living and teaching alone, but by actually dying a felon's death 'for us men and for our salvation,' and by putting his seal on the fact and efficacy of this intervention by rising again from the dead."[12]

Christ is unique in the origin and the nature of His person and life. He walked on earth in normal human situations, yet He was without sin (John 8:46). He never had to apologize or ask forgiveness for anything He did. His contemporaries were astounded by His teaching. "Never did a man speak the way this man speaks" (7:46). "He was teaching them as one having authority, and not as their scribes" (Matt. 7:29). He never asked for advice or permission. His miracles also pointed to uniqueness. "What kind of a man is this, that even the winds and the sea obey Him?" (8:27). "Since the beginning of time it has never been heard that anyone opened the eyes of a person born blind" (John 9:32).

Other religious leaders claimed to *teach* the way of life they had found. Christ claimed to *be* the Way of life (14:6). Muslims (the term means "one who submits [to God's will]") do not want to be called Mohammedans or for people to call their religion Mohammedanism. They explain that Muhammad was only a prophet who brought the revelation of God; he is not the basis of their faith. Buddha pointed away from himself to his teaching. At his death his followers asked him how they could remember him. His response was that "it did not matter much whether they remembered him or not. The essential thing was the teaching."[13] But shortly before His death, when He instituted the Lord's Supper, Jesus commanded His disciples, "Do this in remembrance of Me" (Luke 22:19).

Griffith Thomas pointed out that "Christianity is the only religion in the world which rests on the Person of its Founder."[14] He added, "There is no word in his teaching that he does not in some way make to depend on himself."[15] This, of course, is because no other historical founder of a religion insisted that He is the one and only God. As someone has said, "If it is not superhuman authority that speaks to us here, it is surely superhuman arrogance."[16] A man once told the Scottish writer Thomas Carlyle that he could honestly say of himself the words of Jesus, "I and the Father are one." "Yes," Carlyle responded, "but Jesus got the world to believe him."

Yet in all of His moral perfection, authoritative teaching, and miracle-working, Jesus never conveyed an impression of pride or sanctimonious aloofness. As John Stott notes, there is paradox in Christ that cannot be explained naturally. "There was no touch of self-importance about Jesus. He was humble. It is this paradox that is so baffling, the self-centeredness of His teachings and the unself-centeredness of His behavior. In thought He put Himself first; in deed last. He combined in Himself the greatest self-esteem and the greatest self-sacrifice. He knew Himself to be the Lord of all, but he became the servant of all. He said he was going to judge the world, but he washed his apostle's feet."[17]

Could the Gospel writers have made up such a portrait of a person, or were they reporting what they saw, the unique revelation of God? The very restrained portrait of Him by the biblical writers testifies to the latter. Reading the mythologies of various peoples shows the propensity of people to embellish the truth with fantastic imagination. Even the nonbiblical writings about Jesus, purporting to tell of His boyhood, portray Him as a childhood prodigy instructing His schoolteachers with hidden mysteries in the alphabet and astounding His family and playmates with miraculous works. According to these apocryphal gospels, on one occasion at the age of five, Jesus supposedly fashioned twelve sparrows out of clay on the Sabbath. When questioned by His father, Joseph about such activity on the holy day, Jesus clapped His hands and the sparrows flew away chirping.

In total contrast the Bible portrays the miracles of Christ with straightforward simplicity. Their purpose was not to amuse His audience or entertain the curious, but to demonstrate the glory of His Father in keeping with the goal of His life. Leon Morris points out the astounding fact that none of the writers of the Gospel accounts of Jesus ever praised Jesus. They did occasionally report people praising Him, but they themselves did not offer a word of praise. This is hard to explain if their accounts are exaggerated stories to make Christ something more than a human being. Some have charged that the biblical writers deified Christ even as Buddha was deified by his disciples.[18] But not until centuries after Buddha's death was he regarded as divine and then only in limited circles. But the scriptural portrait of Jesus as the divine Son of God was written while those who knew Him during His earthly life were still living.

All the evidence points to the fact that the Gospel writers gave us an objective report of this unique person in their midst. They did so because they wanted others to believe them. Moreover, the person whom they portrayed is so transcendent that it stretches one's credibility to think that He could have been invented by ordinary human writers, especially Galilean fishermen. Even Jean-Jacques Rousseau (1712–1778), the philosopher who helped pave the way for humanistic liberalism, acknowledged the supernatural origin of the gospel. "The gospel," he said, "has marks of truth so great, so striking, so perfectly inimitable, that the inventor of it would be more astonishing than the hero."[19] If the Gospel writers were devising fiction, then we must admit with Robert Dabney that "liars have composed the noblest and most beautiful model of truth ever seen among men."[20] Furthermore, they "expended all this miraculous art in constructing an imaginary picture of which the only apparent result is to condemn their own falsehood in inventing it."[21]

Perhaps most of all the Christ portrayed by biblical writers is so uncomfortable to natural sinful humans that it is impossible to believe that people could or would concoct the idea of such a person. H. G. Wells, although not an orthodox Christian, says that Jesus "was like some terrible moral huntsman digging mankind out of the snug burrows in which they had lived hitherto. . . . Is it any wonder that men were dazzled and blinded and cried out against him? . . . Is it any wonder that to this day this Galilean is too much for our small hearts?"[22]

THE BIBLICAL ACCOUNT OF MAN

Who would paint such a picture of people as we find in Scripture? The tendency of humans is either to exalt themselves above what they really are or to reduce themselves below their true nature. The Dutch scholar Desiderius Erasmus (1466–1536) once said, "Man is to man either a god or a wolf."

On the one hand human philosophies and theologies often extol humanity to the level of deity. The Greek philosopher Heraclitus (around 540–480 B.C.) proclaimed, "The gods are immortal men, and men are mortal gods." Much later German philosopher Georg Hegel (1770–1831) spoke of the "implicit divinity" of everyone, and theologians spoke of that spark of deity in people which needs to be fanned into flames.

On the other hand the more recent influence of naturalistic evolution, philosophers speak of humans as the aristocrats of animals. According to some evolutionists we are nothing more than complex organisms whose actions are controlled by our environment, much like Pavlov's dogs that were trained to respond to certain stimuli.

The greatness of people—our freedom, creativity, ability to soar above the world by our spirit—and yet our bondage to the natural environment as creatures of the earth leave us perplexed about our own nature. The great questions all humans ask—Who am I? Where did I come from? What is the purpose of my existence?—can never be answered from the study of nature. Only a revelation from our Creator can answer our questions. And nowhere except in the Bible do we find a picture of human nature that accounts for the reality of human existence.

We are creatures of the earth (Gen. 2:7), but we are also formed in the image of God (1:27). We belong to this world, and therefore we must labor to maintain the natural environment as our physical home. But we are also made for fellowship with God, and therefore we can never be satisfied by nature alone.

But the problem of human identity stems not only from our nature as created beings. It also arises from sin. If we are in the image of God, why do we not act like God? Again the Bible provides the answer in a way that we would not expect from people writing on their own. According to the Scriptures our dignity is marred by sin, sin for which we are responsible. To be sure, we recognize our failure to do what we ought. We must recognize our "inhumanity" against others. But without divine revelation people try to explain this flaw by some lack of knowledge or some evolutionary vestige of animal aggression. All such explanations sidestep full responsibility; they do not acknowledge willful rebellion against God. When sin is viewed as the mere pitiful product of our evolutionary environment, then human beings become less than human.

The Bible, however, declares that we are responsible sinners. It upholds the dignity of human freedom, the power to act, and the perversity of human conduct. Human beings are great, but they are fallen in sin. The Scriptures, moreover, present the human condition in perfect candor. While they do not major on depravity, even the heroes of the faith cannot hide their weaknesses. People are presented as sinners in need of God's salvation.

Perhaps the Bible's description of the inner turmoil in our consciousness gives the most profound evidence of its supernatural knowledge of our human nature. Robert Dabney writes of Scripture's picture of "the profound and melancholy revelation of our inner consciousness," including the emptiness of earthly pursuits to which we are impelled by a perverted heart, the sinful transgressions of our own consciences and the desire, yet inability, to realize moral renewal.[23] Then he poignantly asks, "By what wisdom is it that this book hath revealed an insight so much deeper, more honest, and more searching, than any human philosophy, into the abyss of our miserable consciousness? When man's guilty soul avouches its truth in every groan of his remorse and his anguish, does it not appear obviously the utterance of him whose eyes behold, whose eyelids try the heart of the children of men?"[24]

THE BIBLICAL CONCEPT OF SALVATION

All religions offer some means to free human life of suffering and to provide peace and well-being. But the salvation revealed in Scriptures points uniquely to a divine source. The diverse means of "salvation" found in the world's religions are all based on one concept: Deliverance comes through human efforts. This is illustrated in the following story about some Hindus.

> We turned away from the river and came to an open stretch of land, a stony path between fields, hemmed in by low clay walls and thorny shrubs. It began to be hot. Every step kicked up dust. After a short while we came upon a young man, lying flat on the ground and apparently doing some gymnastic exercises. He got up, reached back with his left hand as far as he could, picked up a stone from a small heap lying there, stretched himself flat on the ground, reached with his right forward as far as possible and put the stone there on a similar small heap of stones. . . . Dr. Govindam explained to me that the young man was not allowed to speak as long as he was occupied with this especially meritorious form of parikrama (circumambulation). On a particular spot of 108 pebbles had to be collected and then moved, as shown by the young man, pebble by pebble, the length of the body at a time. After all 108 pebbles have been moved the distance of about two steps, one starts all over again. How long does it take to make the pilgrimage in this manner? Weeks, perhaps months. We passed other devout people who had chosen this penance, among them an old widow.

> Dr. Govindam explained to us that she was probably doing it to gain merit that would profit her husband in the other world. . . . Weeks later I saw her still at it, a few kilometers ahead of the spot where we had first discovered her. She seemed so weak that after every twenty meters she remained lying exhausted next to her small pile of stones.[25]

Whether by the Hindu way of righteousness, the eightfold discipline of Buddhism's "Middle Way," or the praying and fasting of Muslims, all nonbiblical religions seek to earn salvation by works. The popular idea is that entrance into heaven is gained by "doing the best I can." This is easy to understand when we realize that consciously or unconsciously people in their fallen nature are in bondage to sin, the attitude seen in the first sin, "You will be like God" (Gen. 3:5). It is difficult for a "god" to acknowledge that he cannot do anything for himself.

In some religions, however, people believe in savior-gods who give salvation to their adherents. The most widely accepted form of Buddhism in Japan is based on the story of Amita, who accumulated such a vast store of merit on his way to Buddhahood that he vowed to give rebirth in paradise to all who sincerely trust in him and constantly repeat "Hail Amita-Buddha."[26] The concept of savior-gods was also widespread in ancient Egypt and Mesopotamia.

However, even if people believe in gods who save, they still believe that works are necessary to earn the gods' favor. Moreover, they have no means of dealing seriously with the obvious reality of sin. As Leon Morris points out, "The deepest thinkers among mankind have always thought that real forgiveness is possible only when due regard is paid to the moral law. . . . Should we not see this as something God has implanted deep down in the human heart? Faced with a revolting crime even the most careless among us are apt to say, 'That deserves to be punished!' "[27] There is no such satisfying sense of justice in false religions.

How different is the salvation depicted in the Bible! The natural desire of people to earn merit is completely absent; all glory in salvation belongs to God. The historical reality of sin and its punishment are fully upheld. Salvation is worked out by God's infinite love in a way that completely preserves His infinite holiness. God's holiness demands satisfaction in the punishment of sin; and His love provides that satisfaction in the sacrifice of His Son. God "displayed [Christ, His very Son] publicly as a propitiation [satisfaction] in his blood . . . to demonstrate His righteousness . . . that He might be just and the justifier of the one who has faith in Jesus" (Rom. 3:25–26). Thus contrary to remedies for the human misery of sin that attempt to somehow find restoration out of fallen nature itself, which is impossible, or remedies that set aside God's holiness and justice and deem sinful people as blessed, biblical salvation comprehensibly deals with the deep problem of human sin. "It proposes to engage the omnipotence, love and wisdom of God himself, both to satisfy divine justice, and to restore man's ruin in sin; so that the deliverance shall meet fully every demand of offended heaven, and every necessity of fallen humanity, and endow us with a new blessedness as righteous as it is precious, and as everlasting as it is righteous."[28]

The death of the very Son of God, as the means of salvation, is contrary to all other religions. Ajith Fernando, a Christian scholar who has served for years in Sri Lanka, tells of a "well-known Buddhist writer" who informed him that "Buddha was superior to Jesus because even though Jesus lived a noble life, He was defeated through death in His battle for righteousness."[29] *The Jewish Encyclopedia* asserts, "No Messiah that Jews could recognize could suffer such a death; for 'He that is hanged is accursed of God'(Deut. 21:23), 'an insult to God' (Targum, Rashi)."[30] Muslims likewise reject the crucifixion of Christ. The Koran says, "They declared: 'We have put to death the Messiah Jesus, the son of Mary, the Apostle of Allah.' They did not kill him, nor did they crucify him, but they thought they did" (Sura 4:156). Clearly the cross of Christ, as Paul wrote, is "to Jews a stumbling block, and to Gentiles foolishness" (1 Cor. 1:23). But yet it is "the power of God and the wisdom of God" for salvation (1:24).

Moreover, God's salvation is rooted not in mythical stories or enlightening ideas, but in history. Gresham Machen's words summarize the uniqueness of the Bible's teaching of salvation. "Salvation then, according to the Bible, is not something that was discovered, but something that happened. Hence appears the uniqueness of the Bible. All ideas of Christianity might be discovered in some other religions, yet there would be in that other religion no Christianity. For Christianity depends, not upon a complex of ideas, but upon the narration of an event. Without that event, the world, in the Christ view, is altogether dark, and humanity is lost under the guilt of sin. There can be no salvation by the discovery of eternal truth, for eternal truth brings naught but despair, because of sin. But a new face has been put upon life by the blessed thing that God did when he offered his only begotten son."[31]

Such salvation is so strange to the natural man and yet so grand and satisfying to the deep aspirations in the hearts of all people that it cannot have been authored by mere humans. Paul, who had so earnestly attempted to save himself by human works, summed up the supernaturalness of God's salvation: "For God has shut up all in disobedience that He might show mercy to all. Oh, the depth of the riches both of the wisdom and knowledge of God! How unsearchable are His judgments and unfathomable His ways!" (Rom. 11:32–33).

Six

Within this awful volume lies
The mystery of mysteries;
Happiest he of human race
To whom God has given Grace
To read, to fear, to hope, to pray.
To lift the latch, and learn the way;
And better had he ne'er been born
Who reads to doubt, or reads to scorn.[1]

—Sir Walter Scott

Six

How Else Is the Bible Unique?

THE BIBLE'S PROPHECIES, unity, survival, and influence—these four additional factors also demonstrate the unique supernatural character of the Scriptures.

THE EVIDENCE OF PROPHECY

Nowhere is the uniqueness of the Bible more evident than in the supernatural nature of its prophecies. People, ancient and modern, have always sought to know the events of the future. Their diviners, astrologers, psychics, and fortunetellers pronounced what would take place. But in none of these is there any comparison with the prophecies of Scripture. God challenged the false gods to declare the future. "Let them bring forth and declare to us what is going to take place . . . or announce to us what is coming. Declare the things that are going to come afterward, that we may know that you are gods" (Isa. 41:22–23). What the false gods were unable to do, God does: "I declared the former things long ago" (48:3).

True, some people other than biblical prophets have been able to make amazing predictions beyond the ability of mere human guessing. But none compare with the prophets of Scripture. Some have predicted certain events in the near future that came true. But which modern-day prophet or psychic has ever predicted as numerous prophecies about nations, peoples, cities, and individuals as the Bible, some of which looked hundreds and even thousand of years into the future? Or which prophets other than the true prophets of Scripture have made predictions that to date have all been verified by history? The Scriptures boldly label as "false" every prophet whose predictions do not come to pass (Deut. 18:20–22). By this standard the Bible stands alone. As René Pache says, "Prophecy without divine inspiration can be a risky business."[2] Interestingly the sacred books of other religions contain very little prophecy in comparison with the Bible.

Prominent among the prophetic themes of the Bible are the prophecies relating to the nation of Israel. A few of these, predicted in some cases hundreds of years before the fact, include oppression in another land (Egypt) for four hundred years (Gen. 15:13–16), kings from Judah (49:10), distinction from other peoples (Num. 23:9), dispersion and suffering because of unbelief (Deut. 28:64–67; Luke 21:20–24), and continued preservation and final restoration (Ezek. 36–37; Amos 9:9–15; Rom. 11:25–29). These latter prophecies have yet to be completely fulfilled. But the unique historical event of 1948, the reestablishment of the nation Israel after its people had been dispersed for centuries, points to the fact that these biblical prophecies about Israel's being preserved and restored are indeed possible.

Also many prophecies about gentile nations were fulfilled, including the destruction of Nineveh (Zeph. 2:13–15; Nahum) and the fall of Babylon, Medo-Persia, Greece, and Rome (Dan. 2, 7, 8). Ezekiel's prediction about the city of Tyre is amazingly accurate (Ezek. 26:3–12, 14, 21). Ezekiel prophesied that "many nations" like waves of the sea would be brought against the city; Tyre would be made like a "bare rock," "a place for the spreading of nets in the midst of the sea." Nebuchadnezzar, king of Babylon, would besiege the city and destroy it; they would "throw your stones and your timbers and your debris into the water"; and Tyre would "be built no more" and not "found again."

History records the complete fulfillment of these rather complex predictions. Just a few years after Ezekiel's words Nebuchadnezzar besieged the city and after thirteen years he destroyed it. But much of the population of Tyre had moved by boat to an island about one-half mile offshore, where Tyre continued as a strong city for several hundred years. When Babylon declined in power, Tyre again regained her independence but was conquered by the Persians not long after. Her subsequent history gives clear evidence of the fulfillment of the coming of "many nations" against her. Being forced to submit to one conqueror after another until finally she fell to the Saracens in the fourteenth century A.D., Tyre never again regained any importance. The great city was never "built" or "found" again.

An interesting detail in Ezekiel's prophecy pertains to the throwing of Tyre's stones, timbers, and debris into the sea. Nebuchadnezzar besieged the mainland city for more than a decade, demolishing its walls, towers, and "settlements on the mainland" (26:6, NIV). But he passed by the island part of the city. Alexander the Great, on the other hand, was determined to take all of Tyre. To do so, in 332 B.C. he built a causeway out to the island, using material from the old city, throwing its stones, timbers, and debris into the water, leaving the old city like a "bare rock."[3]

Most significant is the detailed predictions pertaining to the Messiah, which are incredible apart from divine inspiration. From the details of the place of His birth in insignificant Bethlehem (Mic. 5:2) to the casting of lots for His clothing at the foot of the cross (Ps. 22:14–18; Matt. 27:35), the events of His life were foretold hundreds of years before they occurred. Daniel Rose, once the head of the Jewish Department of the Bible Institute of Los Angeles and the person for whom the present library building at Biola University is named, told a Jewish friend one day, "I want to read you a portion of the Bible, and when I am finished I want you to tell me from what part of it I have been reading." Rose then read from Isaiah 52 and 53.

When he finished, he closed the book and asked his Jewish friend to tell him from what portion of the Bible he had read. The man replied without hesitation, "The New Testament." Rose then asked, "To whom does the passage refer?" "To Jesus of Nazareth," his friend replied. Then Rose showed his friend that he had been reading from the Old Testament prophecy of Isaiah.[4] The prophecy was so clear that even one who did not at the time believe in Jesus as the Messiah easily recognized this prophecy as fulfilled in Him!

Oxford University scholar H. P. Liddon noted that the Old Testament has 332 distinct predictions that were literally fulfilled in Christ.[5] The probability of that number of predictions concerning one single individual coming true has been calculated as 1 out of 83 billion. With such odds, clearly these prophecies are not the product of human authorship alone. The God who knows the future and directs the course of history is the ultimate source.

Also the purposes of the Bible's prophecies differ from the divinations of people. Curiosity and the desire for power are the mainsprings of fortunetelling. But God discloses the future of nations and people for the purpose of revealing Himself and His will. Biblical prophecy is not designed to help God's people set dates, but to help them understand His plan for history so that they might align their lives with Him and His purposes. Thus prophecy marks the Bible as a unique writing.

THE UNITY OF THE BIBLE

Josh McDowell, a popular Christian speaker on university campuses, tells the story of encountering a representative of the *Great Books of the Western World.* This set includes the writings of many of the outstanding thinkers who shaped Western civilization, beginning with ancient Greek philosophers and continuing to recent times. Referring to these books, Josh challenged the representative to take just ten of the authors, all from the same walk of life, the same time period, the same place, the same language, and pose of them one question, "Would they agree in their views?" The gentleman paused for a moment and then replied, "No! You would have a conglomeration."[6]

When we compare this diversity of human thought by only ten authors with the unity found in the Bible, the evidence for its supernaturalness is overwhelming. The Bible consists of the writings of more than forty people. From all walks of life—including kings, herdsmen, poets, philosophers, statesmen, legislators, fishermen, priests, and prophets—these people wrote over a time span of more than fifteen hundred years. They lived in diverse cultures, and wrote in a variety of literary styles. But the message of the Bible is one great drama in which all the parts fit together.

From "Paradise Lost" in Genesis to "Paradise Regained" in Revelation, the Bible presents the unfolding of God's great purpose for the human race that is worked out through His Son. Jesus Himself said that the Scriptures bear witness of Him (John 5:39). Christ and His work form the cord that ties all of Scripture together.

The Bible may be compared to the human body in which every part can only be explained in reference to the whole. So the great variety of books of the Bible have their meaning only as they are parts of the book. Such a work, encompassing the lives of generations of individuals, can only be accounted for by another Author, the Spirit of God, who is forever the same. The psalmist wrote, "The sum of Thy Word is truth, and every one of Thy righteous ordinances is everlasting" (Ps. 119:160).

THE SURVIVAL OF THE BIBLE

No book in human history has been preserved as well as the Bible. The preservation of its text alone is unique, especially when we realize that it was copied without the benefit of printing presses or copy machines. No ancient manuscript has been preserved in the way the Jews preserved the Old Testament writings. Special classes of men kept tabs on every letter, syllable, word, and paragraph in order to preserve and transmit these documents faithfully. No other ancient work comes close to this attestation.[7] Much of the New Testament can be reproduced from quotations from the early Christian writers. In fact, the text of the Bible is more sure today than the text of Shakespeare's plays.[8]

When compared to other books, the simple fact that the Bible has survived and continues to be the most popular book in the world after thousands of years is unique. But this is doubly so when we realize that since it was written, many people have attempted to get rid of it. Jehoiakim, the king of Judah, threw the scroll of Jeremiah's prophecy into a fire. But God simply had His prophet write the same words again with additional material (Jer. 36:21–32). Jehoiakim's action is illustrative of many attempts to destroy God's written Word, only to have it flourish more.

In the persecution of the Jews under Antiochus Epiphanes in the second century B.C., the Pentateuch, the first five books of the Old Testament, was torn up and burned. "Anyone found possessing the book of the covenant . . . was condemned to death by the decree of the king" (1 Maccabees 1:56–57). We have already noted in the Introduction the attempt by Emperor Diocletian early in the fourth century of the church to rid the Roman Empire of the Bible, only to have it exalted a few years later by Emperor Constantine. Since that time the Bible has faced opposition in many places. As late as the nineteenth century the government of Korea tried to keep the Bible out of that land, but the presence of a vital church there today demonstrates its failure. Only decades ago the Bible had to be smuggled into the Soviet Union, but today the Scriptures are welcomed there.

The story of a patient in the American hospital in Turkey about the middle of the twentieth century depicts the amazing unstoppable nature of the Word of God. When he was dismissed from the hospital, he took the Bible someone had given him back to his town and proudly displayed it to his friends. A Muslim teacher snatched it from him, tore out its pages, and threw them into the street. The young man was afraid to pick them up. But a passing grocer did and used the pages for wrapping paper. Before long they were scattered all over town. His customers read the pages and returned for more. In a few days the entire Bible was distributed to interested readers. When a Bible colporteur came to the town sometime later he was surprised to find one hundred persons eager to buy the Bible.[9] History demonstrates over and over the truth of God's promise in Isaiah 55:11: "My Word . . . shall not return to Me empty, without accomplishing what I desire, and without succeeding in the matter for which I sent it."

At times the attack against the Word took the form of restricting its dissemination. Thinking that they were serving God, church leaders attempted to keep the Bible out of the hands of ordinary people. When Jerome completed his translation of the Bible from Hebrew and Greek into Latin in A.D. 405 so that the ordinary person of his day could read it, he was assailed by the bishop of his time. People accused him of tampering with the Word of God and promoting his own ideas. But his Latin version became the Bible of Europe.

Ten centuries later Oxford University professor John Wycliffe (1320–1384) sought to give the English people a Bible they could read. Both church and state leaders did everything they could to prevent it, because they said ordinary people could not understand it. Archbishop Arundel, in a letter to the pope, described Wycliffe as "that Pestilent wretch, John Wycliffe, the son of the old Serpent, the forerunner of Antichrist, who has completed his iniquity by inventing a new translation of the Scriptures."[10] Those who possessed copies of Wycliffe's Bible were hunted down and burned at the stake with their Scriptures about their neck. But its quickening power spread through Britain and continental Europe.

Later, after the invention of the printing press, William Tyndale (around 1494–1536) put the Bible into the language of his time which had changed considerably since Wycliffe's day. Priests and bishops burned thousands of copies of his translation as "a burnt offering most pleasing to Almighty God." Tyndale was finally strangled and burned at the stake. His last words were, "Lord, open the King of England's eyes!" In less than three years King Henry VIII authorized the publication of the Great Bible, a combination of Tyndale's version and that of Miles Coverdale (1488–1569). A copy of the Great Bible was chained in every parish church in England so that all of the people might read it.[11] Tyndale's prayer was answered. For many centuries and in many countries, simply reading a translation of the Bible meant the person would be excommunicated, or possessing a copy of the Bible would result in death. But even this attempt to restrict the spread of God's Word was futile.

The same blatant frontal assaults attempting to squelch the Word of God through physical destruction did not continue in the "civilized" cultures of the modern Western world. But the attack continued in the form of undermining and ridiculing the trustworthiness of the Scriptures by so-called enlightened skeptical and atheistic philosophers and liberal biblical scholars. Although more subtle, the goal was the same—to discredit the Bible so that it would be neglected and discarded.

French humanist Voltaire (1694–1778) boastfully proclaimed, "Fifty years from now the world will hear no more of the Bible." Yet in the year of his boast the British Museum purchased a manuscript of the Greek New Testament from the Russian government for $500,000, while a first edition of Voltaire's book was selling for eight cents a copy! Fifty years after the death of Voltaire, Bibles were being printed by the Geneva Bible Society in the very house where Voltaire had lived and on his own printing presses!

Atheist Thomas Paine (1737–1809) predicted that the Bible would soon be out of print. "When I get through," he announced, "there will not be five Bibles left in America." With the current variety of translations and editions available, many individuals today have more than that number themselves. Criticism of the Bible from the highest learned scholarship continues unabated, but the Word of God runs free throughout the world as never before.

"No other book has been so chopped, knived, sifted, scrutinized, and vilified. What book on philosophy or religion or psychology or *belles lettres* of classical or modern times has been subject to such a mass attack as the Bible? With such venom and skepticism, with such thoroughness and erudition? Upon chapter, line, and tenet?"[12] "A thousand times over, the death knell of the Bible has been sounded, the funeral procession formed, the inscriptions cut on the tombstone, and the committal read. But somehow the corpse never stays put."[13]

The French Protestants known as Huguenots portrayed the Bible and Christianity as an anvil surrounded by three blacksmiths. Beneath the picture they inscribed these words: "The more they pound and the more they shout, the more they wear their hammers out!" From kings to critics the attackers wear different faces, their assaults take different strategies, but they all pass from the scene to be replaced by others who shall likewise be gone. But as the Word of God itself affirms, it remains forever.

- Forever, O Lord, Thy word is settled in heaven. (Ps. 119:89)
- Of old I have known from Thy testimonies, that Thou hast founded them forever. (119:152)
- Heaven and earth will pass away, but My words shall not pass away. (Matt. 24:35)
- The grass withers, and the flower falls off, but the Word of the Lord abides forever. (1 Pet. 1:24–25)

THE INFLUENCE OF THE BIBLE

No book compares with the influence of the Bible in human history. It has impacted every important realm of human society, as evident in its presence in every sort of writing—historical, juridical, legislative, social, moral, and biographical. "If every Bible in any considerable city were destroyed," McAfee writes, "the Book could be restored in all its essential parts from the quotations on the shelves of the city public library."[14] Ralph Waldo Emerson, a wide reader of the best writings of the world, though far from an evangelical believer, described the Bible as "the most original book in the world," and he said that "all elevation of thought clothes itself in the words and forms of thought of that book."[15]

The only explanation for this supremacy of stature lies in the unique influence of the Bible in numerous human societies. It is the "living and active" Word of God (Heb. 4:12), and the instrument God uses to transform a life radically, as one is "born again . . . through the living and abiding Word of God" (1 Pet. 1:23). It is "the Word of life" (Phil. 2:16), and its message of the gospel is "the power of God for salvation" (Rom. 1:16). Its truths promise to set men free from bondage (8:31–32).

Throughout history the Bible verifies these claims. No other book has had comparable impact for good. The great books of human learning have helped us to understand better the world in which we live, but none has helped to change individuals themselves. Many have pointed out the tragic fact that while the extent of our knowledge has exploded in the last century, we seem less capable than ever before of loving one another and finding peace among nations. The endless parade of wars and revolutions is evidence that human learning does not change the heart when it enlarges the mind.

Even the influential writings of other religions have never resulted in lifting and transforming the lives of individuals. For the most part, they give people rules of life, but the power to effect these rules is absent. In many cases they only produce a kind of stoic acceptance of present miseries.

The Bible's influence on human societies produces unique results, as seen in the changes in the fundamental laws of Western societies since Roman times, the social reforms, the raised status of women, the freeing of slaves, and other transformations. As someone has said, "The gospel in the world is freedom's immortal seed."

But more important than its influence for political freedom is its ability to bring freedom from the power of sin. As noted in chapter 1, the

Bible has power to bring life to individuals, as seen in the examples of Augustine and Luther. This could be multiplied by countless people from all walks of life who have testified and given proof in their lives that studying and meditating on God's Word has a transforming effect that no other writing produces.

Even entire societies have been transformed by the Bible. For example, in 1790 the crew of an English vessel named *The Bounty* took over the ship and put their officers adrift. Nine of the mutineers along with six men and twelve women from Tahiti sailed off to Pitcairn Island, which had been discovered only twenty-three years earlier and was uninhabited. There they learned to distill alcohol from a native plant, and as a result the island became a hell on earth. Drunkenness brought disease, wild orgies, and brutality. It also brought bloody massacres so that by 1800 all six Tahitian men and all the English mutineers except one, Alexander Smith, who later changed his name to John Adams, had perished.

A remarkable thing then happened. Going through a dead sailor's chest on the wrecked *Bounty*, Adams came across a Bible. Reading it, he became convicted of his sins. He repented and determined to live a godly life. He began teaching the Bible to the Tahitian women and their children. A few years passed, and in 1808 an American ship called on the island and found a prosperous peaceful Christian society free of disease, immorality, and crime. The offspring of mutineers, drunken revelers, and murderers had been transformed into people of kindness and gentleness, living together in a community of peace as a result of nothing but the teaching of the Word of God.

An honest evaluation of human history will inevitably have to conclude with Tiplady's words. "No other book has ever so completely changed the course of human destiny. In light and power the Bible stands by itself. . . . Where it shines, life and beauty spring to birth. It is the Supreme Book of power."[16]

CONCLUSION

The evidences discussed in this and the preceding chapter leave little question about the uniqueness of the Bible among all human writings, including the most revered scriptures of other religions. Sir Monier-Williams's comparison of the Bible with the sacred books of the East sums up the Bible's uniqueness in comparison to all other writings. As a professor of Sanskrit, Monier-Williams spent forty-two years studying the sacred books of Eastern religions. He said that at first he was impressed by the flashes of truth he found scattered among these writings and began to think they shared the message of the Scriptures of Christianity, but to a lesser degree. After further study, however, he completely reversed his thinking, concluding that the main ideas were radically different. "They all begin," he said, "with some flashes of true light, end in utter darkness."[17] He said you could pile them all on the left side of a desk but place the Bible on the right side with a wide gap between them. This would illustrate, he pointed out, the difference between the Bible and all other religious writings and the Bible's uniqueness and superiority.[18]

As Lewis Sperry Chafer, the founder and first president of Dallas Theological Seminary, observed, "The Bible is not such a book a man would write if he *could*, or could write if he *would*."[19] But beyond its content, the Bible is recognized as the most influential book in human history because it has a unique ability to grip the human soul at its deepest level. All this demands the conclusion that the Bible is not the product of human minds, but is a revelation from beyond us—from God Himself.

Seven

How can I close without expression of thanks to him who has loved us so as to give us so pure a record of His will,—God-given in all its parts, even though cast in the forms of human speech,—infallible in all its statements,—divine even to its smallest particle! . . . Let us bless God . . . for His inspired Word! And may He grant that we may always cherish, love and venerate it, and form all our life and thinking to it! So we may find safety for our feet, and peaceful security for our souls.[1]

—Benjamin B. Warfield

Seven

Is the Bible the Inspired Word of God?

IN CONTRAST to the pagan idol gods who "have mouths, but . . . cannot speak" (Pss. 115:5; 135:15–16), "whose devotees cry to them, but they cannot answer" (Isa. 46:7), the God of the Bible communicates with His people through words. The very nature of God involves self-expression through speech. "In the beginning was the Word, and the Word was with God, and the Word was God" (John 1:1). It is not surprising, therefore, that He communicated with His people throughout history in word, as the writer to Hebrews declared. "God, after He spoke long ago to the fathers in the prophets in many portions and in many ways, in these last days has spoken to us in His Son" (Heb. 1:1–2). Since the Christian God is a speaking God, does He still speak to His people today? And if so, where or how can we hear His voice?

According to the writer of Hebrews, prophets under the control of the Holy Spirit spoke and wrote God's words. This climaxed in God's Son, who not only spoke the word as a prophet, but was Himself the very Word of God manifest in history. As we will see in this chapter, God's prophetic word was written down and preserved in sacred writings known as the Scriptures. As a result God's people both in the Old and New Testaments have identified the Scriptures as "the Word of God."

Throughout church history believers have seldom questioned this fact. But with the Enlightenment, which exalted human reason in the search for truth through the so-called scientific method, this fact came to be denied by many. To some the Bible is only a record of human religious experience. Others identify parts of the Bible as God's Word, portions such as those introduced by the formula "Thus says the Lord," or "The Word of the Lord came to . . . , saying." Many people say the Bible only contains or witnesses to the Word, but is not the Word itself. They say that only when the Holy Spirit speaks to them through the Word does the Bible then *become* the Word of God.

This is a critical issue. For if the Bible is the very Word of God, then despite its human form, we have God's Word in objective, concrete form and as His creatures we must obey it. On the other hand, if the Bible is only a human word, perhaps exalted in some way, then we must somehow search for the Word of God in and behind the fallible human words, or perhaps, as some suggest, even in other religious writings.

This chapter discusses the Bible's own testimony about its nature. This may seem like circular reasoning, seeking to determine the nature of the Bible by its own claims. More will be said about this method in our discussion of inerrancy in chapter 10. But two points in response may be noted here.

First, if we permit a person to speak for himself and do not offhandedly dismiss his testimony as false, can't we also permit the Bible to speak for itself? Even though Jesus had other witnesses, He testified for Himself. "Even if I bear witness of Myself," He told the Pharisees, "My witness is true" (John 8:14). The truthworthiness of the Bible is attested by external and internal proofs. It deserves to be heeded, therefore, in its claims for itself.

Second, Christians know that the Bible is the basis of all the great doctrines of the faith, such as the deity of Christ and salvation through His death and resurrection. If we accept the Scriptures as our guide to truth in these areas, should we not also accept the teachings of the Bible about its own nature?

THE MEANING OF "THE WORD OF GOD"

To say "the Bible is the Word of God" is not to say that the Word of God is limited to Scripture. God's speech is manifest in various forms. For example, the psalmist wrote, "He sends forth His command to the earth; His *word* runs very swiftly. He gives snow like wool; He scatters the frost like ashes. He casts forth His ice as fragments; who can stand before His cold? He sends forth His *word* and melts them; He causes His wind to blow and the waters to flow" (Ps. 147:15–18, italics added). Clearly the "word" in this passage is not the Bible. And in the statement "The Word became flesh, and dwelt among us" (John 1:14), the Word refers to Christ.

The Word of God is thus broader than oral or written revelation. It can be defined as God's self-expression, which according to Scripture takes a variety of forms. First, it is the *power* of God by which he effects and controls all things according to His will (for example, creation, Gen. 1:3; Ps. 33:6–9; judgment, 46:6; Is. 30:30; healing, Matt. 8:8). Second, it is the *authoritative speech* of God by which He communicates with His personal creatures. Interestingly, after using "word" for the exertion of God's will over nature in the statement above from Psalm 147, we read, "He declares His words to Jacob, His statutes and His ordinances to Israel" (147:19). Third, the word of God is the personal *presence* of God with His creatures. One's person is, of course, revealed in his or her speech (see Matt. 12:34). So Scripture informs us that "the LORD revealed Himself to Samuel . . . by [His] word" (1 Sam. 3:21). But this third usage goes beyond words to the manifestation of God in the person of His Son, Jesus Christ, the Word (John 1:1, 14; Rev. 19:13). This last use brings us to the profound truth that the "word" of God is nothing less than the self-revelation of the triune God. "God the Father is the one who speaks; the Son is the word spoken; the Spirit is that mighty breath . . . that drives that word to accomplish its purpose."[2]

THE TESTIMONY OF THE OLD TESTAMENT

As the Bible records the history of God's relationship with people, it is not surprising that in the Old Testament we find frequent mention of God's word as *verbal communication*. He not only speaks, but His word is conveyed through human instruments, so that what they say and write are God's words.

God's Word Spoken

Several Hebrew words are used in the Old Testament to express God's speech or words. God's "mouth" is mentioned about fifty times as the organ of speech, emphasizing not only the direct source of His words but also their nature as speech. Jeremiah's message came from "the mouth of the LORD" (Jer. 9:12). A "prophet" is one who speaks the words from the mouth of another. This is made clear in the incident when Moses complained of his lack of fluency of speech and Aaron became his spokesman. "You are to speak to him," God told Moses, "and put the words in his mouth . . . he shall speak for you to the people; and it shall come about that he shall be as a mouth for you, and you shall be as God to him" (Exod. 4:15–16). God later identified this ministry of Aaron with Moses in these words: "your brother Aaron shall be your prophet" (7:1).

In the same way God told Jeremiah, "All that I command you, you shall speak. . . . Behold, I have put My words in your mouth" (Jer. 1:7–9). Later Jeremiah said a true prophet is one who "has stood in the council of the Lord that he should see and hear His word" and thus announce "My words to My people" (23:18, 22).

Prophets spoke as the Lord's "spokesmen," or as God said to Jeremiah, "as My mouth" (15:19, KJV). His warnings of judgment and promises of salvation are sure because "the mouth of the LORD has spoken" (Isa. 1:20; 40:5). The "mouth of the Lord" is often translated "word" or "command," thereby emphasizing the verbal nature of God's revelation. "So Moses numbered them according to the word [literally, 'mouth'] of the LORD" (Num. 3:16). "Then all the . . . sons of Israel journeyed by stages . . . according to the command [literally, 'mouth'] of the LORD" (Exod. 17:1). The actions of the tribes of Israel that stayed on the east side of the Jordan were "according to the command [literally, 'mouth'] of the LORD through Moses" (Josh. 22:9). Of interest in this last example is the fact that we have no record of God commanding Moses about the leaders of the tribes of Reuben, Gad, and the half-tribe of Manasseh. Moses simply gave his own instructions to them (see Num. 32:20–24). But as the prophet of God, the words from his mouth were also from the "mouth" of the Lord; they were God's words.

God's speaking in the Old Testament is also frequently expressed by the verb *ʾāmar* ("to speak or say") and its related nouns, *ʾēmer*, *ʾemrâ*, and *ʾimrâ*, translated variously as "speech," "utterance," or "word." The verb *ʾāmar* always expresses a personal relationship in which a person utters "reasonable statements . . . which may be heard and understood by others."[3] When used of God, it refers to revelation. "The expressions 'God has spoken (said),' 'God speaks (says),' and 'God will speak (say),' imply that God can be heard in the realm of nature and history, the arena of human experience and understanding. . . . [He] has the power to speak so that he can be understood."[4] Thus God often conveyed His will to people by the spoken word (for example, "God spoke to Noah"; Gen. 8:15). "Thus says [*ʾāmar*] the LORD," is a common formula in the prophets (over 130 times in Jeremiah alone), signifying that they are conveying a message much like a human messenger carrying a message.[5] The related nouns for "speech" or "word" are also used for the *content* of God's speaking (for example, Job 22:22; 23:12; Ps. 77:8; Isa. 41:26). Of particular interest is the fact that *ʾimrâ* ("word") occurs nineteen times in Psalm 119. Used with other terms like "statutes," "commandments," "testimonies," and "precepts," it is clear that the psalmist meant more than some personal subjective revelation from God. The "word" of God was the written Scriptures by which many blessings had been passed on to the psalmist.

The most common Old Testament word for "speaking" is the verb *dābar.* Its corresponding noun, "word," also means "thing," "matter," "affair," as in the "matter about which one speaks."[6] The verb *dābar* focuses on the activity of speaking, that is, the producing of words and sentences. But this does not detract from the importance of *what* is spoken. This is evident from the content of such "speaking," for in the Scriptures these terms are the most common ones used of God speaking His word. About four hundred times statements like "the LORD said," "the LORD promised," and "the LORD commanded" occur, in which the verb translates *dābar.*

Dābar is especially prominent in relationship to God's word through the prophets. God spoke to His prophets as Isaiah testified. "And again the LORD spoke to me" (Isa. 8:5; see also Jer. 36:2, 4; Ezek. 3:10). But His speech came not simply *to* the prophets. It also came *through* them to others (for example, the Lord spoke "through Isaiah . . . saying" (Isa. 20:2; see also Exod. 9:35; 1 Kings 12:15; Jer. 37:2; Ezek. 38:17). Thus the reception of God's word by the prophets and its proclamation can be seen as a speech-act by God. As David said, "The Spirit of the LORD spoke by me, and His word was on my tongue" (2 Sam. 23:2). Isaiah spoke to Ahaz the word that he had received from God, but the same process is described when we read, "Then the LORD spoke again to Ahaz, saying" (Isa. 7:10; see also 7:3–4).

The "words" that the prophets spoke were therefore "the word of the LORD." Occurring approximately 240 times in the Old Testament, this phrase describes both the word of God to the prophets and the word that they proclaimed to the people (for example, "The word of the LORD which came to Hosea" [Hos. 1:1; see also Mic. 1:1; Zeph. 1:1], and "Hear the word of the LORD" [Isa. 1:10; Amos 7:16]). The phrase is thus "a technical term for the prophetic word of revelation."[7]

Other uses of *dābar* for God's word are also found. Speaking to Moses, Aaron, and Miriam, God declared, "Hear now My words" (Num. 12:6). According to the psalmist, God "remembered His holy word" to Abraham (Ps. 105:42). Of significance is the description of the Ten Commandments as "the words of the covenant, the Ten Commandments [literally, 'the ten words']" (Exod. 34:28; see also Deut. 4:13; 10:4), and God's commands in general (for example, Ps. 50:17).

Clearly, then, God revealed Himself through verbal communication. God spoke to people, and their responsibility was to "hear" or "listen" to His voice.

God's Word Written

God's Word was also written. God Himself wrote down the fundamental principles of His covenant with His Old Testament people in the Ten Commandments, which "were all the words which the LORD had spoken" with Moses (Deut. 9:10; see also 10:4; 4:13; Exod. 24:12; 31:18; 32:15–16; 34:1). Frequently God commanded others to write. After Israel defeated Amalek, God told Moses, "Write this in a book as a memorial, and recite it to Joshua, that I will utterly blot out the memory of Amalek from under heaven" (Exod. 17:14). And God instructed Moses to write "this song," that is, "the Song of Moses," "that this song may be a witness for Me against the sons of Israel" (Deut. 31:19). Writing, as these instructions demonstrate, was for the purpose of preserving the words for future generations.

Moses wrote down the covenant provisions that God gave to Israel through him. After recounting "all the words of the LORD and all the ordinances" to the people, "Moses wrote down all of the words of the LORD" (Exod. 24:3–4). Again God said, "Write down these words, for in accordance with these words I have made a covenant with you and with Israel" (34:27). At the end of his earthly journey Moses repeated the words of the covenant with the people as they were about to cross the Jordan into the Promised Land (Deut. 29:1; 30:1). "And it came about when Moses finished writing the words of this law in a book until they were complete, that Moses commanded the Levites . . . 'Take this book of the law and place it beside the ark of the covenant of the LORD your God, that it may remain there as a witness against you' " (Deut. 31:24–26; see also 31:9). "This book of the law" was more than just various commandments and statutes. As we have seen, Moses wrote the account of the defeat of Amalek. And he also recorded the journey of the people from Egypt to Israel (Num. 33:2). "The book of the covenant," as it came to be known (2 Kings 23:2, 21; see 2 Chron. 34:14), was not simply the stipulations of the covenant; it also included the record of the activities of the members of the covenant. In his farewell Joshua recorded the renewal of the covenant with the people at Shechem, writing "these words in the book of the law of God" (Josh. 24:25–26). Later, historical records of the acts of Israel's kings were written by the prophets Samuel, Nathan, and Gad (1 Chron. 29:29).[8]

Instructions to write the Word of God were also given to the later prophets. The command to Isaiah is particularly instructive in that the purpose for writing is made explicit. "Now go, write it on a tablet before them and inscribe it on a scroll, that it may serve in the time to come as a witness forever" (Isa. 30:8). Isaiah's generation was a "rebellious people" (30:9) who rejected God's voice. But the speech of God through the prophet would retain its power as the Word of God in addressing later generations after Isaiah was dead (Isa. 8:1). Also Jeremiah and Habakkuk were instructed to write their prophecies (Jer. 30:2; 36:2–4, 27–32; Hab. 2:2). Other references indicate that the prophets wrote as well as spoke their messages (for example, Jer. 15:13; 45:1; 51:60). Even entire prophetic books are described as "the word of the LORD" (for example, Hos. 1:1; Mic. 1:1; Zeph. 1:1).

The Old Testament thus clearly testifies to the truth that God speaks His word through writing as well as by speaking. Moreover, entire writings, not just certain parts, are identified as God's Word. This becomes even clearer when we consider the attitude of Jesus and others in the New Testament toward the Old Testament writings. But the principle is already evident in the Old Testament itself. All the Pentateuch, not just some statements, are God's Word. Joshua was to do all that is written in "the book of the law" (Josh. 1:8), in which he himself had written words. Ezra read from "the book of the law of God daily" (Neh. 8:13). And the introduction of entire prophetic books with the statement, "The word of the Lord which came to . . . implies that the whole book is regarded as ['the word of the Lord']."[9] No distinction is made between statements in the book directly attributed to God and the historical comments of the prophet. "We have here a transition to the final view that not merely the prophetic book, but in the last resort the whole of the Old Testament, is the Word of God."[10]

THE TESTIMONY OF THE NEW TESTAMENT

Jesus as the Word of God

The Word of God reaches its climactic meaning in the New Testament when it is used for the person of Christ, the Son of God (John 1:1). More than a spoken or written word that conveys a conceptual message, God's Word is the very action of God Himself. For example, Christ came to fulfill the Law and the Prophets, not just by giving them their full meaning in His teaching but also by His life and death (Matt. 5:17). Thus He is "the end of the law for righteousness" (Rom. 10:4). The New Covenant is not present in His words, but in His blood (Matt. 26:28), in "what takes place in His person, in the life lived by Him."[11] Jesus is the prophesied Servant of the Lord who would be "a covenant for the people" (Isa. 42:6; 49:8, NIV). He brought the message of salvation, but more than that, He is our "righteousness and sanctification, and redemption" (1 Cor. 1:30), and "He Himself is our peace" (Eph. 2:14). Christ is therefore not simply the One who brings God's final Word; He "incorporates it in His person, in the historical process . . . of His life and being."[12]

Apostolic Preaching as the Word of God

The truth of Jesus being God's Word, however, does not eclipse the verbal word or make it any less the Word of God. Jesus Himself spoke "the words of God" (John 3:34: see also 7:16; 8:26–28). But more commonly the "word of God" (or the synonymous expressions "the word of the Lord" or "the word") is used, as noted in chapter 1, in the New Testament for the message that the early witnesses proclaimed. They spoke "the word of God with boldness" (Acts 4:31). Paul and Barnabas proclaimed "the word of God" in the synagogues at Salamis, where they were summoned by "the proconsul, Sergius Paulus, a man of intelligence" who "sought to hear the word of God" (13:5, 7). Later they returned to "visit the brethren in every city in which [they] proclaimed the word of the Lord" (15:36).

Paul settled in Corinth for eighteen months "teaching the word of God among them" (18:11). The believers at Thessalonica received "the word of God's message" that Paul proclaimed to them as "the word of God" (1 Thess. 2:13). The "living and abiding word of God," by which believers are "born again," was "the word which [Peter] preached" (1 Pet. 1:23, 25). "The word of God," "the word of the Lord," or "the word," are used almost eighty times of the message the early-church witnesses proclaimed about Jesus. In addition other verses refer to the apostles' teaching as "sound words" (1 Tim. 6:3) or "the word of truth" (Col. 1:5).

The Old Testament as the Word of God

The New Testament writers also testified to the written form of God's Word. Reminding Timothy that he had "known the sacred writings" from his childhood, the apostle Paul stated, "All Scripture is inspired by God" (2 Tim. 3:15–16). The words "all Scripture" could also be translated "every Scripture," referring to individual parts. But here, used in parallel with "sacred writings," the common name for the Old Testament among Greek-speaking Jews, Paul probably meant all Scripture as a whole. This would accord with his frequent personification of Scripture collectively in the phrase "Scripture says . . ." (for example, Rom. 4:3; 9:17; Gal. 4:30).

The word "inspired" here can be misleading. Two of its meanings in English are "to fill with an animating, quickening, or exalting influence" and "to produce or arouse (a feeling, thought, etc.)."[13] Both of these primary meanings suggest that "inspire" has the sense of producing or generating something in something else, suggesting in this case that God filled the Scriptures with His life and energy. While this is true and is taught in Hebrews 4:12, Paul was referring here not to the dynamic of the Scriptures, but to their source—from God.

"Inspired by God" translates *theopneustos*, a Greek word that combines the noun "God" (*theos*) and the adjective *pneustos* formed from the verb "to breathe" (*pneō*).[14] *Theopneustos* always has the passive meaning of "God-breathed" (NIV), not "God-breathing." The sense then is that the Scriptures are the product of the breath of God; they were breathed out by Him. The verse thus emphasizes the source of the Scriptures. But it also says something about their nature. Having their source in God, they are His words. It should be noted that although "all Scripture" in 2 Timothy 3:16 refers specifically to the Old Testament, the apostle's teaching also applies to the New Testament writings. They too were considered "Scripture" by the New Testament writers.

The New Testament often combines references to the Old Testament with the new message about Christ, calling both of them "the word of God." The writer of Hebrews no doubt included the entire Old Testament writings when he said God's Word is living and powerful (Heb. 4:12). Also when Paul preached, he often quoted the Old Testament to show that Jesus is the promised Messiah. His preaching of the Word of God therefore included the Old Testament (Col. 1:15).

Although the New Testament writers did not refer to the Old Testament as a whole as the "word of God," evidence abounds in the New Testament that they did consider the entire Old Testament as the very words of God. The New Testament often states that God spoke through human authors, who wrote the Old Testament. And of course the New Testament writers often said God spoke through human authors. For example, Matthew introduced the Old Testament prophecy of Jesus' virgin birth by writing, "Now all this took place that what was *spoken by the Lord through the prophet* might be fulfilled, saying, 'Behold, the virgin shall be with child'" (Matt. 1:22–23; italics added). In this instance and others, the Old Testament was said to be a communication directly from God (compare 2:15).Yet the Old Testament was God's Word even when the citation was the words of the Old Testament writer. For example, in Acts 4:25 Peter and John referred to God speaking "by the Holy Spirit" in Psalm

2:1–2, but these were actually David's words, for God spoke "through the mouth . . . of David." Christ came in fulfillment of what God spoke "by the mouth of His holy prophets from of old" (Luke 1:70). And Psalm 95:7–8 was words spoken by God "through David" (Heb. 4:7).

Sometimes portions of the Old Testament were said to have been spoken by God directly without any reference to the human author. One example is the Ten Commandments, which, Matthew and James said, were spoken by God, with no reference to Moses (Matt. 15:4; James 2:11). Also Paul said that God's Word that was addressed to Pharaoh (Exod. 9:16) was "the Scripture" (Rom. 9:17).

Conversely the Old Testament Scriptures are the Word of God even when God is not recorded as the speaker. An interesting illustration of the New Testament understanding of all Scripture as the speech or words of God is provided by the writer of Hebrews when he cited six Old Testament passages (Heb. 1:5–13). In introducing each of those quotations he wrote that God said those words. Yet in four of them (1:6, 7, 8–9, 10–12) the speaker in the Old Testament was actually someone else. Because these verses are part of the Old Testament Scriptures, they are all the words of God.

The New Testament as the Word of God

The Scriptures which the New Testament cites as "the word of God" are, of course, the sacred writings of the Old Testament. Can we also call the New Testament the Word of God? Since the process of writing and gathering together the New Testament writings was still going on, no statements describe the entire New Testament as "Scripture" or "the Word of God." However, several factors indicate that the New Testament authors saw their writings in the same category as the Scriptures of the Old Testament, that is, as the Word of God.

They often recorded God's direct speech. God's words were heard at the baptism and transfiguration of Jesus (Matt. 3:17; 17:5). The risen Lord spoke to Paul on the Damascus Road (Acts 9:4) and later (19:9–10; 23:11) as well as to others (9:11–16; 10:13), and Jesus Christ spoke to the apostle John (Rev. 1:17–3:22).

The parity of the New Testament with the Old Testament as the Word of God is also behind the exhortation to "read" (that is, to read aloud) the apostolic letters in the churches (Col. 4:16; 1 Thess. 5:27; see also 2 Cor. 1:13). In Jewish synagogue meetings the Old Testament Scriptures were read publicly (Luke 4:16; Acts 13:15; 15:21; 2 Cor. 3:15). The reading of New Testament writings in the church along with the Old Testament demonstrates that from the very first they were ranked equally with the Old Testament.[15] Peter made this explicit when he referred to Paul's letters along with "the rest of the Scriptures" (2 Pet. 3:16).

When Paul quoted in 1 Timothy 5:18 from Deuteronomy 25:4 and Luke 10:7, he referred to them as "the Scripture," thus putting the Old and New Testaments in the same category.

The last book of the Bible is called "the revelation of Jesus Christ, which God gave . . . to His bond-servant John" (Rev. 1:1). John then testified that he "bore witness to the word of God and to the testimony of Jesus Christ" (1:2). The entire Book of Revelation is thus a word from God which is witnessed to by Christ (22:16, 18, 20).[16] The pronouncement of blessing on the one "who reads [the public reader] and those who hear the words of the prophecy [the book of Revelation]" are reminiscent of Jesus' words in Luke 11:28: "Blessed are those who hear the word of God, and observe it." The warning of the plagues of God against anyone who would add to the "words of the prophecy of this book" are also similar to the Old Testament warnings against adding words to God's commandments (Deut. 4:2; 12:32). Thus the Book of Revelation is unambiguously presented as God's Word.

THE WRITTEN WORD AND THE PERSONAL WORD, JESUS CHRIST

Theologians influenced by rationalism have consistently rejected the Bible as the Word of God and have affirmed instead that only Jesus Christ is the Word of God. At the end of the nineteenth century, the influential dean of Canterbury, F. W. Farrar, cited the words of another to express his own opinion: "Take away this persecuting, burning, cursing, damning of men for not subscribing to the words of men as the Words of God; require of Christians only to believe Christ, and to call no man master but Him only."[17] More recently John Barton argues that "it is only in a loose sense that 'the Bible' is Paul's source of authority at all. What matters to him is God's action in Christ."[18] As Karl Barth says, "The equation, God's Word is God's Son, makes anything doctrinaire in regarding the Word of God radically impossible." To these men, the Word of God is the revelation of God in Christ and is *not* any verbal proposition.

Even some evangelical writers place more emphasis on Christ as God's Word than on the Bible. Donald Bloesch, for example, writes, "We must bear in mind that the ultimate, final authority is not Scripture but the living God himself as we find him in Jesus Christ. . . . The Bible is authoritative because it points beyond itself to the absolute authority, the living and transcendent Word of God. . . . Just as the church is subordinated to the Bible, so the Bible in turn is subordinated to Jesus Christ, who embodies the mind and counsel of God."[19] Alister McGrath, a British evangelical, asserts that the Scriptures must not be identified as "revelation itself," for they are "a channel through which God's self-revelation in Jesus Christ is encountered."[20] However, this runs counter to the fact that the Scriptures, as we have seen, are clearly the Word of God.

True, a person is more than words. But we must be careful that we don't inordinately divide a person from his words. Several things should be noted about the relationship of the written Word of God, the Scriptures, and the personal Word, Jesus Christ.

First, the truth that Christ is the final and ultimate revelation of God does not make God's previous forms of revelation something other than His revelatory Word. As the writer to the Hebrews affirmed, God spoke both "in the prophets" and "in His Son" (Heb. 1:1–2). As we have seen, the words of the prophets were God's speech. In fact, Scripture itself refers to both Christ and the written Scriptures as the Word of God, with no qualitative distinction between them. For example, the Scriptures are "living and active" (Heb. 4:12), and Jesus said His own words are "spirit and . . . life" (John 6:63; see also 1 Pet. 1:23).

Some writers argue that the Bible is a "testimony" or a "witness" to the living Word, and not the Word itself. They point out that Jesus Himself said that the Scriptures "bear witness" of Him (John 5:39). Does the fact that Scripture is witness to Christ make it less than the Word of God? The answer to this question is seen when we remember that Jesus bore witness to Himself (5:31; 8:14). Also the heavenly Father and the Holy Spirit also bore witness to Him (5:37; 8:18; 15:26). His own self-witness and that of the Father and the Spirit are surely the "words of God." The testimony of the writers of Scripture writing under the inspiration of the Spirit is simply the continuation of this witness and thus nothing less than the Word of God. As Jesus said to His apostles, the Spirit "will bear witness of Me, and you will bear witness also" (15:26–27; see also Luke 24:18; Rev. 1:1).

Second, an individual's word cannot be separated from him or her, for they "reveal" the person. "The mouth speaks out of that which fills the heart" (Matt. 12:34), and the "heart" refers to what we really are inwardly (Prov. 27:19; 1 Pet. 3:15). Our words are thus the expression of ourselves. If a person speaks coarse or foolish words, we are apt to think that he himself is coarse or foolish. If we respect a person's words, we are respecting him or her. Obeying God's words shows that we respect and love Him. For Jesus said, "He who has My commandments and keeps them, he it is who loves Me" (John 14:21; see also 14:23–24; 15:10, 14).

Words, in fact, are the most significant way by which we communicate. Of course, we can communicate through bodily actions, but the primacy of speech is evident even in this when we call it body "language." As Walter Ong observes, we cannot sit and look steadily into the face of another person silently without it feeling very unnatural and even embarrassing. But looking at the other person as we converse with that individual is perfectly natural.[21]

As human beings we are designed to share ourselves with others in verbal communication. Our words express what we are and think.

In a similar way God's words are nothing less than the extension of Himself in communicating with us. Jesus' words were a means of communicating Himself, "the Word." The human authors of Scripture were controlled by the Holy Spirit as they wrote and thus, as already noted, their words were the product of the "breath" of God (2 Tim. 3:16). And so those words are nothing less than the words of God expressing His person.

This fact is seen when toward the close of His earthly life Jesus told His disciples, "I have many more things to say to you, but you cannot bear them now. But when He, the Spirit of truth comes, He will guide you into all the truth; for He will not speak on His own initiative, but whatever He hears, He will speak . . . . All things that the Father has are Mine; therefore I said, that He takes of Mine, and will disclose it to you" (John 16:12–15). The Holy Spirit would continue to teach what Christ had taught the disciples. He would unfold for them the full meaning of Christ's death and resurrection, which the disciples would be able to understand only after those events occurred. Those early witnesses, therefore, proclaimed the gospel of Christ as the Word of God because it was in reality Christ's teaching through the Spirit. The letters to the seven churches in Revelation 2–3 are clear examples of this process. Christ spoke the words of each letter, and yet each one concludes with the statement, "He who has an ear, let him hear what the Spirit says to the churches" (2:7, 11, 17, 29; 3:6, 13, 22). The apostle John's words were Christ's words, that is, the *words* of God expressing and communicating the person of God through his Son, the *Word* of God. *Therefore the verbal word of God written in Scripture cannot be divorced from the personal Word.* The Bible, the written Word, is the expression of Christ, the living Word.

THE SIGNIFICANCE OF THE BIBLE AS "GOD'S WORD"

Does it really matter whether the Bible is God's revelatory word or fallible human writings that only bear witness to Jesus Christ? Of what significance is the belief that the Bible is the very Word of God? Further responses to these questions will be evident in later chapters, but a few crucial implications are worth noting here.

First, if the Bible is the Word of God, then we have an objective, verbal revelation of God in human history today. His Word is not simply His inner speech to human hearts that could easily be confused with our own thoughts. Of course, God by His Spirit does speak His word to our hearts, for only then can we really receive it. But His Word is given to us in the Scriptures.

Without the Scriptures as an objective revelation of God in history, we would be at a loss to know the real content of His Word. If Scripture is only a witness to the Word, then what is the Word? The usual answer is

Christ. But who is Christ and what is revealed about Him? If the writings of Scripture are only the fallible words of humans, if they are only a human document that must be submitted to the historical-critical method of human scholarship in order to know what really happened, then how do we know the true content of their witness? That is, how can the content of God's Word be ascertained if the words of Scripture are fallible, human words?

If the biblical record of the death and resurrection of Christ, for example, is only a fallible human witness to a divine word that is never objective in human history, then we can never be sure that the Bible records the true meaning of those acts. But if the Bible is the objective Word of God, then our responsibility is to seek to understand it and to receive it in obedience.

Second, if the Bible is God's Word, then we must hear the Bible as God's speech to us. Much as we reveal ourselves to others through our words, God reveals Himself to us through the words of the Bible so that we can come to know Him. Because the words of the Bible are not simply the words of human writers of past history but the words of the living God, they continue to speak just as when they were first written. The words of the prophet Isaiah may have been rejected by his contemporaries, but in writing them in Scripture they will "serve in the time to come as a witness forever" (Isa. 30:8; see also 8:16). The Word of God still speaks, and someday people will listen. God is still "saying" His Word of warning against hardening one's heart, a warning that was first addressed to Israel in the wilderness (Num. 14:22–23), was then written again by the psalmist (Ps. 95:11), and was later addressed to the readers of the Book of Hebrews (Heb. 4:7). God did give some specific instructions to certain people, instructions that are not applicable to us today, but God's words of instruction in the Bible still speak God's truth now. Parents give their children specific instructions, such as the time to go to bed, but those instructions are no longer applicable when the children become adults. But the point of those instructions—that people need proper rest—is still valid for adults. Similarly God speaks His truth to us anew each day through the words of Scripture.

Third, since the Bible is the objective Word of God, it is always that. It is therefore wrong to say that the Bible *becomes* the Word of God when He uses it to speak to someone. The Scriptures are the living Word of God, whether people recognize it as such or not. Jesus spoke the words of God, yet many people did not recognize them as such because, as He said, they could not "hear My word" (John 8:43). So instead of waiting for the Bible to become God's Word, we recognize that it *is* His Word. Therefore we pray with the psalmist, "Open my eyes, that I may behold wonderful things from Thy law" (Ps. 119:18). That is, we ask God to enable us to understand what He has *already* said in the Bible. It is our responsibility to obey Jesus' words to "take care how you listen" (Luke 8:18).

CONCLUSION

As words are the basis of our relationship with other people, so they are in our relationship with God. His Word is embodied in the person and work of Christ. But it is also given in verbal, written form so that we may know Him and what He requires of us. God thus confronts us in Christ through His written word, the Bible, and it is to this that we respond. The mark of Jesus' disciples, Jesus said to God the Father, is that "they have kept Thy word" (John 17:6; see also 8:51; 15:10). God's Old Testament people were bound to Him in covenant as they heard His words and spoke in response, saying, "All that the LORD has spoken we will do" (Exod. 19:8; see also 24:7). The identity of God's people thus resides in the conversation they carried on with God, listening to His Word and obeying it. According to the testimony of both the Old and New Testaments, these written Scriptures are God's Word. Thus our relationship to Him depends on our having the very Word of God.

Eight

Christ absolutely trusted the Bible; and though there are in it things inexplicable and intricate that have puzzled me so much, I am going, not in a blind sense, but reverently, to trust the Book because of Him.[1]

—Bishop H.C.G. Moule

Eight

How Did Christ View the Scriptures?

CHRISTIANS have always believed Jesus' words are fully authoritative and reliable. While He was on earth, He claimed to speak only the words of God the Father, who sent Him. "My teaching is not Mine, but His who sent Me" (John 7:16; see also 8:28; 12:49). The Gospels record that the "multitudes were amazed at His teaching; for He was teaching them as one having authority" (Matt. 7:28–29). Of His own evaluation of His words He said, "Heaven and earth will pass away, but My words will not pass away" (Mark 13:31). The words He spoke will judge men at the last day (John 12:48). Only those who hear His words and put them into practice will pass the final test of life (Matt. 7:24–25).

Some people have the idea that Jesus' words, printed in red in some Bibles, are somehow more authoritative than the rest of Scripture. All Scripture is authoritative, because, as discussed in the previous chapter, God is its Author. Nevertheless the teachings of Jesus remain particularly important because of who He is—the Son of God. Since He is our Lord, it is important that we take special notice of what He said about the Scriptures. His attitude toward God's Word must also be ours.

THE PROMINENCE OF SCRIPTURE IN THE LIFE OF JESUS

Jesus' Frequent Use of Scripture

Whether He was struggling with Satan in His temptation, teaching the crowds by the sea, or instructing His disciples, Jesus' words were punctuated with citations from the Old Testament Scriptures. They were on His lips in prayer, even in His suffering on the cross. His mind was so saturated with the words of Scripture that He used them to express His own feelings. The anguish of David centuries earlier became the expression of His own agony as He cried from the cross, "My God, My God, why hast Thou forsaken Me?" (Matt. 27:46). And as He died, He said in the words of the psalmist, "Into Thy hand I commit My spirit" (Ps. 31:5; Luke 23:46). Even after His resurrection, He expounded the Scriptures (24:44–45).

In the King James Version the four Gospels include 3,779 verses. According to Graham Scroggie, 1,934 of these verses, in whole or in part, contain the words of Christ.[2] Out of these 1,934 verses approximately 180, or almost one out of ten, cite or allude to the Old Testament. Even this does not give us the full picture, for as John W. Wenham notes, "In many passages there is simply no way to distinguish between Jesus' conscious allusion to the Old Testament and His normal, habitual use of Old Testament words and thought forms. The Holy Scriptures penetrated the warp and woof of Christ's mind."[3]

Jesus' Use of the Entire Old Testament

The Lord's many references to Scripture encompass the entire scope of Old Testament history. Among the many people and events Jesus mentioned are the creation of Adam and Eve and the institution of marriage (Matt. 19:4–6), the death of Abel (23:35), the days of Noah and the Flood (24:37–38), the destruction of Sodom (Luke 17:29), Abraham (John 8:56), Isaac and Jacob (Matt. 8:11), the appearance of God in the burning bush (Mark 12:26), the life of David (Matt. 12:3), Solomon (12:42), the ministry of Elijah (Luke 4:25), and the martyrdom of the prophet Zechariah (Matt. 23:35). He also referred to God's miraculous provision of the manna

(John 6:49), the death of Lot's wife (Luke 17:31–32), the bronze serpent (John 3:14), and Jonah and the great fish (Matt. 12:40).

Jesus' mention of these events and people from the Old Testament were not simply side comments in His teaching. Many of these persons and events prefigured His own messianic ministry and future events of the last days. David, Solomon, Jonah, and others, were types of Himself, and the bronze serpent was typical of His salvation through the cross. The days of Noah were typical of the coming eschatological judgment.

Some people say that Jesus' references to these events do not mean that He considered them historical. After all, it is argued, one can use legends as illustrations of spiritual truths. However, the way Jesus cited these events in His teaching supports their historical reality. His reference to monogamy (Matt. 19:4–5; Mark 10:6–8) surely implies the historicity of the early Genesis account of Adam and Eve. Jesus' statement that "the men of Nineveh shall stand up with this generation at the judgment, and shall condemn it because they repented at the preaching of Jonah" (Matt. 12:41) would be meaningless unless there were actual "men of Nineveh" who heard a historical person named Jonah. As T. T. Perowne wrote, it is impossible "to suppose Him to say that imaginary persons who at the imaginary preaching of an imaginary prophet repented in imagination, shall rise up in that day [of judgment] and condemn the actual impenitence of those His actual hearers."[4] The similar declaration that it will be more tolerable in the day of judgment for Sodom than for the people of Capernaum, who saw His miraculous works but refused to repent (11:23–24), clearly shows the historicity of the incident at Sodom. The same must be said of His reference to the Flood as a picture of the coming judgment. The comparison of His own death and resurrection with Jonah's "three days and three nights in the belly of the sea monster" (12:40) depends on the reality of Jonah's experience.

These examples and others, such as the references to Abraham (John 8:56–58) and Elijah and Elisha (Luke 4:25–27), suggest that Jesus, contrary to many critics of the Bible, accepted the historicity of all the Old Testament. According to Jesus' words, God did create the first two human beings, Adam and Eve (Matt. 19:4), Cain and Abel existed (Luke 11:51), and there was a flood in the days of Noah. Sodom and Gomorrah were destroyed by fire, and the incident of Lot's wife is historical fact (17:29–32). Similarly the miracles of Elijah (4:25–26) and the much ridiculed record of Jonah and the great fish (Matt. 12:40–41) are reliable history. There is no record that Jesus ever hinted that any of the persons and events that the Old Testament presents in a straightforward way as history are anything but truthful records of reality.

Contrary to the views of many modern scholars, Jesus affirmed the Mosaic authorship of the first five books of the Bible, often referred to in Scripture as the Law. Jesus mentioned Moses as the writer of the Law about two dozen times, and He quoted Moses sixteen times. He asked rhetorically, "Did not Moses give you the Law?" (John 7:19). Also the liberal theory that the Book of Isaiah was written by two or more authors is contrary to Jesus' teaching. According to liberal scholars Isaiah 1–39 was written by one person and chapters 40–66 were penned by a second or deutero Isaiah (and some ascribe chapters 56–66 to a third "Isaiah"). However, Jesus ascribed statements from all sections of the book to Isaiah. In one instance Jesus cited from both Isaiah 53 and Isaiah 6, ascribing both to the prophet Isaiah (John 12:38–41).

Jesus' concept of the Scriptures encompassed the entire Old Testament, as seen in His reference to "the Law of Moses and the Prophets and the Psalms" (Luke 24:44). At that time, one way of referring to the Old Testament was to speak of its three-part division: the Law, the Prophets, and the Writings. The Psalms were the first book in the Writings. Jesus thus spoke of the entire Old Testament, referring to all of them as "the Scripture" (24:45). The entire Scriptures were also described as the Law and the prophets (Matt. 5:17), or simply as the "Law" (5:18; John 10:34).[5]

Jesus' wide acquaintance with Scripture and especially its central place in all of His teaching and ministry leads to the conclusion that He fully believed and practiced in His own life His first recorded scriptural citation, "Man shall not live on bread alone, but on every word that proceeds out of the mouth of God" (Matt. 4:4; see Deut. 8:3). Charles Haddon Spurgeon once said to his people, "It is blessed to eat into the very soul of the Bible until, at last, you come to talk in scriptural language, and your spirit is flavoured with the words of the Lord, so that your blood is *Bibline* and the very essence of the Bible flows from you."[6] No one exemplified this as did Jesus.

JESUS' RECOGNITION OF THE AUTHORITY OF SCRIPTURE

Jesus' Personal Submission to Scripture

Jesus' respect for the Scriptures is not only manifest by the number of times it is found on His lips. It is also seen in His submission to its authority. Beginning with Satan's temptation, Jesus recognized that the Scriptures gave commands contrary to what the devil was asking, and He was determined to obey the Word of God (Matt. 4:4, 6–7, 10). He knew that God's will for the Messiah foretold in the Old Testament was for Him to suffer and die. So He resisted Peter's rejection of this truth, recognizing it as a temptation from Satan (16:23).

His actions frequently brought charges by the religious leaders that He was breaking the commandments of the Law (Mark 2:24–28; 3:4; Luke 13:14–17). But Jesus' reply was always the same. If they understood the true meaning of the laws, they would recognize that He was not violating them in any way (John 7:21–24). These problems arose, according to Jesus, because the teachers had developed traditions that actually perverted God's Word (Matt. 15:6). For example, Jesus saw that the restrictions of the Halakah, the rules set forth by the rabbis for keeping the commandments, actually had the effect of preventing people from keeping the commandment to love one's neighbor on the Sabbath (Mark 3:1–4). Because He perfectly submitted to God's Word, Jesus could say to His opponents, "Which one of you convicts Me [proves Me guilty] of sin?" but none could do so (John 8:46; see also 18:23). New Testament scholar Adolph Schlatter correctly noted, "Jesus saw his entire life-calling in the Scripture—it was not marginal but absolutely central to his life. . . . His whole will was consumed with this: to do what each commandment commanded. Here is the One Man—the first in history—who not only knew the Word but did it."[7]

Perhaps even more than His obedience to the righteous commands of God's Law for His people, Jesus' submission to Scripture is evident in the way He saw Himself as the fulfillment of that Scripture. The Scriptures, He said, "bear witness of Me" (John 5:39). And to the two in Emmaus He said, "These are My words which I spoke to you while I was still with you, that all things which are written about Me in the Law of Moses and the Prophets and the Psalms must be fulfilled" (Luke 24:44).

His submission to Scripture is also seen in the way its prophecies compelled Him to walk the road of suffering to death. At His baptism He told John the Baptist, "It is fitting for us to fulfill all righteousness" (Matt. 3:15), that is, it is necessary for you to baptize Me so that I may in obedience fulfill My work as the Servant of the Lord. Toward the end of His earthly life, Jesus told His disciples, "Behold, we are going up to Jerusalem, and all things which are written through the prophets about the Son of Man will be accomplished. For He will be delivered to the Gentiles, . . . and after they have scourged Him, they will kill Him, and the third day He will rise again" (Luke 18:31–33). "This which is written must be fulfilled in Me, 'And He was numbered with transgressors'; for that which refers to Me has its fulfillment" (22:37). His submission to the suffering role that the Old Testament prophesied is seen at His arrest in Gethsemane. When one of His disciples attempted to defend Him with a sword, Jesus told him to put the sword back in its place, saying that He could call on his Father and have twelve legions of angels at His disposal to defend Him. He refused such aid, explaining, "How then shall the Scriptures be fulfilled, that it must happen this way?" (Matt. 26:54).

"No array of explicit statements in which He acknowledges His acceptance of the Old Testament Scriptures as the word of God can equal in force this implied subordination of Himself and of His word to the one great scheme of which the ancient revelation given to Israel formed the preparatory state."[8]

Jesus' Use of Scripture in His Teaching

Besides demonstrating His belief in the authority of the Scriptures by submitting to them in His own life, Jesus used them as the final authority in His teaching. Though He was Himself God's final Word of revelation (Heb. 1:3) and though He received revelation from the Father (Matt. 11:27), much of His teaching was based on the words of Old Testament Scripture. This is particularly apparent in His discussions with His questioners:

> Have you not read what David did? (Matt. 12:3)
> Or have you not read? (12:5)
> Have you not read? (19:4)
> Have you never read? (21:16)
> Did you never read in the Scriptures? (21:42)
> Have you not read that which was spoken to you by God? (22:31)
> What did Moses command you? (Mark 10:3)
> What is written in the Law? How does it read to you? (Luke 10:26)
> What then is this that is written? (20:17)
> In your law it has been written. (John 8:17)
> Has it not been written in your Law? (10:34)

Many of Jesus' other teachings are introduced by similar statements in which He explicitly called attention to the Old Testament. But these by no means tell all of the story, for much of the Old Testament forms the basis of His teaching without *specific* reference to it.

The fundamental themes of Jesus' teaching as well as those of a more incidental nature were founded on the Old Testament. His proclamation of the kingdom of heaven was derived from Daniel's prophecy that "the God of heaven will set up a kingdom" (Dan. 2:44). In His conversation with Nicodemus, Jesus hinted that the truth of the new birth by the Holy Spirit (John 3:3–8) should have been known to him, a ruler in Israel, because Ezekiel and others had spoken about it (Ezek. 36:25–27). Jesus referred to the future Tribulation (Mark 13:14) that Daniel wrote about (Dan. 9:27; 11:31; 12:11). And Jesus' description of eternal punishment as the condition "where their worm does not die, and the fire is not quenched" (Mark 9:48) comes from Isaiah 66:24.

In response to the Pharisees' question on divorce, Jesus based His theology of marriage on the Genesis account of Creation. God had made male and female and the two became one flesh. This was the teaching of Scripture, and so this was the will of God (Matt. 19:4–6). On another occasion Jesus summed up His understanding of man's ultimate duty before God in the words of Deuteronomy 6:5: "You shall love the LORD your God with all your heart, and with all your soul, and with all your mind" (Matt. 22:37). Even the so-called Golden Rule—whatever you want others to do for you, do so for them—was, Jesus said, the teaching of "the Law and the Prophets" (7:12).

The words spoken by the prophet Isaiah centuries earlier to the people of His day applied also to the scribes and Pharisees of the first century: "This people honors Me with their lips, but their heart is far away from Me. But in vain do they worship Me, teaching as doctrines the precepts of men" (Matt. 15:8–9; quoting Isa. 29:13). The divine judgment of spiritual blindness for rejecting truth pronounced by the prophet Isaiah (Isa. 6:9–10) was still applicable to the generation that was rejecting His teaching (Mark 3:12).

Sometimes it was only a brief phrase or thought that was applicable to a given situation. Jesus said that the phrase "sheep without a shepherd" (which was used several times in the Old Testament) was a very appropriate description of the multitudes in His own day (Num. 27:17; Ezek. 34:5; Matt. 9:36). He warned against grabbing a place of honor lest someone be present who deserves it more (Luke 14:7–11), a truth already found in Proverbs 25:6–7. His well-known statement, "The poor you have with you always" (Matt. 26:11) was based on a statement to that effect in Deuteronomy 15:11. Jesus' words about a stone being rejected by builders and yet breaking those who stumble over it and crushing those on which it falls were taken from the Old Testament (Matt. 21:42, 44; Isa. 8:14–15; Dan. 2:34, 44). Such citations and allusions to the Old Testament could be multiplied many times.

Above all, Jesus used the Scriptures to interpret His own person and mission in the world. We have already noted how, after the Resurrection, He used the entire Old Testament to instruct His disciples on the things concerning Himself. But long before this He had referred to the fulfillment of Scripture in Himself. He had come, He said, "not . . . to abolish" the Law or the Prophets," but to fulfill them (Matt. 5:17). The ministry of John the Baptist, which pointed to Him, was in fulfillment of Isaiah's prophecy that a messenger would be sent to prepare the way before the Lord (Matt. 11:10; Isa. 40:3). And Jesus inaugurated His ministry at Nazareth by taking up the scroll in the synagogue and reading from Isaiah 61:1, "The Spirit of the Lord GOD is upon Me, because the LORD anointed me to bring good news to the afflicted" (Luke 4:18). He then said these words were fulfilled in Himself (4:21).

On one occasion, when the disciples of John questioned whether He really was "the Coming One," Jesus validated His identity by pointing to His miracles, which fulfilled the prophecy Isaiah had given for the Messiah and His times (Matt. 11:1–6; Isa. 35:5–6).

Nowhere is Jesus' interpretation of His actions as the fulfillment of Scripture more evident than in the events surrounding the Crucifixion. His rejection by the Jewish leaders (Matt. 21:42; Ps. 118:22); His betrayal by one of His disciples (John 13:18; Ps. 41:9); the scattering of His disciples when He was arrested (Matt. 26:31; Zech. 13:7); His substitutionary death (Mark 10:45; Is. 53:10–11)—all these Jesus said fulfilled the prophetic Word of God about Himself.

Only a short time before His death, "Jesus, knowing that all things had already been accomplished, in order that the Scripture might be fulfilled, said, 'I am thirsty' " (John 19:28). Even the rather incidental statement of the psalmist about the distasteful drink which God's Suffering Servant would receive from His persecutors had to be fulfilled in Him (Ps. 69:21). When Jesus had drunk, "He said, 'It is finished!' And He bowed His head and gave up His spirit" (John 19:30). All the prophecies of the Scriptures that spoke of His life and death were fulfilled. As the obedient Servant, He had to fulfill them for they were the Word of His heavenly Father.[9]

What Jesus believed about the Scriptures is especially evident in His response to those who challenged His teaching. On some occasions He sought to open their eyes to truth by using probing questions.[10] In these confrontations with opponents, Jesus always appealed to Scripture as His final authority.

In the parable of the vineyard He told a story that clearly pricked the consciences of His hearers, who were rejecting Him as the Son of God (Luke 20:16–17). In the story the result of the rejection was the transfer of the vineyard, which represented the kingdom, from the unbelieving Jews of His day to others who would receive God's true messenger. When His listeners rejected the implications of the story with the cry, "May it never be!" (20:16), Jesus countered with an appeal to Scripture: "What then is this that is written, 'The stone which the builders rejected, this became the chief corner stone'?" (20:17). For Jesus, this Old Testament verse applied to His present situation, and because Scripture is absolutely authoritative, His hearers' objection was overruled.

His antagonists frequently sought to trap Him with subtle questions.[11] On one occasion the Sadducees, who did not believe in the Resurrection, thought they had disproven the Resurrection with the question about the hypothetical woman who had married seven brothers successively (Matt. 22:23–33). They wanted to know whose wife she would be after the Resurrection.

Jesus responded with the statement, "You are mistaken, not understanding the Scriptures, or the power of God" (22:29), and proceeded to give them a brief lesson in the proper understanding of Scripture: "Regarding the resurrection of the dead, have you not read that which was spoken to you by God, saying, 'I am the God of Abraham, and the God of Isaac, and the God of Jacob'? God is not the God of the dead but of the living" (22:31–32). Abraham, Isaac, and Jacob had long ago passed from the earth when God told Moses at the burning bush that He is their God (Exod. 3:6), indicating that they still existed and there is life after death. It is interesting to note that, according to Jesus, God spoke in words that could be "read," that is, the Scriptures.

On another occasion, when the Pharisees challenged Jesus about the action of His disciples on the Sabbath, Jesus responded with the words, "have you not read in the Law?" (Matt. 12:5). Their error was not only in ignoring the Scriptures, but also in failing to understand its meaning. So the Lord instructed them, "But if you had known what this means, 'I desire compassion, and not a sacrifice,' you would not have condemned the innocent" (12:7; quoting Hos. 6:6).

Again and again when challenged by His opponents, Jesus cited Scripture as His final court of appeal. When the Pharisees tested Him with the question, "Is it lawful for a man to divorce his wife for any cause at all?" Jesus replied, "Have you not read . . . ?" and then He cited the Genesis account of the first marriage which gave God's intent (Matt. 19:4–6). Even in response to the serious charge of blasphemy ("You, being a man, make Yourself out to be God," John 10:33) Jesus appealed to the Old Testament, asking, "Has it not been written in your Law?" (10:34).

For Jesus the Scriptures were the final authority. The right use of Scripture could not be refuted, nor did He ever question that any portions were authoritative. If the Scriptures said it, that was sufficient.

CHRIST'S TEACHING ON THE INSPIRATION OF THE SCRIPTURES

To Christ the Old Testament Scriptures were the words of God Himself. Interestingly we have no record of any of Jesus' contemporaries, including His opponents, ever questioning this reliance on the Scriptures, for they too had a high view of them, believing them to be sacred writings. As a result, we do not have any long teaching by Christ on the nature of the Scriptures, for this was well known and accepted. However, He did make several statements about the Scriptures that give us further insight into His understanding of their inspired nature.

Two Key Statements

Matthew 5:17–18. Because Jesus placed a greater emphasis on the attitude of the heart and less on the outward observance of the details of the Law than did the teachers of His day, the question of His scriptural orthodoxy was no doubt raised in the minds of many. He therefore set the record straight with words that clearly reveal His viewpoint on the Scriptures: "Do not think that I came to abolish the Law or the Prophets; I did not come to abolish, but to fulfill. For truly I say to you, until heaven and earth pass away, not the smallest letter or stroke shall pass away from the Law, until all is accomplished" (Matt. 5:17–18).

"Law" and "Prophets" (5:17) or simply "Law" (5:18) in Jesus' day were two ways of referring to the entire Old Testament writings.[12] These writings, which looked forward to Him, were absolutely true and would be completely accomplished. To emphasize His point, Jesus referred to the smallest letter in the Hebrew alphabet, *yod*, which is smaller than our English letter *i*, and to a tiny stroke that distinguishes one Hebrew letter from another, smaller but comparable to the stroke that differentiates E from F, or possibly just a small embellishment of a Hebrew letter. Our English equivalent of Jesus' words might be, "not one *t* will be uncrossed or an *i* undotted."

This points to the authority of the Scriptures down to the smallest detail. Everything written in the Scriptures is true.

John 10:34–36. What Jesus thought about the Scriptures is clearly evident in His statement made in defense of His claim to be God. In response to His opponents, Jesus as usual answered the charge of blasphemy by appealing to Scripture: "Has it not been written in your Law, 'I said, you are gods'? If he called them gods, to whom the word of God came (and the Scripture cannot be broken), do you say of Him, whom the Father sanctified and sent into the world, 'You are blaspheming'; because I said, 'I am the Son of God'?" (John 10:34–36).

Jesus' citation comes from Psalm 82:6, where the psalmist referred to the human judges of Israel as "gods." Though Jesus did not cite the parallel expression in the psalm, "sons of the Most High," He may have assumed that His hearers would be acquainted with the passage and would know that the "gods" and "sons of the Most High" go together. In citing this passage Jesus was reasoning from the lesser to the greater. He said in essence, "If the Scriptures call the human judges who served as vehicles of the Word of God 'gods,' then how can you charge Me with blasphemy when I claim to be the Son of God?" Jesus certainly claimed to be the Son of God in a far higher sense than the judges of old, but this Scripture that called men "gods" should have caused His opponents to back off from the immediate charge of blasphemy. He desired to make them stop and consider more fully His right to claim that He is the Son of God (John 10:37–38).

The point for our discussion, however, is in His statement "the Scripture cannot be broken" (10:35). This quotation about "gods" comes, as noted, from Psalm 82:6, which Jesus called "Law" (10:34), thus showing that He viewed all the Old Testament as authoritative. The "Law" and "the Scripture"—terms He used synonymously—cannot be "broken," that is, they will not lose their force and be no longer binding. Scripture cannot be voided or annulled.

God as the Author of Scripture

For Jesus the authority of the Scriptures rested on His conviction that God was their ultimate Author, even though human authors were involved. Responding to a question related to marriage and divorce, Jesus quoted words that were written by the author of Genesis. But these words were ultimately God's words, for Jesus stated, "He who created them . . . said" (Matt. 19:4–5).

Several times Jesus referred to Scripture as the product of prophecy, which the Old Testament stated was God's speech through human instruments. For example, in Mark 7:6 Jesus introduced His quotation of Isaiah 29:13 by saying, "Rightly did Isaiah prophesy." The "abomination of desolation," Jesus said, was "spoken of through Daniel the prophet" (Matt. 24:15). That is, Daniel was the means through whom God spoke this prophecy. Often Jesus simply introduced quotations from Scripture with such words as "Moses said" (Mark 7:10). Other times Jesus noted that some Old Testament statements were spoken directly by God, thus affirming their absolute divine authority.

Jesus also taught that the writings that were yet to form the New Testament would be inspired by the Holy Spirit. Speaking to His disciples who would be the apostles of the early church, He promised that the Holy Spirit would "bring to your remembrance all that I said to you" (John 14:26). Then He said, "I have many more things to say to you, but you cannot bear them now. But when He, the Spirit of truth comes, He will guide you into all the truth . . . and He will disclose to you what is to come. He shall glorify Me; for He shall take of Mine, and shall disclose it to you" (16:12–14). While these promises of the Spirit's teaching can be applied in a derivative sense to the illuminating work of the Spirit in believers' lives, their real import, as D. A. Carson explains, is "not to explain how readers at the end of the first century may be taught by the Spirit, but to explain to readers at the end of the first century how the first witnesses, the first disciples, came to an accurate and full understanding of the truth of Jesus Christ."[13]

The Inerrancy of Scripture

The Bible gives no indication that Jesus distinguished between those portions of Scripture that discuss spiritual truth and other matters that might seem to be more peripheral, such as details of history or science. While at times Jesus used the term "Scripture" in reference to specific passages, He also, as we have seen, referred to the whole of Scripture when declaring that its every "jot" and "tittle" would be fulfilled (Matt. 5:17) and that it could not be "annulled" (John 10:35). His continual reference to "Scripture" with

God as the implied author (for example, Matt. 21:42; Luke 4:21; John 5:39) and His statements that "Scripture" must be fulfilled (for example, Matt. 26:54) indicate that the entire Old Testament, and not just certain parts of it, is inerrant.

Two things were sacred to the Jews at the time of Christ—the Scriptures and the temple. When He predicted the destruction of the temple, Jesus was accused of speaking against it. But He was never accused of uttering one word against the Scriptures, which the Jews held to be absolutely authoritative with every word characterized as "the revealed truth of God."[14]

OUR ATTITUDE TOWARD CHRIST'S TEACHING

Clearly Jesus held a high view of the Scriptures. Although written by human authors, they were ultimately authored by God and were thus the very Word of God.

Some try to dodge the evidence presented in this chapter by saying that writers recorded their own views of the Scriptures rather than the belief of Jesus. In other words the Gospel writers, these scholars assert, put their own views in the mouth of Jesus. Therefore we really do not know what Jesus thought about the Scriptures. Two points should be noted in response to this explanation. First, given the way in which Jesus' view of Scripture pervades everything He taught and did, to deny that it is authentic leads to total pessimism regarding any historical knowledge of Him. Second, the way Jesus used the Old Testament, sometimes in very original ways, to interpret Himself and His work makes it far more likely that the disciples who wrote the Gospels were following Jesus' understanding rather than making it up themselves.

Others believe Jesus' attitude toward the Scriptures was simply an accommodation to the belief of His contemporaries. He appealed to the authority of the Old Testament because His audience believed it was inspired, not because He did. Such an explanation fails on at least two counts. First, the Gospel records make it clear that Jesus did not hesitate to challenge His contemporaries when He disagreed with them. Why should He accommodate their alleged error in the case of the Scriptures? Second, it is impossible to believe that He could repeatedly relate Himself and His ministry as the fulfillment of the Old Testament and at the same time believe they were only human writings filled with fallacies.

Still others seek to account for the teachings of Jesus by declaring that when He became a man His knowledge was limited. This limitation included the possibility of mistaken ideas. Much could be said in reply to this suggestion, but again two comments must suffice. First, limitation does not necessarily involve error. But second, and more importantly, Jesus claimed to speak the truth. If He was mistaken about the Scriptures on which He grounded His teaching, it is difficult to see why His words on other matters should be trusted.

There is no way around the implication of these clear teachings of Christ. We come to know Christ and believe in Him for our eternal destiny only through the Scriptures. Our faith in Him is therefore intrinsically linked to our faith in the truthfulness of the Bible. If we believe the Bible's record of Christ—that He is who He said He was, namely, the very revelation of God, the truth incarnate—then we must accept Him as our authoritative Teacher in all things, including the nature of the Bible. As someone has said, "The Incarnate Word sets His seal on the Written Word. The Incarnate Word is God; therefore, the inspiration of the Old Testament is authenticated by God Himself." With Christ, therefore, we must believe that the Scriptures are the inspired Word of God and that all it teaches is true and authoritative.

Nine

"The Bible," says Dr. [B. F.] Westcott, "is authoritative, for it is the Word of God; it is intelligible, for it is the word of man." Because it is the word of man in every part and element, it comes home to our hearts. Because it is the word of God in every part and element, it is our constant law and guide.[1]

—Benjamin B. Warfield

Nine

Is the Bible a Human Book?

THE SCRIPTURES, as we have seen, emphasize again and again their nature as God's Word. The divine authorship of the Bible, however, has frequently been denied by critical scholars. As a result, evangelicals in their study of the nature of Scripture have tended to focus on the divine character of the Bible and its consequences of absolute truthfulness and inerrancy. But it is important to recognize that along with being the Word of God the Scriptures are also the words of man. Moreover, the humanity of the Bible contributes to its value.

THE HUMANNESS OF THE BIBLE

Muslims hold that their sacred writing, the Koran, was dictated to Muhammad from heaven. But aside from a few people in the past, no Christian scholar makes such a claim for the Bible. Beyond the many references to its human writers, the humanness of the writings is patently evident. Written over centuries of time, its scope of human experience and variety of content and literary form is unmatched by any other book. Prose, poetry, history, theology, narrative, parable, proverb, apocalyptic, genealogy, law, and letter—all these and more are in the Bible, and all are forms of typical human writings of their time. The covenant forms of the Old Testament, for example, resemble ancient Hittite treaties. Also the instructions for the conduct of believers in various positions in the home, the so-called house tables, in the New Testament epistles (for example, Eph. 5:22–33, 6:1–9; Col. 3:18–4:1) bear similarity to earlier nonbiblical codes of conduct.

As we have seen, the Bible records the words of God that were addressed to people with introductory statements such as "Thus says the Lord," as well as inspired interpretations of these words and God's deeds in history. But the meditative responses to God's words and actions by His people are also part of Scripture. The psalmist's pleas for God's deliverance from his enemies, as well as his exclamation, "I love Thee, O Lord, my strength" (Ps. 18:1), are all part of the Bible.

Far from serving as human word processors, the writers of the Bible were real people expressing thoughts through their own minds and personalities. The poetic style of the psalmists stands in contrast to the analytical and logical structure of the apostle Paul's writings. The writings of the apostle John and of Luke differ in vocabulary and literary style. Jeremiah is often called the "weeping prophet" because of the mournful and melancholic strains that are felt in his writings. As Paul said, Isaiah "cries out" his message (Rom. 9:27), and in another instance Isaiah was "very bold" (10:20). Isaiah was communicating God's Word, but the full humanity of the prophet—mind, emotion, and will—was involved in the process.

In addition to differences in style and vocabulary, the personalities of the biblical writers were often directly involved in their messages as they wrote of firsthand experiences. Isaiah's vision of "the Lord sitting on a throne, lofty and exalted" (Isa. 6:1) was directly related to his own call to the ministry (6:7–8). David expressed his experience when he wrote, "I have been young, and now I am old; yet I have not seen the righteous forsaken, or his descendants begging bread" (Ps. 37:25). The cultures in which the writers lived show through their writings. Paul's numerous references and illustrations from Greco-Roman life—military, athletic, and legal—reflect his personal historical setting. The humanity of the writers was also involved in the very content and purpose of their writing. In the words of J. I. Packer, Holy Scripture has "been shaped by its writers' didactic aim, personal interest, and overall theology."[2]

The double truth that the Bible is God's Word and also human words calls for an explanation of the relationship of God and the human writers in its production, in what is generally termed "the inspiration of the Bible." The "inspiration" of the Bible has been explained in a number of ways. All but the "dictation" view agree on the full humanness of Scripture. The differences concern the degree and nature of divine involvement.

THE VIEW THAT THE BIBLE IS PRIMARILY HUMAN WORDS

The human characteristics of the Bible lead many to emphasize it as the words of men, which cannot be equated with "the Word of God." Some of this stems simply from the idea that there are errors in its content. Writers are said to contradict each other and to misstate certain facts of history and science. In the minds of some, however, it is not primarily the presence of errors but simply the humanness of the Bible that precludes it from being equated with God's Word. God is seen as so different from us humans, so "wholly other," that His Word spoken in Christ can never be expressed in human language. As Karl Barth, a noted exponent of this position, expressed it, "In the Bible we are invariably concerned with human attempts to repeat and reproduce in human thoughts and expressions, this Word of God [i.e., the Word in Christ] in definite human situations. ... In the one case *Deux dixit* [God speaks], in the other *Paulus dixit* [Paul speaks]. These are two different things."[3]

For many others humanness is simply incompatible with absolute truth. They argue that everyone is conditioned by his or her cultural context. Our perception of truth is relative to our limited historical context and therefore is always imperfect. In this view the humanness of the writers of the Bible, despite the presence of the Holy Spirit with them, results only in a fallible witness to divine revelation. Although there is disagreement as to the extent that human fallibility affects the reliability and truthfulness of Scripture, those who hold this position would agree with the statement by Roman Catholic scholar Hans Küng that the Bible "is unequivocally man's word: collected, written down, given varied emphasis, sentence by sentence by quite definite individuals and developed in different ways. Hence it is not without shortcoming and mistakes, concealment and confusion, limitations and errors."[4]

Some liberal rationalists have stressed the humanity of the Scriptures to the point that they essentially deny divine inspiration. They hold the notion that the writers of the Bible were individuals who were naturally gifted with insight in religion, and that their "inspiration" is comparable to what we might associate with an "inspired" artist, poet, or musician. Most Christian scholars, however, recognize some divine activity in the production of the Scriptures, although many emphasize its humanity at the expense of accepting its full divine character. The following views are three variations of this approach to inspiration.

First, some say that the writers of the Bible were inspired in the same manner that all believers are inspired to do God's work. According to this view, inspiration refers primarily to God's work in the writers of the Bible which is similar to His providing spiritual gifts to believers. As one might suppose, there is considerable variety in the way this view is stated. Some speak of it as "the stirring of the prophetic spirit."[5] The same prophetic spirit, however, continues in the church today and thus does not indicate a special work unique to the writers of the Scriptures. Most refer to different "kinds" or "degrees" of inspiration usually related to the nature of the biblical materials. The great hymns of the church, such as those written by Isaac Watts, Charles Wesley, Augustus Toplady, and Reginald Heber, are said to have the "same kind of inspiration" as that of some of the psalms that simply encourage the praise of God. If these hymns had been written during the times of David and his successors (although their content would have been different because the coming of Christ was still future) "there is little doubt but that . . . [they] would have found their way into the Hebrew canon."[6]

One recent explanation of inspiration that falls in this category likens inspiration to "a good teacher inspiring his students." Thus God inspired the writers of Scripture through His relationship with them and the community of which they were a part, and especially through His great acts of salvation, including the redemption of Israel from bondage and the life, death, and resurrection of Jesus Christ. This inspiration heightens natural abilities but is "no guarantee of inerrancy, since agents, even when inspired by God, can make mistakes."[7] In this view the same kind of inspiration continues today in the church. But because the Bible records the special revelatory actions of God in history, it is normative for Christian theology.[8]

This concept of inspiration fails to do justice to the abundant scriptural testimony that although the Scriptures are written by humans and are therefore human writings, they are also God's Word. Moreover, inspiration relates not only to the divine influence on the human writers but also characterizes the end product. The sacred writings ("all Scripture") are breathed out by God (2 Tim. 3:16). In short, this view of inspiration confuses the unique work of the Spirit in the inspiration of the Scriptures with His universal work of illuminating and teaching the inspired writings. It confuses the giving of God's Word, His revelation, with the ministry of illumination to understand that revelation. The greatness of Christian hymns, writings, or sermons by individuals other than biblical writers is the result of this latter work and is determined solely by the way they faithfully express God's revealed truth in Scripture.

Second, the Bible is said to be inspired because it "becomes" the Word of God. This view of God's inspiring activity in the writers of Scripture is similar to the previous one. However, it places greater emphasis on the distinction between God's revelation of His Word in personal encounter and the writings of Scripture. The Bible is not directly the revealed Word of God in any of its statements. Rather God *uses* the Scriptures to reveal Himself to individuals. Karl Barth expresses this concept of inspiration. "Verbal inspiration does not mean the infallibility of the Biblical word in its linguistic, historical and theological character as human word. It means that the fallible and faulty human word is as such used by God and has to be received and heard in spite of its human fallibility."[9]

The followers of this view believe that God influenced the writers of Scripture to be special witnesses of His great acts in the world, especially His revelation in Christ. This influence led those authors to write about those events and their own encounter with God through the events. God continues to use their words to reveal Himself through personal encounters with people today. When individuals hear the voice of God through the Scriptures, it "becomes" the Word of God.

The prophets and apostles, according to some scholars, used myths such as miracle stories to convey spiritual truth. Much of what seems to be historical reporting must be "demythologized" or stripped of its mythical dress to get at the spiritual truth that is really being conveyed.

Since it is impossible, according to this view, to equate any of the actual statements of the Bible with the Word of God, it is difficult to see how we can really know what God is saying. Theodore Engelder says that those who advocate this view of the Bible "refuse to believe that God performed the miracle of giving us by inspiration an infallible Bible, but [they] are ready to believe that God daily performs the greater miracle of enabling men to find and see in the fallible word of man the infallible Word of God."[10] It is obvious that such an interpretation of inspiration, outside of having no support in Scripture, makes the hearing of God's Word a very subjective matter. Different people can hear it differently, and we have no way to decide who is hearing it correctly. Again, like the previous position, this explanation of inspiration confuses the special work of inspiration related to conveying revelation with the work of illumination.

A third view is that the Bible is inspired sufficiently to accomplish its purpose of infallibly conveying saving truth. The actual nature and extent of God's work in the composition of the Bible varies somewhat among the exponents of this view. They tend to speak of God's "inspiration" of all of the Bible, but their focus is not so much on the truthfulness of the Bible as it is on its adequacy to accomplish its saving purpose. The Bible is inspired and thus infallible, they say, in the sense that it is trustworthy for accomplishing what God intended it to accomplish.[11]

A problem with this position is that it becomes difficult to know which portions of the Bible are pertinent to this saving purpose and which ones are not. Generally matters of science and history are considered peripheral to the saving message of Scripture and thus are not infallible. This view, which some called "limited inspiration," has several problems. First, the Scriptures explicitly declare that "*all* Scripture is inspired" (2 Tim. 3:16, italics added). Nowhere does the Bible say that inspiration or infallibility is limited to matters of only "faith and practice." Second, no one has been able to show how we can clearly determine the line between matters of faith and non-faith. Is Jesus' resurrection, for example, a matter of history or of "faith"? If, for example, there are several historical difficulties in harmonizing the accounts of the four Gospel writers, can we simply say that the record is fallible in its history and yet maintain that somehow the fact of His resurrection comes under the infallible inspiration of God? Such a separation seems impossible. If the historical record is not true, how can we maintain that Jesus' resurrection is a matter of "faith"—except on some basis other than the record of Scripture?

One of the reasons Christianity is superior to other religions is that it is rooted in history rather than myth. To exclude history from inspiration because of some yet-unsolved problems is to weaken this truth. Why should God supernaturally influence the biblical writers in their religious interpretation of His historical saving acts, giving us their meaning infallibly, while at the same time those writers recorded historical errors?

Most important is the fact that the Bible is concerned about our spiritual needs, but it also teaches us to understand and live all of life to the glory of God—"humanity, the world, nature, history, their origin and their destination, their past and their future."[12] What the Bible says about all matters is therefore related to the overall redemptive message of Scripture and is God's Word to us.

THE VIEW THAT THE BIBLE IS BOTH HUMAN AND DIVINE

Until the Enlightenment of the eighteenth century the almost universal understanding of the Bible by believers since the early church was that the Bible is the Word of God and also the words of man. A biblical doctrine of inspiration must account for the fact that the divine and human authors are both involved, with the result that the Bible bears the genuine characteristics of both.

The Biblical Concept of Inspiration

According to the Bible itself the inspiration of Scripture focuses on two truths—its process and result. As noted earlier, when the apostle Paul wrote that "all Scripture is inspired" (literally, "God-breathed," 2 Tim. 3:16), the emphasis is on the result of inspiration or the nature of the Bible itself. It is God-breathed writings. But in order to produce this result, God must also have worked in the human writer. The concept of the inspiration of the Scriptures therefore also speaks of this divine control.

Putting together these two concepts of the process and the result, we may define inspiration as "the supernatural work of the Holy Spirit on the writers of the Scriptures so that, fully using their own personalities and writing styles, they wrote precisely what God intended them to write and therefore are God's words as well as man's words." Benjamin B. Warfield, who strongly defended the evangelical concept of inspiration in the late nineteenth and early twentieth centuries, put it this way: "The Bible is the Word of God in such a sense that its words, though written by men and bearing indelibly impressed upon them the marks of their human origin, were written, nevertheless, under such an influence of the Holy Ghost as to be also the words of God, the adequate expression of His mind and will."[13]

This understanding of inspiration has often been falsely characterized as "the dictation theory," as if the human writers simply functioned as secretaries of the Holy Spirit. While a few people who stress the divine side of the words of the Bible have held this view, this has never been the ordinary view of the church. Some in the early church spoke of the Holy Spirit working on the biblical writers as a musician plays on a harp or lyre, and the great church father Augustine wrote that the Lord used the human writers "as if they were His own hands."[14] Similarly John Calvin referred to the biblical writers as "penmen"[15] and "scribes"[16] of the Holy Spirit. However, these writers did not intend for these metaphors to teach a dictation theory of inspiration, for that would have denied God's use of the full humanity of the biblical writers. Rather, they sought only to stress the end product as the infallible Word of God.

> This "dictation theory" is a straw man. It is safe to say that no Protestant theologian, from the Reformation till now, has ever held it; and certainly modern Evangelicals do not hold it. . . . It is true that many sixteenth- and seventeeth-century theologians spoke of Scripture as "dictated by the Holy Ghost." But all they meant was that the authors wrote word for word what

> God intended. . . . The use of the term "dictation" was always figurative. . . . The proof of this lies in the fact that, when these theologians addressed themselves to the question, What was the Spirit's mode of operating in the writers' mind, they all gave their answer in terms not of dictation, but of *accommodation*, and rightly maintained that God completely adapted His inspiring activity to the cast of mind, outlook, temperament, interest, literary habits and stylistic idiosyncrasies of each writer.[17]

The Spirit's Control of the Human Authors

The view that the Bible is both the word of man and the infallible Word of God calls for explanation. As noted earlier, the reason many people reject the Bible as the Word of God is its human characteristics. If it is human, they say, it is inevitably fallible. So how can it also be the infallible Word of God? Perhaps even more than the problem of infallibility or inerrancy is the question of how the words of Scripture can be human and divine at the same time. The answer requires both an understanding of human nature and the acknowledgment of the mystery of divine miracle.

The idea that "humanity means fallibility" must be rejected. The statement "To err is human" is no more correct than "To sin is human." For if these statements are true, then Christ, who did not sin, was not human and believers will not be human in heaven. But, of course, Christ was fully human, and we will still be human in glory. In reality sin and error are not part of the essence of human nature; instead, they are defects in it as a result of the Fall. They are to the personal dimension of human nature as sickness is to the physical—*disorders* of nature rather than *parts of its essence.* As our Lord demonstrated in His life on earth, true human nature in fellowship with God, as it was intended by Creation, does not involve either sin or error. Created in the image of God in fellowship with Him, humanity was designed by nature to communicate with God in truth.

As the Bible teaches, the writers of Scripture were not left to themselves in the process of writing God's Word. The Holy Spirit uniquely and miraculously worked in the process of inspiration to overrule their defect of sin, guiding them to say and write exactly what God desired.

This special controlling influence of God is perhaps most clearly seen in Peter's statement that "prophecy never had its origin in the will of man, but men spoke from God as they were carried along by the Holy Spirit" (2 Pet. 1:21, NIV). By the term "prophecy" Peter meant the entire Old Testament and not simply the prophets proper.[18] The Scriptures, according to the apostle's teaching, were never the result of the prompting of the human writer's own mind. In Eugene Peterson's paraphrase, they were "not something concocted in the human heart."[19] They originated as men were "carried along" by the Spirit of God. The Greek word translated "carried along" was used of a sailing ship carried along by the wind (Acts 27:15, 17). When the wind blows, the ship moves; when it stops, the ship stops. We may also think of a piece of driftwood carried along by a stream of water. Its rate of travel and its direction are totally at the mercy of the water that "carries it along."

The words "carried along by the Holy Spirit," then, suggest that the writers of Scripture were instruments in the hands of the creative Spirit of God. He directed them in what they wrote. This is not to suggest they were passive, like typewriters. But their activity was under the controlling power of the Holy Spirit. When they wrote under the influence of the Spirit, they knew that they were not expressing simply the thoughts of men. As Warfield noted, the prophets "knew that the Spirit by which they were inspired was not the natural spirit of their nation."[20] God's thoughts transcended the thoughts of sinful man as "the heavens are higher than the earth" (Isa. 55:8–9). Scripture testifies repeatedly that it is the word spoken by God through humans. The human authors wrote what God wanted them to write, so that in a very real sense He was the author of the writings as much as the humans who penned them.

The nature of the Spirit's work with the writers of Scripture was varied, or as the writer of Hebrews says, God spoke in "many ways" (Heb. 1:1). In some instances the operation of the Spirit was experienced more extraneously than at other times. To some, God conveyed His Word to the writers of Scripture in an audible voice as He did with Moses who "heard the voice [of God] speaking to him from above the mercy seat" (Num. 7:89; see also Exod. 4:12; 19:3–6; 1 Sam. 3:4–14; Is. 6:8–9; Rev. 14:13). At times He revealed His Word as He did to Daniel, in dreams, visions, or by sending an angel to speak His Word (Dan. 7:1; 8:1; 9:21–22). On other occasions the recipients of His Word experienced a state of spiritual exaltation that might be described as a trance (Rev. 1:10; see also Acts 10:10; 22:17; 2 Cor. 12:2–4). Most often, however, the writers of Scripture retained complete lucidity when entering into dialogue with God (Isa. 6:11; Jer. 14:13). Typically the prophets received God's Word through what has been termed "internal suggestion," which was probably true of dreams and visions as well.[21]

These descriptions of the Spirit's working speak especially to the portions of the Scriptures in which the human writers were primarily receptive, such as a typical prophetic utterance. But the Spirit was also involved in those portions of Scripture in which the human writer was more actively involved and the divine influence was not experienced in such an extraneous way. The psalms that express the personal experiences of the writers and the historical portions that involved the writers' research represent this category. In the Epistles the apostles simply taught the Word of God without mentioning that the Word of God was coming to them. In general it might be said that the Spirit's influence is different than in the previous category where His work was more obvious. However, it is a mistake, commonly made among higher critical scholars, to deny His involvement in these instances when the total powers of the human personality were actively creative in the production of the Word or when the authors used other sources including nonbiblical ones. Bruce Demarest and Gordon Lewis term this error "the single-cause fallacy," namely, "that if an author researched and used other sources, his message was not ultimately from God."[22] In response they state that "God works not only providentially in everything that comes to pass, but also miraculously in overseeing the production of, say, Luke's Gospel (1:1–4) and in the use of other canonical and noncanonical sources."[23]

The process in these instances has been called "concursive operation," in which the Spirit of God works "in, with, and through" the human activity "in such a manner as to communicate to the product [i.e., the Scriptures] qualities distinctly superhuman."[24] In other words the Spirit controlled the prophet or apostle as they spoke or wrote so that what was written by them was also the words of God. It is not that He stood outside of the human powers, only entering in at certain times to avoid errors or other inadequacies. Instead, as Warfield says, the Spirit was continually "working confluently in, with and by them, elevating them, directing them, controlling them, energizing them, so that, as His instruments, they rise above themselves and under His inspiration do His work and reach his aim."[25]

How this process of inspiration took place is not fully known, but that it is possible must readily be acknowledged. Augustine's comments on the devil's ability to put it into the heart of Judas to betray Jesus (John 13:2) are worth pondering in this connection. "Such a putting (into the heart) is a spiritual suggestion and entereth not by the ear, but through the thoughts; and thereby not in a way that is corporeal, but spiritual. . . . But how such things are done, as that devilish suggestions should be introduced, and so mingle with human thoughts that man accounts them his own, how can he know? Nor can we doubt that good suggestions are likewise made by a good spirit in the same unobservable and spiritual way."[26]

The question of the process of inspiration seems related to the question of how God works in us as humans to accomplish His will. When Scripture teaches us to "work out" our salvation, because God "is at work" in us (Phil. 2:13), it clearly teaches that somehow we and God can be active together without denying the validity of each. In relation to speech, the words of Jesus provide an interesting example. He claimed to speak words taught to Him by His Father (John 7:16; 8:28), and He claimed that He did so without any error. This process is explained in John 3:34: "For He whom God has sent speaks the words of God; for He gives the Spirit without measure." This pictures Jesus gifted with the Spirit in full measure (that is, beyond that of any other prophet) so that He perfectly spoke God's words. The gift of the Spirit, of course, related to Jesus in His humanity. So in His humanity He spoke actively and freely with no sense of "dictation" from His Father. His words were thus human words and the words of God at the same time.

Something similar may be true of believers in their glorified state of perfection in heaven. They will be so related to God and empowered by Him that the words of our Lord, "not My will, but Thine be done" (Luke 22:42) will be true forever. Apparently, then, their will and actions will also be God's will and works. In a similar way they will speak only truth, which can only be thought of as expressions of God's truth since He is the source of all truth. Thus truthful words spoken in true human freedom will also be His words of truth.

The incarnation of the Son of God—His coming to earth in a sinless human nature—provides an interesting analogy to the miracle of God's work in producing the Scriptures. The Holy Spirit came on Mary, who was truly human and fallible. Yet through her, by means of a normal development following supernatural conception, the Son of God was born with a true human nature. He bore fully the characteristics of a man as well as of God. Even as the sinful element in Mary was overruled so as not to contaminate the Lord, so the sinful fallibility of the human authors was overruled and what was produced was without flaw.

THE IMPORTANCE OF THE HUMANNESS OF SCRIPTURE

The common marks of the humanness of the Bible—the seeming mundaneness of much of its history and storytelling, the human expressions of problems and blessings in life, its very simplicity—all combine to make us wonder that this is also the Word of God. Should God's Word have been more regal, more profound, more mystical, more transcendent, more doctrinal (something like a good systematic theology)?

The nature of the Bible, however, perfectly fits the purpose of God's revelation, which is not cognitive knowledge, but redemption and real life. As Richard Gaffin explains, "Revelation is not so much divinely given gnosis to provide us with knowledge concerning the nature of God, man, and the world as it is divinely inspired interpretation of God's activity of redeeming men so that they might worship and serve him in the world."[27] Thus the Bible, as the revelatory Word of God, is first and foremost a historical book unfolding the story of God's redemptive purposes in history. Salvation is not an abstract philosophical or ethical system, but the historical reality of God's saving actions. The humanness of the many writers of Scripture representing various cultures demonstrates this fact.

By speaking His Word through the fullness of human experience in diverse historical situations, God has adapted to our human understanding. The knowledge of divine truth is conveyed through didactic teaching.

Thus we find doctrinal portions in the Bible such as much of the Book of Romans. But knowing God is attained only through engaging the whole person—intellect, feeling, and action. Such knowledge is conveyed only through concrete life. So the Scriptures do more than reveal God to us. They also reveal the experiences of His people with Him so that we might see how truth can be lived out in our lives. Jesus' parables serve the same purpose. The various literary genres in the Bible also serve the same learning purpose, for truth is communicated not only through doctrinal propositions and historical narrative, but also through poetry, proverbs, stories, prophecy, and so forth.

The human form of the words of the Bible is thus perfectly fitting for conveying God's message of redemption. The humanness of its history allows us to grasp something of the grandeur and scope of God's redemptive program from beginning to end. Its historical unfolding allows us to learn truth not only from verbal teaching but also from others' experiences. After reading the historical record of God's people, no one can doubt the reality of sin and the need for redemption. The varied kinds of literature in the Bible and its historical form also make it a fit instrument to speak to all peoples. The simplicity of the message of its story can be grasped by the simple beginner. But the profundity of its teachings continually entices the most mature toward greater understanding. In short, the reality of the Bible as the Word of God and the word of man completely meets our needs as humans.

Also the humanness of Scripture must be taken into consideration in its interpretation. It is not a homogenous book dropped from heaven, but a book written by humans living in various cultural settings. And although the message of the Word of God is not culture-bound, it nevertheless is expressed in the language, literary modes, and thought forms of specific cultures. Being aware of these human dimensions of the Bible can help us understand it better.

CONCLUSION

The Bible as the Word of God and the word of man is truly a miraculous book. As discussed, its divine and human nature may be likened to the union of the divine and the human natures in Jesus Christ, who was both truly man and truly God. The analogy is not exact, however, in that Christ's divine and human natures were united in one person, whereas the Holy Spirit does not *personally* unite with human nature in the inspiration of Scriptures. But as Warfield explains, the Scriptures and Christ *are* similar in that both are a union of the human and divine that resulted in an inerrant product. "In the case of Our Lord's person, the human nature remains truly human while yet it can never fall into sin or error because it can never act out of relation with the Divine nature into conjunction with which it has been brought; so in the case of the production of Scripture by the conjoint action of human and Divine factors, the human factors have acted as human factors, and have left their mark on the product as such, and yet cannot have fallen into that error . . . because they have not acted apart from the divine factors, . . . but only under their unerring guidance."[28]

Perhaps the most accurate way to think of the Bible is to think of its words as the words of our Saviour spoken through His humanity under the control of the Spirit. While red-letter editions of the Scripture can be helpful in noting the recorded words of our Lord, they can also be misleading in suggesting that the historical words of Jesus are somehow different in quality than those of the other inspired human writers. As we have seen, *all* Scripture written under the control of the Holy Spirit is equally the words of God and the words of humans. This is not in any sense to lower the significance of Jesus' words. Instead it exalts the supernatural character of the Scriptures. Christ, though having a human nature, is supernatural. And in a similar way, the Bible, though written by humans, is supernatural because of the Holy Spirit's superintending control over the writers.

Ten

I have learned to yield this respect and honor only to the canonical books of Scripture: of these alone do I most firmly believe that their authors were completely free from error.[1]

—Augustine

Ten

Is the Bible Reliable?

SINCE THE SCRIPTURES are the Word of God expressed in human words, does this mean that they are true and without error? Yes, because God is the "God of truth" (Ps. 31:5). If the Scriptures are truly His words, then they are completely true and without error.

Although Christians acknowledge the truthfulness of God, this conclusion that the Scriptures are completely true and without error is denied by many today, even among those who speak of them as God's Word and affirm the inspiration of all Scripture. In some instances they apply the terms "infallibility" and "inerrancy" to the Scriptures, but they say that these words mean that the Bible can include factual errors in matters not directly related to the faith and practice of the Christian life. I. Howard Marshall, for example, explains that "the purpose of the Bible was to guide people to salvation and the associated way of life." He then says, "'Infallible' means that the Bible is entirely trustworthy for the purposes for which God inspired it.'"[2] Some scholars apply the term "inerrancy" to what the author intended to teach. In other words, as Clark Pinnock writes, "The Bible *contains* errors but *teaches* none. . . . Inerrancy refers . . . to the *teaching* rather than to all the *components* utilized in its formulation."[3] The Scriptures, according to Donald Bloesch, "did not err in what they proclaimed, but this does not mean that they were faultless in their recording of historical data or in their world view, which is now outdated."[4]

So we need to examine closely the matter of the Bible's truthfulness. The question is this: Is the Bible inerrant in all that it asserts in all areas or only in those matters directly related to our salvation and Christian walk?

THE BIBLE'S TEACHING ON ITS TRUTHFULNESS

Because the terms "inerrant" and "inerrancy" are not used in the Scriptures to describe their own nature, some people object to their use, arguing that such terms are going beyond the teaching of Scripture. It should be noted, however, that terms that are not actually used in Scripture can nevertheless convey biblical truth. The word "Trinity," for example, is never found in the Bible, and yet orthodox believers throughout church history have recognized it as an accurate description of the biblical God.

Similarly, the question of whether the Scriptures contain errors or are "inerrant" is conveyed through other terminology. The positive side of the concept of "inerrancy" has to do with "truth," which is clearly a biblical term. If the Bible is inerrant, it is completely true. Therefore the question is, Does the Bible teach its truthfulness, that is, that it is "wholly true"?

How do we go about answering this question? Two methods of approach lead to opposite conclusions. One proposes that we examine all the data of the Bible in determining our doctrine of inspiration and inerrancy. The scriptural teachings on the nature of the Bible and all of what is often termed the phenomena of the Bible must be brought together in determining the nature of the Bible's inspiration.

The other method begins with the teachings of the Scriptures on the subjects of their own inspiration and truthfulness. Careful interpretation is made of everything that Scripture teaches about its nature. The summation of this teaching then becomes essentially our doctrine of inspiration.

The difference in the two approaches can be illustrated in the way they deal with certain problems in the Scriptures. For example, Jesus referred to the mustard seed as "smaller than all other seeds" (Matt. 13:32). Botany, however, knows of seeds that are actually smaller than mustard seeds. Coming across this biblical statement, which is not strictly true scientifically, the first approach declares that the inspiration of the Bible must be of such a nature that it includes some "errors" such as this one.

Paul's statement that "all Scripture is inspired" (2 Tim. 3:16) must therefore be interpreted in some limited fashion in order to allow for this kind of "mistake." In other words if we find inaccuracies of history and science in the Bible or statements made by one writer that we cannot harmonize with those of other writers, we must define inspiration in harmony with these assumed errors.

The problem with this approach is that human research and knowledge is the criterion of truth by which a statement of Scripture is declared correct or erroneous. God's speech must correspond with our contemporary knowledge. But the history of biblical scholarship demonstrates that many things that were viewed as errors in earlier days have been shown to be accurate as new information has been received from archaeology and the study of the biblical languages and manuscripts. Thus it seems presumptuous to make final judgments on these things today when more information tomorrow may throw new light on them.

The second approach, which seeks to understand the doctrine of inspiration from the direct biblical statements on the subject, must also deal with problems like the mustard seed. But this approach first determines what the Bible teaches about itself, then seeks to harmonize problems such as the mustard seed with that teaching. Assuming for the moment that a careful study of the Scriptures reveals that Christ and the biblical writers teach the full inspiration of all Scripture, this approach seeks an explanation of the problem which is consonant with this teaching. If a problem is found for which there is no adequate solution, it is not considered an adequate basis for changing the explicit teaching of the Scripture. A recognition of the limitation of our present human knowledge must be acknowledged.

The way we approach other doctrines of the Bible can help determine which of these two views is correct. Evangelicals have always affirmed the full deity and sinlessness of Christ, based on direct statements, such as John 1:1, where He is explicitly identified as God. But suppose we sought to determine whether He was truly God by examining all the statements about Him. Jesus said to the rich young ruler, "Why do you call Me good?

No one is good except God alone" (Luke 18:19). Such a statement might be interpreted as making Jesus someone less than God, or even making Him a sinner.

On another occasion Jesus confessed ignorance of the day of His coming again, stating that "the Father alone" knows this information (Mark 13:32). Since one of the attributes of God is omniscience, some might conclude from this verse that Jesus is not God. But the church did not use verses such as these to modify their belief in the full deity of Christ. Believing scholars interpreted these verses in ways that harmonized with the clear teaching of the deity of Christ and His sinlessness.

The usual method of understanding the teaching of the Scriptures on a given subject has always been to start with the explicit statements pertaining to that topic. After coming to an understanding of what is explicitly taught, other data may help in further clarifying the basic teaching, but must not be allowed to deny that teaching. The statements discussed above that seem to raise questions about Christ's deity help us understand Him more fully as both God and man. Similarly the phenomena of Scripture help us to understand more fully its nature. Paul's statement that the Scriptures are breathed out by God (2 Tim. 3:16) could suggest that the Scriptures were dictated by Him. But the Scriptures clearly reveal the differing personalities of the writers and other human characteristics, which cause us to reject the dictation theory of inspiration in favor of an understanding that encompasses genuine human participation. Additional understanding from other data, therefore, can lead us to a better understanding of the basic teaching, but it cannot be allowed to negate that teaching.

The Meaning of "Truth" in Scripture

Before we look at the testimony of the Scriptures to their truthfulness, it is necessary to define what Scripture means by "truth" or "true." The Old Testament Hebrew word for truth (*ʾemet*) has the basic idea of "firmness" or "certainty." On the basis of this meaning, many say that truth in the biblical sense means reliability or faithfulness. It denotes one who can be depended on, one in whom a person can place complete confidence, much like the meaning of "true" in the statement, "I will be true to you." The opposite of true is thus unfaithful, unreliable, or deceitful. Truth, it is argued, thus relates to people in relation to others (one can count on their word or actions), and not objective facts or propositions. In this view the focus is on reliability, not factuality. The Scriptures are said to be true, that is, reliable and trustworthy in accomplishing God's purpose of leading people to salvation. According to this understanding, therefore, the biblical concepts of truth and error do not focus on whether something objectively corresponds to reality.

In response it must be noted that although the original meaning of a word provides information about its past history, it does not determine its meaning in a subsequent period of history. In examining the use of the word "truth" in the Scriptures, we find that it refers not only to faithfulness but also to factuality in the sense of conforming to facts or reality.

It is true that in many places in the Old Testament *'emet* means faithfulness. Truth is a characteristic of God: "His faithfulness is a shield and bulwark" (Ps. 91:4); He "remains faithful forever" (146:6, NIV); "In my faithfulness I will reward them" (Isa. 61:8, NIV; see also Gen. 24:27; Exod. 34:6; Ps. 31:5; Jer. 4:2; Zech. 8:8). His actions are faithful or reliable: "The work of his hands are faithful and just" (Ps. 111:7, NIV). The same meaning of *'emet* is applied to humans, although much less frequently. Joshua exhorted the Israelites to "fear the LORD and serve him in sincerity and truth [or faithfulness]" (Josh. 24:14, see also Exod. 18:21, "men of truth," or "trustworthy men," NIV). With something of the same meaning "truth" is applied to objects. In these cases faithfulness means reliability or certainty. Rahab's request for a "pledge of truth" (Josh. 2:12) signified one on which she could rely. Similarly the "true reward" (Prov. 11:18) is one that is certain.

The last two uses are clearly moving toward a meaning of "truth" that signifies factual reality. The "true reward" is one that will prove to be true or actual in the future. This meaning of "truth"—something that corresponds to reality, as opposed to what is false, erroneous, or deceitful—is clear in numerous uses of *'emet*. "Truth" is called for in judicial matters. "Judge with truth" (Zech. 8:16), and "dispense true justice" (7:9). In both instances the call is for "judgments that are in accordance with *'emet*, with the actual facts, so that they prove to be right and just."[5] In matters of judgment thorough investigation is called for to see "if it is true and the matter established" (Deut. 13:14; see also 17:4, "it is true and . . . certain"; and 22:20). Witnesses are thus commended for their truthfulness (Prov. 14:25; Jer. 42:5).

One's speech is also to be characterized by truth. "Speak the truth to one another" (Zech. 8:16; see also Prov. 8:7; Dan. 11:2). In Psalm 15:2 speaking "truth" is contrasted with slandering or giving false and malicious reports. Similarly Jeremiah lamented over Jerusalem, saying, "Everyone deceives his neighbor, and does not speak the truth, they have taught their tongue to speak lies" (Jer. 9:5). The prophet Micaiah was summoned to speak "nothing but the truth in the name of the LORD" (1 Kings 22:16). "Truthful lips" are commended, but "a lying tongue" and "lying lips" are condemned (Prov. 12:19, 22). Clearly in these verses truth has to do with factuality or correspondence to reality as opposed to what is fictitious.

The concept of truth in the Old Testament thus includes the fundamental idea of something that is firm and can be relied on. It is primarily a personal attribute, denoting faithfulness and reliability. But it also denotes the idea of conformity to reality, that is, truth as opposed to what is false. Actually these two thoughts merge. As Roger Nicole points out, "It is because truth is conformity to fact that confidence may be placed in it or in the one who asserts it, and it is because a person is faithful that he or she will be careful to make statements that are true."[6]

The New Testament idea of truth carries over from the Old Testament, although the meaning of conformity to reality is the primary emphasis. In Greek literature the word *alētheia* ("truth") refers to things as they are, that is, what corresponds to reality. However, this same word translates the Hebrew *'emet* in the Septuagint, the Greek translation of the New Testament. The New Testament writers used this Greek term with the same meanings it had in the Old Testament.[7] The intellectual element is prominent, but the idea of truth in the sense of constancy or reliability is also present in many uses. This latter thought, however, was also commonly expressed in the New Testament by a group of words related to *pistos* ("trustworthy," "faithful," "dependable").

Which idea is dominant in each occurrence of the word "truth" in the New Testament is often difficult to determine. Several broad senses, however, may be distinguished, even though these may overlap.[8] Truth as reliability or dependability is still apparent in some uses, especially those referring to God, but also at times in reference to people. "Let God be found true" (Rom. 3:4), a statement about God's covenant promises with Israel, signifies His reliability, His faithfulness to His Word, which is analogous to the statement in the previous verse about the faithfulness of God (3:3). A similar meaning is seen in the words about Christ's servant ministry "on behalf of the truth [reliability, faithfulness] of God to confirm the promises given to the fathers" (15:8). As "children of light" believers are to produce the "fruit of light [which] consists in all goodness and righteousness and truth" (Eph. 5:9). This meaning of "truth" is clearly analogous to *ʾemet* in the Old Testament record of Hezekiah's "faithfulness": He did "what was good and right and faithful [*ʾemet*] before the LORD his God" (2 Chron. 31:20, NIV).

The primary emphasis in the occurrences of the word "truth" in its various forms (i.e., noun, adverb, adjective), however, is on what conforms to reality. Truth distinguished what is actual, real, or genuine from what is false. "Here is a true Israelite, in whom there is nothing false" (John 1:47, NIV; see also 1:9, "true light"; 4:23, "true worshipers"; 8:31, "then you are truly disciples"). It describes the real versus the imaginary. "What was being done by the angel was real, but [Peter] thought he was seeing a vision" (Acts 12:9). Ministering "in truth" stands in contrast to serving in pretense (Phil. 1:18). God is "the only true [genuine] God," as opposed to false gods (John 17:3).

Factuality is evident when the word "true" is used of one's witness or testimony. A true witness speaks according to reality (5:31–32; 8:13–14; Titus 1:13). Correspondence to facts is also seen in the contrast between truth and falsehood. Paul declared, "I am telling the truth . . . I am not lying" (Rom. 9:1; see also Acts 26:25 and 1 Tim. 2:7). "Therefore, laying aside falsehood, speak truth" (Eph. 4:25). And "speaking the truth" (4:15) is in contrast to "deceitful scheming" (4:14). The "liar" does not have "the truth" in him (1 John 2:4; see also 1:6 and James 3:14). Truth as opposed to lies is clearly seen in Jesus' words concerning the devil: "He was a murderer from the beginning, and does not stand in the truth, because there is not truth in him. Whenever he speaks a lie, he speaks from his own nature; for he is a liar, and the father of lies" (John 8:44). Even when the opposite is not mentioned, it is clear that truth means what is not false or in error. When Jesus asked who touched Him, the woman who was healed "fell down before Him and told Him the whole truth" (Mark 5:33).

This concept of truth as correspondence to reality is prominent throughout the New Testament. The writers claimed that their message was true because it was based on things that actually happened. They repeatedly asserted that they were eyewitnesses of Christ and His saving works (Acts 1:22; 2:32; 3:15; 5:32; 10:39; 1 Pet. 5:1–2; 2 Pet. 1:16–18; 1 John 1:1–3). Paul's affirmation of the resurrection of Christ rests on the truth that He actually appeared to people. And this could easily be verified, for most of them were still alive when the assertion was made (see 1 Cor. 15:1–8, esp. v. 6).

The New Testament concept of truth also includes the idea of ultimate reality. In this sense the thought is not truth in distinction to the unreal or false, but in distinction to something that is symbolic or a mere shadow of the heavenly or divine reality. The earthly Old Testament tabernacle was only a copy of the "true" heavenly tabernacle (Heb. 8:2; 9:24). Most importantly truth in this sense came with Christ. John wrote that "grace and truth came through Jesus Christ" (John 1:17, NIV). This is not to deny that grace and truth were already present in God's dealings in the Old Testament. But with the coming of Christ the divine reality of truth that was present in the Old Testament became fully disclosed. He was "the only begotten from the Father, full of grace and truth" (1:14). Since He is the full reality of the truth of God manifest in the world, He spoke truth, and He could also say, "I am . . . the truth" (14:6). And as Paul wrote, "truth is in Jesus" (Eph. 4:21).

From these various uses of "truth" in the Old and New Testaments, it is evident that truth involves several ideas—reliability or faithfulness, conformity to reality or factuality, and divine reality. Although one idea may be primary in a particular passage, these various threads are bound together. A reliable or truthful person will speak in conformity to reality, that is, he will not lie. Even the final revelation of God's "truth" in Christ is not unrelated to the truth revealed before through the prophets (Heb. 1:1–2).

Truth in the scriptural sense is ultimately a perfection of God Himself. All truth comes from God. His actions are manifestations of His truth, of His unchangeable constancy. So also His word is dependable; He always acts in accord with what He speaks, that is, His speech always accords with reality; it is factual. Thus He cannot lie (Titus 1:2; Heb. 6:18). Since everything is created by God and finds its end in God's purpose, truth is to be reflected in human life. God's commands are manifestations of His will. They reflect the truth of God, and are, as the apostle writes, "the embodiment . . . of the truth" (Rom. 2:20). People are therefore called to "[walk] in truth" (2 John 4; 3 John 3–4), to practice truth (John 3:21; 1 John 1:6), and to speak truth (Eph. 4:15, 25). Such a concept of truth whose definition is finally derived from God Himself suggests the perfection of its characteristics—reliability, conformity to fact, and ultimate divine reality.

The Bible's Testimony to Its Truth

The Bible frequently witnesses to its truthfulness. The identification of the Scriptures as the Word of God is clearly a claim to truthfulness, for God is the God of truth. And Paul's statement about the inspiration of the Scriptures by the Spirit of God (2 Tim. 3:16)—and Jesus' statements that "not the smallest letter or stroke [of the Law or Scripture] shall pass away" (Matt. 5:18) and that "the Scripture cannot be broken" (John 10:35)—clearly imply truthfulness.

Also several statements in the Bible refer explicitly to its being truthful. For example, the psalmist in his great meditation on the value and delights of Scripture in Psalm 119 declared, "Thy law is truth" (119:142), "all Thy commandments are truth" (119:151), and, "the sum of Thy word is truth" (119:160). The word "sum" in the last statement indicates that "truth" is a characteristic of all of Scripture. As Derek Kidner says, the use of the same word for the total of a census count (for example, Exod. 30:12; Num. 1:2) "shows that 'the sum of' is not a way of saying 'by and large,' but rather, 'every part of' God's word is truth."[9] To be sure, the psalmist's delight in the Word of God throughout the psalm (119:16, 24, 47, 70, 77, 143, 174) shows that "truthfulness" had a personal or existential meaning for him. He has found them to be faithful and reliable in the struggles of his life. But as Anthony Thiselton notes, "The same Psalmist sees the law of God as a lamp and a light (v. 105) which shows the believer the true state of affairs,"[10] and therefore the meaning of truth as conformity to reality cannot be excluded from these statements. Believers find Scripture personally reliable in life because they are true factually and they express reality. In God's attack against the false prophets of Jeremiah's day the issue was clearly truth versus falsity. The false prophets "prophesy falsely in My name" (Jer. 23:25), "but let him who has My word speak My word in truth" (23:28, see also 1 Kings 17:24).

In the New Testament the gospel is frequently said to be characterized by truth. It is "the word of truth" (Eph. 1:13, NIV; Col. 1:5). The Old Testament Scriptures are the "embodiment of knowledge and of the truth" (Rom. 2:20). Most significant is Jesus' affirmation that "Thy word is truth" (John 17:17). In Thiselton's words, "This word from God is valid, effective, in no way false, indeed in accord with reality. It is all these things precisely because it is the revealing word of God himself."[11]

In addition to explicit statements on the truthfulness of the Scriptures, other statements in the Bible refer to its perfection. As the psalmist declared, "The words of the LORD are pure words; as silver tried in a furnace on the earth, refined seven times" (Ps. 12:6). The Hebrew word translated "pure" is used elsewhere to describe a metal, such as gold, that is free of impurities (Exod. 25:11, 17, 24, 29). It is also used of a pure heart (Ps. 51:10; Ezek. 36:25) or of ritual purity or cleanness (Lev. 10:10, 14; 13:13, 17; Deut. 14:11, 20; Mal. 1:11). To emphasize the purity of God's Word, David wrote that it is like silver "refined seven times" (Ps. 12:6). The number seven probably expresses "in a forceful way the concept of absolute purity, total freedom from impurity or imperfection."[12]

David also wrote, "As for God, His way is blameless; the word of the LORD is tried; He is a shield to all who take refuge in Him" (18:30). The Hebrew word translated "tried" ("flawless," NIV) is commonly used for refining, smelting, testing, or proving metals. God's Word has been tested and shown to be completely pure and entirely reliable. As the verse suggests, God's Word corresponds to His actions. His "way" is "blameless" or "perfect" (NIV); His word is likewise "tried" or "free of blemish."[13] This tested and proven quality of God's Word is heightened in 119:140, where it is described as "very pure" (or "tried," as in 18:30). Proverbs 30:5 says, "Every word of God is tested [or, flawless, NIV]." To the purity of God's Word, Agur cautioned, "Do not add to His words lest He reprove you, and you be proved a liar" (30:6). The contrast with lying shows that the purity of God's tested and tried Word refers not only to the fact that the believer finds it reliable in life, but also that it is truth as opposed to falsehood.

In Proverbs 8:8 wisdom, personified as an individual, said, "All the utterances of my mouth are in righteousness; there is nothing crooked or perverted in them." The use of "right" in 12:17 and Psalm 52:3 in opposition to falsehood and deceit indicates that "righteous" speech includes truthful speech.

Interestingly the Scriptures never limit their claim of truthfulness to some teachings (such as those that relate directly to salvation) while not affirming the truthfulness of other teachings. But does this mean that the Scriptures are inerrant? Truthfulness, especially in the sense of reliability, is applied to humans whose lives are predominantly characterized by this attribute, but not perfectly. This, however, cannot be said of God. Since the very concept of truth is grounded in Him, the meaning of "truth" does not encompass imperfection. Unreliability or lack of conformity to reality are never part of truth itself. Because God is true, the truthfulness of His revelation in actions and speech is never characterized by falsehood. The Holy Spirit, through whom the Word of God came into being, is also called the Spirit of truth (John 14:17; 15:26; 16:13; 1 John 4:6). Since the Scriptures were written by those who were "moved by the Holy Spirit" (2 Pet. 1:21) so that what they wrote is the Word of God, it is difficult to conclude anything other than that the Scriptures are true in every part.

THE MEANING OF THE INERRANCY OF THE SCRIPTURES

In the past the traditional term used to describe the truthfulness of Scripture was "infallible." However, since "infallible" can carry the meaning of "unfailing in effectiveness or operation," some people, as noted earlier, use this word of the Scriptures to suggest that they are unfailing in accomplishing their purpose of bringing salvation. Thus in this view, infallibility does not mean without error. For this reason most who refer to the truthfulness of Scripture refer to its inerrancy.

The Definition of "Inerrancy"

Following the Scriptures' own language, inerrancy is best defined as "truthfulness." It means that the Scriptures in their original writings are true in everything that they said regarding all matters. David Dockery defines inerrancy this way: "The Bible (in its original writings) properly interpreted in light of which culture and communication means had developed by the time of its composition will be completely true (and therefore not false) in all that it affirms, to the degree of precision intended by the author, in all matters relating to God and his creation."[14]

Because the Scriptures are true, they are not only reliable or trustworthy; they also conform to reality. Of course, many sentences in the Bible are not factual statements whose truth can be measured by conformity to external realities such as historical facts. Prayers, commands, and exhortations, for example, do not directly assert propositions that can be directly verified except in the sense that the statements were actually made. Calling all forms of utterances "speech acts," Kevin Vanhoozer explains how even those speech acts that are not propositions nevertheless can be said to be true if certain realities are implied in them.[15] For example, the exhortation "Praise the Lord" implies the existence of God, His worthiness of praise, and a certain relationship between Him and His people that makes praise the right thing to do. The truthfulness of the exhortation to praise the Lord thus rests on implied realities. Because all the Scriptures are the Word of God, His "speech acts" are inerrant, including commands, promises, warnings, prayers, and so forth.[16]

Some Necessary Qualifications of "Inerrancy"

To avoid a misunderstanding of inerrancy, it is necessary to ask several questions when we examine statements in Scriptures. First, was the human author portraying the statement as true, or was he simply reporting what someone said that may have been untrue? The inclusion of Satan's statement to Eve, "You surely shall not die" (Gen. 3:4), demonstrates that the Bible includes things that are actually false. And the Bible accurately records the speeches of Job's friends, though they were wrong in accusing Job of some serious sin. Usually the context makes clear whether a statement is to be understood as truth or not. Yet the Bible is still inerrant in that it truthfully and accurately reported what was said or what occurred.

Second, did the author intend to speak in popular language or in technical scientific language? We speak of the sun rising and setting, but scientifically we know that the earth moves, not the sun. We don't charge our newspaper writers or television weather reporters as being in error when they report the times of sunrises and sunsets.

Third, was the author speaking in round numbers? If the number is a reasonable approximation, then no untruth is involved. In many situations—the population of cities, the size of crowds, mileage distances—people use round numbers, but we don't say those statements are in error. The same principle applies to quotations of others. They may be exact word-for-word quotes, or they may be paraphrases that give the gist of the original meaning without including error.

Fourth, was the author intending to speak literally or through a figure of speech? Some would say that the biblical writers held an erroneous cosmology in speaking of "the four corners of the earth" (Isa. 11:12) or the "windows of heaven" (Gen. 7:11, KJV). However, when such language is understood in a figurative sense, as it was undoubtedly intended, no error is involved.

Some people object to the doctrine of inerrancy by calling attention to some grammatical constructions in Hebrew or Greek that do not follow the usual patterns. As Nicole explains, "We have sentences that are suspended [not completed as begun]; we have verbs where the subject is in doubt; we have forms of speech which might have fallen under the condemnation of a classical Hebrew or Greek grammarian."[17] Grammar, however, is not an issue of truth but of conformity to human convention of language, which is variable and fluctuates over time. In any case, whether one speaks and writes with good grammar has nothing to do with the truthfulness of a statement. Moreover, good reasons can often be found for those instances in which the biblical writers varied from normal grammatical expressions. In some cases it resulted from bringing Hebrew constructions over into the Greek language, constructions that did not conform to standard Greek grammar.

Inerrancy therefore means that when full consideration is given to the statements of Scripture in light of their intended meaning and use by the human authors, the Bible is fully trustworthy in all it states. Its primary teaching is related to God's great redemptive program through Jesus Christ. But in providing this salvation, God invaded our world to deal with us in our history and geography. Thus the record of God's salvation touches other areas of knowledge as well as spiritual truth. It is this record, in its entirety, that is the inspired, inerrant word of God. This does not mean the writers knew more about history and science than people do today, nor does it mean that they were experts in all fields of knowledge. Instead it means that God preserved them from misleading us in any statement, no matter how seemingly insignificant.

THE SIGNIFICANCE OF THE INERRANCY OF THE BIBLE

Since the Enlightenment of the eighteenth century, the question of the inerrancy of the Scriptures has been debated among Christians. Much energy has been expended and ink spilt even among evangelicals who have struggled over this issue in the last several decades. Is the inerrancy or truthfulness of the Scriptures really that significant for the Christian faith? Of course believing in inerrancy does not guarantee that a person will interpret the Bible accurately, as evidenced by the fact that inerrancy is affirmed by some cults such as the Jehovah's Witnesses. But the Scriptures, not our interpretations of them, are inerrant. Inerrancy, however, does provide a necessary logical basis for the full authority of all the Bible.

Inerrancy Means All of the Bible Is Authoritative

If the Bible contains errors, its authority is limited. Of course, one can say, as many do, that Scripture is authoritative only in teachings that relate to salvation. However, by saying this, a person limits the authority of the Scriptures.

J. I. Packer's words about the significance of inerrancy in relation to the exposition of the Scriptures are well worth thoughtful consideration. When we affirm the inerrancy of the Bible, Packer notes, "We may not 1) deny, disregard, or arbitrarily relativize, anything that the biblical writers teach, nor 2) discount any of the practical implications for worship and service that their teaching carries, nor 3) cut the knot of any problem of Bible harmony, factual or theological, by allowing ourselves to assume that the inspired authors were not necessarily consistent either with themselves or with each other."[18]

By affirming the inerrancy of the Scriptures, we place ourselves under the authority of all the teachings of the Bible. To say that the Bible has errors limits its authority and can "lead to reduced and distorted versions of Christianity."[19]

If we accept errors in some parts of Scripture, this raises questions about the whole. True, an error in one statement does not necessarily mean that errors exist throughout the Bible. But the existence of one error in the Scriptures does open the possibility for other errors. Thus to say the Bible has errors undermines our confidence in the whole of Scripture.

Some Bible students say inerrancy pertains only to matters of faith and practice, the truth of which cannot be verified. But logically this raises the question of how spiritual matters can be reliable. Why should an unbeliever accept as true those spiritual parts of the Bible about God and Christ's death as a substitute for sinners, teachings that cannot be checked, when he is told that the very areas that can be confirmed, such as matters of history or science, contain inaccuracies?

Once errors are admitted in even a very limited area, the tendency is for more alleged errors to be admitted. At first some theologians questioned matters of historical reliability, but soon they challenged aspects of the Bible's theology and ethics. As Carl Henry writes, "It was soon apparent that scholars who abandoned the trustworthiness of biblical history had furnished an entering wedge for the abandonment of doctrinal elements."[20] For example, in 1905 William Newton Clark wrote that only Jesus' theological and moral teachings are authoritative.[21] Following that, the reality of demons in Jesus' ministry—a theological and moral issue—

came to be rejected as prescientific. The rationalistic criticism of the Bible then led to Harry Emerson Fosdick saying that only Jesus' life is "abidingly valid."[22] Going even further, some came to view Jesus as only a source of inspiration.

This is not to say that everyone who denies the truthfulness of all the Bible limits the authority of the Bible. It does point out, however, that affirming even some errors in Scripture makes it difficult, on principle, to preclude other individuals from finding more.

Inerrancy Means That the Bible Is the Final Authority

Not only does adherence to the Bible's inerrancy mean that the Scriptures are *all* authoritative. Perhaps even more importantly, it affirms that God's Word and not human reason is the *final* or ultimate authority. To accept errors in the Bible immediately raises the question, Who decides what is true and what is erroneous in the Scriptures? Is not the biblical critic who says that a certain scriptural statement is in error placing himself as an authority over the Scriptures? The International Council on Biblical Inerrancy aptly noted this reality in the closing of its "Chicago Statement on Biblical Inerrancy": "The result of taking this step [the denial of the total truthfulness of Scripture] is that the Bible which God gave loses its authority, and what has authority instead is a Bible reduced in content according to the demands of one's critical reasonings and in principle reducible still further once one has started. This means that at bottom independent reason now has authority, as opposed to Scriptural teaching."[23] The Chicago Statement then asserts that a denial of inerrancy leads to an unstable subjectivism.[24] Nicole's words deserve the attention of every believer: "What is supremely at stake in this whole discussion is the recognition of the authority of God in the sacred oracles. Are we going to submit unconditionally to the voice of God who has spoken? Or, are we going to insist on screening the message of the Bible, accepting only what appears palatable and remaining free to reject what does not conform to our preconceived criteria?"[25]

CONCLUSION

The Scriptures lay claim to their total truthfulness and flawless purity, that is, to their inerrancy. Nowhere does the Bible indicate that these teachings pertain only to certain parts or certain themes. Submission to the teachings of Scriptures, therefore, entails recognition of its inerrancy. Moreover, this doctrine logically upholds the final authority of all of Scripture. Only truth has authority, and because the Scriptures are completely true they command ultimate authority.

Eleven

All your words are true. (Ps. 119:60, NIV)

Every word of God is flawless. (Prov. 30:5, NIV)

If a Scripture which appears to be of such a kind [contradictory to another Scripture] be brought forward, and if there be a pretext (for saying) that it is contrary (to some other), since I am entirely convinced that no Scripture contradicts another, I shall admit rather that I do not understand what is recorded, and shall strive to persuade those who imagine that the Scriptures are contradictory, to be rather of the same opinion as myself.[1]

—Justin Martyr, second-century church father

Give me the plenary, verbal theory of inspiration, with all its difficulties, rather than doubt. I accept the difficulties and humbly wait for their solution. But while I wait I am standing on the rock.[2]

—J. C. Ryle

Eleven

Does the Bible Contradict Itself?

ONE MIGHT THINK that since the Bible is true, then all its contents would readily harmonize perfectly. The careful student of the Bible, however, inevitably comes across problems in the study of the Scriptures that seem incompatible with their divine inspiration. One portion of Scripture may seem difficult to harmonize with another, and some scriptural data may seem out of step with secular scholarship. If the Scriptures are what they claim to be—the inspired Word of God, how do we account for these apparent problems and what should our response be?

THE CAUSE OF BIBLICAL PROBLEMS

When we consider the nature of the Bible, it is not difficult to understand why we might encounter some problems. According to the writer of Hebrews, God's revelation contained in the Scriptures came into history from "long ago" until "these last days" (Heb. 1:1–2). The writing of the Scriptures spanned centuries of time in which God spoke to His people in their historical settings and diverse cultures. Despite great strides in archeological and historical studies in bridging the historical and cultural gaps that exist between us and Bible times, our knowledge of the ancient world is not complete. The very human characteristics of the Bible necessary for the understanding of God's people throughout history, therefore, make it likely that we will encounter some data in Scripture that are still difficult for us to understand and harmonize to our complete satisfaction.

The impression is sometimes given that these problems are of recent origin, stemming from the use of modern scientific methodology or scientific and historical discoveries. Bible-believing scholars, however, have been aware of these problems for centuries and have sought to resolve them in accord with the inspiration of the Scriptures. Given this fact, it will be helpful to consider briefly the impetus behind much of the modern tendency toward the denial of biblical inerrancy.

Antisupernatualistic Presuppositions

The exaltation of human reason as the ultimate criterion of truth in the eighteenth-century Enlightenment led to the flowering in the nineteenth century of what is known as the historical critical method of studying the Scriptures.This approach held "that reality is uniform and universal, that it is accessible to human reason and investigation, that all events historical and natural occurring within it are in principle comparable by analogy, and that man's contemporary experience of reality can provide the objective criteria by which what could or could not have happened in the past is to be determined."[3] This principle has subsequently been modified in some respects. For example, it is acknowledged that all historical events are in some sense unique and therefore cannot be completely analogous to previous events. Moreover, there may be meaning in an event that is not objectively verifiable, such as the highest values in life, including, for example, justice and love.[4]

Nevertheless the underlying principle that human reason alone can determine what is real and true, and the consequent antisupernaturalistic world-view, remains at the center of much biblical criticism today and provides the criterion for many charges of scriptural error even today. As Richard Purtill explains, "If the biblical narratives did not contain accounts of miraculous events or have reference to God, angels, etc., biblical history would probably be regarded as much more firmly established than most of the history of, say, classical Greece and Rome. But because the biblical accounts do mention miracles and do involve reference to God, angels and demons, etc., considerations other than purely historical ones come into the picture. . . . [Modernists] are convinced as part of their general worldview that miracles don't happen."[5] Howard Vos pointedly summarizes the issue. "The excessive skepticism of many liberal theologians stems not from a careful evaluation of the available data, but from an enormous predisposition against the supernatural."[6]

The belief that human reason is the means of determining truth affects not only history, but also moral and religious matters. While asserted in rather bald terms, the underlying principle of a nineteenth-century writer is still applied by may people today: "If we find even in the Bible anything which confuses our sense of right and wrong, which seems to us less exalted and pure than the character of God would be; if after the most patient thought and prayerful pondering it still retains this aspect, then we are not to bow down to it as God's revelation to us, since it does not meet the need of the earlier and more sacred revelation He has given us in our own spirit and conscience which testify of Him."[7]

Because some regulations of the Mosaic Law recorded in Exodus 21–23 reveal a reflection of the status quo in Israel's society at that time (e.g., slavery) and also the "mercy and justice of God," Paul Achtemeier concludes that this scriptural passage derives from two sources, one natural (from Hebrew life) and the other revelation (from God).[8] Evangelicals have always understood that this passage is the inerrant revelation of the loving God, who wisely suited His regulations to His people at that time in history. But Achtemeier rejects this and proposes instead his own opinion of what God's revelation should be.

All this reveals the fact that *our religious commitment does in fact affect how we view the Bible.* Critics, however, seek to deny this reality. For example, John Barton has asserted that the "ground rules for effective biblical criticism are dependent only on good reasoning. . . . The religious commitment of critics is entirely irrelevant to evaluating their work."[9] However, the following words of evangelical J. I. Packer are difficult to deny. "*When you encounter a present-day view of Holy Scripture, you encounter more than a view of Scripture.* What you meet is a total view of God and the world, that is, a total theology, which is both an ontology, declaring what there is, and an epistemology, stating how we know what there is. . . .

Every view of Scripture . . . proves on analysis to be bound up with an overall view of God and man."[10]

True, there are genuine difficulties in the Scriptures which Bible-believing students cannot avoid. However, many of the modern attacks against the Bible's truthfulness stem not from data that prove that scriptural statements are contradictory or contrary to reality, but from philosophical and theological presuppositions on the part of interpreters. While various explanations can be given for the underlying presuppositions that influence our attitude toward Scripture, Jesus suggests that the fundamental desire of our hearts is what plays the key role. "If any man is willing to do His will, he shall know of the teaching, whether it is of God, or whether I speak from Myself" (John 7:17). Knowing whether His teaching is true or not, Jesus said, cannot be decided by so-called objective rational debate, but depends on a moral choice. What D. A. Carson says about knowing God's will applies to the whole of divine revelation. "The faith commitment envisaged here, this moral choice, is properly basic, and renders impossible any attitude that sets us up as judges of God's ways. . . . Finite and fallen human beings cannot set themselves up on some sure ground *outside* the truth and thus gain the vantage from which they may assess it. Divine revelation can only be assessed, as it were, from the inside."[11]

To the extent that we do not approve of the teachings of Scripture and submit to them, to that same extent we will inevitably find reason for denying that the Bible is God's revelation. We inevitably seek to harmonize our thoughts with the way we choose to live. It is well to remember this principle when thinking about biblical difficulties, for as has been said, "The reason why we find so many dark places in the Bible is, for the most part, because there are so many dark places in our hearts."[12]

Genuine Causes of Biblical Problems

As already noted, many biblical difficulties arise because the Bible is an ancient document, written in cultures that differed from our own. For example, different methods of computation may have been used. This is especially true with regard to chronologies. Weights may change over time, causing difficulty in harmonizing one account with another unless the change is known. We may not yet fully understand the meaning of certain words, idioms, grammatical constructions, or other aspects of the ancient biblical languages and writing styles.

Thus it should not surprise us that certain problems exist. The Spirit of God worked through real people to produce the Scriptures. He did not obliterate their personalities or lift them out of their historical situations to place them on some kind of special plane where they all thought and expressed themselves alike. It should not be surprising if everything does not immediately appear in perfect agreement. In fact, such agreement might be taken as evidence against the authenticity of the Scriptures, suggesting that there was collaboration and forgery on the part of those who wrote it.

A LOOK AT SOME BIBLICAL DIFFICULTIES

It is beyond the scope of this work to discuss all the apparent problems in the Scriptures. Several works dealing with most of the difficulties, especially those often raised against the doctrine of inerrancy, may be consulted. One of the most extensive is Gleason Archer's *Encyclopedia of Bible Difficulties.*[13] Discussions of difficulties may also be found in many commentaries authored by evangelical inerrantists. A brief look at some representative examples and the responses that have been proposed will be helpful.

Historical Problems

Some historical difficulties arise from information outside the Bible, and others stem from alleged internal contradictions. Allegations from outside the Bible have generally come from presuppositions against the supernatural. For example, assuming the evolution of man and culture, some writers insisted that the first five books of the Bible (the Pentateuch) could not have come from the time of Moses because most people then were illiterate and Moses was unable to write. But then the Code of Hammurabi was discovered, and since it was written about 1728 B.C., objections to Moses' authorship of the Pentateuch were dropped.

Similar objections to the Bible's historical reliability have been overcome by archeological research. According to the noted archaeologist William F. Albright, "Until recently it was the fashion among biblical historians to treat the patriarchal sagas of Genesis [11–50] as though they were artificial creations of Israelite scribes of the Divided Monarchy or tales told by imaginative rhapsodists around Israelite campfires during centuries following their occupation of the country. . . . Archaeological discoveries since 1925 have changed all this. Aside from a few die-hards among older scholars, there is scarcely a single biblical historian who has not been impressed by the rapid accumulation of data supporting the substantial historicity of patriarchal tradition."[14]

The existence of the Hittites, mentioned many times in Scripture, was treated with great skepticism until excavations in 1906 at a place ninety miles east of Ankara, Turkey, which turned out to be the capital of the Hittite Empire. The size of Nineveh, "an exceedingly great city, a three days' walk" (Jon. 3:3) was ridiculed by Voltaire as a blatant error. But archeology later confirmed this scriptural statement.

Again and again objections, often based "on false assumptions and unreal, artificial schemes of historical development,"[15] are overturned by the hard evidence of archaeological research. One of the most respected archaeologists of the last half of the twentieth century, the Jewish scholar Nelson Glueck, forthrightly states his findings concerning the historical reliability of Scripture: "As a matter of fact . . . it may be stated categorically that no archaeological discovery has ever controverted a Biblical reference. Scores of archaeological findings . . . confirm in clear outline or in exact detail historical statements in the Bible."[16] Some historical problems remain, but these are unanswered questions calling for more information. None are proofs against the inerrancy of the Bible.

Plausible explanations are also possible when all information is known in relation to alleged historical contradictions in the Scriptures. Variations in the Gospel accounts of the same incident have been the source of problems for a number of people. One of the most popular concerns is Peter's denial and the crowing of the cock. According to Mark's account the cock crowed twice (14:30, 72), while Matthew and Luke simply made the statement that before the cock would crow Peter would deny the Lord three times (Matt. 26:34, 74–75; Luke 22:34, 60–61).

However, no contradiction exists here. Matthew and Luke did not say the cock crowed only once as opposed to Mark's twice. They simply referred to the cock crowing. When we remember that "cockcrowing" was a proverbial expression for early morning, these accounts can be easily harmonized. According to Mark 13:35 the third of the four Roman night watches was designated the "cockcrow" or "cockcrowing." But roosters are also apt to crow earlier, from midnight on. Matthew and Luke gave us the main point of Jesus' prediction that Peter would deny the Lord three times before early morning, signaled by the well-known cockcrowing. On the other hand Mark reported the greater details of Jesus' words. So both accounts are true.

A similar problem is often raised with regard to the number of angels at Jesus' tomb. Critics have pointed out that Matthew and Mark mentioned only one angel at Jesus' tomb (Matt. 28:2–5; Mark 16:5), whereas Luke and John referred to two angels (Luke 24:4; John 20:12). Again no contradiction is involved, because the presence of two surely does not contradict the fact that one is present. The two accounts can easily be seen as complementary.[17]

Problems of variation in accounts, such as these, can generally be solved if we keep in mind the principle that differences can be present without there being a contradiction. The writers may have been led by the Holy Spirit to bring out a different emphasis or a different part of a conversation.

Problems may also be solved when we realize that two statements may not be speaking of something in the same sense. The story is told of a skeptic who was annoyed by supposed errors in the Bible. When asked to name a specific error, he replied that as a lumberman he had figured out the dimensions of Noah's ark and how many feet of lumber went into it. He was surprised at its size. Later, however, he opened his Bible and happened to read where the Levites took the ark on their shoulders and carried it around in the wilderness. "Such foolishness," he said, "made me angry, and I have never looked inside the book again."[18] Obviously, he had not asked himself whether "ark" had the same sense in each passage.

A more serious example occurs in relation to whether John the Baptist was Elijah. When asked whether he was Elijah, John the Baptist replied, "I am not" (John 1:21). However, Jesus explicitly declared that John was Elijah (Matt. 11:14). This dilemma is solved when we recognize that John the Baptist and Jesus were not referring to Elijah in the same sense. The Jews, remembering that Elijah had left the earth in a chariot of fire without dying (2 Kings 2:11), expected the same Elijah to return in fulfillment of Malachi's prophecy (Mal. 4:5). John was not Elijah in this sense, and so he rightly answered no. On the other hand, in connection with the birth of John the angel declared that he would come "in the spirit and power of Elijah" in fulfillment of Malachi's prediction. Knowing that John had fulfilled in a preliminary way Malachi's prediction of Elijah as a forerunner of the coming of the day of the Lord, Jesus could rightly identify him as Elijah.[19]

When facing an apparent discrepancy, we must also ask whether the Bible is speaking of the same event or a similar but different one. Because the disciples still questioned where they could get enough food to feed the four thousand (Matt. 15:32–33) after they had earlier witnessed the miracle of the feeding of the five thousand, many critics view the story of the four thousand (15:32–38) as nothing more than a "doublet," or repetition, of the earlier report of the feeding of the five thousand (14:15–21), which, they say, amounts to a clear contradiction. There is nothing, however, that precludes understanding that Matthew was reporting two somewhat similar, but different incidents. In the first report there were five loaves and two fish, twelve baskets left over, and five thousand men fed. In the second report there were seven loaves and a few small fish, seven baskets left over, and four thousand men fed. The disciples' concern about where the food would come from after Jesus had miraculously fed the five thousand can be accounted for by their continual difficulty in understanding and believing Jesus.[20]

It is also important to recognize that the biblical writers often used methods of computation different from methods used today. This is particularly true with regard to dates. There is some evidence that the New Year was first reckoned as beginning in autumn and was later changed to the spring. However, the religious New Year that began with the Passover in the spring did not completely replace the civil New Year that began in the fall.[21] We, of course, do something similar when we employ fiscal and civil calendars that do not coincide.

The ancients also used different methods in counting the years of the reigns of their kings. According to one system, any part of a calendar year was considered as one year's reign. Thus, for example, using our calendar, if a king assumed the throne in December of one year, he completed his first year at the end of December and began his second on January 1. According to the other system the first year of rule commenced with January no matter what portion of the previous year the king had already reigned.[22]

The ancient scribes of the Near East also did not draw up chronological lists of their rulers as we do today. They simply listed the reigns of each king in succession without synchronizing them with each other. The reigns of a number of kings of Israel overlapped. When these coregencies are recognized, alleged chronological problems disappear. An example of this is seen in the Turin Papyrus of the kings of Egypt. Dynasties XIII–XVII list over 150 rulers whose reigns totaled at least 450 years. But from other sources it is known that these 150 rulers and their 450 years of reign actually fit into around 216 years because several of the kings reigned contemporaneously. As Kitchen and Mitchell note, "It must be stressed that in no case, biblical or extra-biblical, is it a question of inaccuracy, but of the methods current in antiquity."[23]

The biblical chronologists were concerned "to make plain the inner meaning of history as opposed to a listing . . . . It wishes to detail the relationship of a people to its God and to show the inevitable effect *in history* of the character of that relationship."[24] The biblical writers sometimes moved back and forth chronologically in recording historical events; they did this for the purpose of developing particular themes. The fact that chronology was of secondary interest to them does not imply, however, that they were not concerned with accuracy. As Craig Blomberg says, "A careful analysis shows that no two Gospels contradict each other's chronology."[25] The claim of Israel in the Old Testament that they had actually encountered God in history would surely suggest careful concern for historical accuracy. Moreover, biblical accuracy has been increasingly verified by recent scholarship.[26]

Some problems may also stem from our inadequate understanding of the ancient biblical language in either the meaning and use of words or grammatical usage. For example, according to 1 Samuel 28:6 Saul "inquired of the LORD," but received no answer and therefore sought out a medium at Endor. First Chronicles 10:13–14, however, states that he made inquiry of the medium "and did *not* inquire of the LORD" (italics added). This apparent contradiction is quickly solved when we note that different Hebrew words for "inquired" are found in these passages. The one in Samuel simply means "to ask, inquire, or request." The word used by the chronicler, while carrying the meaning "to inquire," also had a predominant theological use, especially in 1 and 2 Chronicles, denoting "a loyal, positive, devoted commitment to Yahweh."[27] Thus while Saul did ask the Lord for information before turning to the medium of Endor, as the writer of 1 Samuel wrote, the chronicler was also correct in that Saul's entire attitude in this incident was not one of "seeking" the Lord in the sense of a committed loyalty.

The apparent contradiction concerning whether those traveling with Paul "heard the voice" of the Lord speaking to Paul (Acts 9:7, NRSV) or "did not hear the voice" (22:9, NRSV) is easily solved when the Greek grammatical constructions of the two statements are considered. In 9:7 the grammatical form (genitive case) of what was heard, that is, "the voice," indicates simply that sounds were heard with no indication that anything was understood. In 22:9, however, "the voice" is in a grammatical form (accusative case) that indicates apprehension of the message heard. While this apparent discrepancy, still apparent in some modern translations, is easily solved with an understanding of the grammar of the biblical language, it is possible that other problems still remain because of our inadequate linguistic understanding of the meaning of words, phrases, and grammar in the biblical languages.

Other biblical difficulties result from copyists' mistakes. As discussed later, the manuscripts from which our present Bibles are translated are very close to the original writings, but they are still copies. Not having printing presses and other modern means of duplication, the Scriptures were first copied over and over by hand. Unless we posit the miraculous superintendence of the copyists similar to the inspiration of the original authors, it is impossible for a human to produce even one perfect copy. Even with our technical skills of computer spell-checkers and other aids including skilled proofreaders, mistakes slip through. One has only to think of reading handwritten documents, some well-worn and stained with use, and copying them perfectly to realize the impossibility of perfect copies.

Careful consideration of the earliest copies of the Scriptures gives evidence of typical mistakes that were made in copying a document.[28] The omission of letters or words that should be present (haplography) or mistaken repetition (dittography) could easily occur as a copyist's eye moved back and forth from the document he was reading to the new one he is writing. Words were omitted as his eye slipped down from one line to another or were repeated or were erroneously joined together or split into two. The transposition of words could also easily occur, as is probable in 2 Samuel 8:17, where Ahimelech is said to be the son of Abiathar whereas 1 Samuel 22:20 has the reverse—Abiathar is the son of Ahimelech.

The very form of the documents written by hand by various individuals adds to the difficulty of making perfect copies. For example, several letters in the Hebrew alphabet are quite similar in appearance. In handwriting it could be easy to confuse some of these letters, much as the "r" and "n" are sometimes difficult to distinguish in the handwriting of some English-language writers. Although numbers are written in words in our Hebrew text, there is evidence of an early system of numerical signs within the Old Testament period. Vertical strokes were used to represent digits and horizontal strokes to represent tens, which were written one above the other for multiples of ten. In such a decimal system, it is easy to see how inadvertent mistakes could be made even as we can easily leave off or add a zero to a large number. Later, letters of the alphabet were also used for numbers, thereby making it possible for numbers to be erroneously copied as one letter was confused with another in a worn or smudged document.[29]

An obvious instance is found in the numbers recorded in 2 Kings 24:8 and 2 Chronicles 36:9. According to the Kings account, Jehoiachin became king when he was eighteen years old and he reigned three months before he was taken captive. The Chronicles verse, however, states that he was only eight years old when he began reigning, and that he reigned three months and ten days. This is obviously a contradiction caused by a copyist's error. Since eighteen is written in Hebrew as "eight" and "ten," it seems clear that the "ten" was misplaced. It was correctly joined to the eight in Kings—making eighteen—but it was omitted in Chronicles and picked up later as ten days. In fact, some of the manuscripts of the Greek and Syriac translations of 2 Chronicles 36:9 do record that Jehoiachin was eighteen, as in 2 Kings 24:8.

In some instances copying was done by a scribe as someone else read the text aloud. The problem of some words sounding the same when verbally pronounced, but having different spellings and meanings (for example, "weigh" and "way"; and "there" and "their") is also present in Hebrew and Greek and could easily account for some copying mistakes.

Most alleged discrepancies in the Bible involve names, dates, or numbers. These are most easily subject to corruption in that they cannot be determined from the context. That is, "specific names, dates, and numbers are items which cannot be grammatically predicted in a sentence, or be remembered by reason of the word order or the general meaning."[30] For example, if we were copying a sentence naming a mayor of a city, we could as easily write "Joe" as "John" if we didn't know him personally. Both would fit the sentence. On the other hand, if we were copying a sentence about a queen, we would not likely write "Joe" or "John" because we would immediately sense something illogical and recheck what we were writing. The same is true with numbers and dates. We could easily write the year 1046 instead of 1064 for an event with which we are not personally acquainted. Many of the errors in transmitting the Old Testament documents are in these areas that had little particular meaning to a copyist. Even so, compared to most other ancient writings of significant length the Scriptures contain relatively few questions even in these areas.[31]

Scientific Problems

Most of the so-called scientific problems in the Bible stem from an approach to reality that rules out the supernatural. Miracles are rejected as myth because they contradict natural laws. When the existence of God is accepted, however, we have no legitimate reason for denying His supernatural intervention in His creation as He wishes. To insist that what the

Bible calls demonic activity is unscientific superstition is to base belief on *unproven presuppositions* and not on true science.

Since evolution has never been demonstrated scientifically, there is no basis to charge the Bible with error in relation to creation. Bible-believing scientists—and an increasing number of advocates of evolution—affirm that evolution is only an unproven theory. Some years ago Gerald A. Kerkut, who is not a biblical creationist, wrote *Implications of Evolution* (Elmsford, N.Y.: Pergamon, 1960). In it he set forth seven fundamental principles of the evolutionary theory. None of these seven, according to Kerkut, has ever been proven. More recently, with the increasing understanding of the amazing design of life forms and the finely calibrated interdependence of their parts, the validity of the concept of naturalistic evolution is even more questioned and its lack of factual support exposed.[32]

Certain isolated statements are sometimes raised as examples of the Bible's lack of accurate scientific knowledge. One of the classic instances is Jesus' statement that the mustard seed "is smaller than all other seeds" (Matt. 13:32). Since botanists know that the orchid seed is smaller, they say Jesus was in error. However, among the seeds the Jews sowed in their gardens or fields, the mustard seed *was* the smallest. According to Gleason Archer, "No one yet has proved that ancient Palestinians planted anything that bore a smaller seed than that of the black mustard." So it became proverbial to speak of it as the smallest of seeds (17:20; Luke 17:6), and Jesus' statement is to be understood within this framework. His statement could be charged with error only if He were intending to make a scientific statement covering all seeds of all creation.

Some also see an error in the statement in Leviticus 11:6 that the rabbit "chews cud." Several explanations are possible. True, rabbits do not chew the cud by swallowing food without chewing it much and then later regurgitating it to chew it more thoroughly. However, the movement of its jaws is similar to that of animals that do chew their cud. It is also possible that the Hebrew term translated "chew the cud" does not mean exactly what our phrase means. Camel and rock badgers (also called coneys) are also said to chew the cud, but technically they do not do so. Finally some have noted that rabbits engage in "refection." At times they pass droppings of a different texture which they then eat. Certain foods difficult to digest are acted on by bacteria during the first pass through the intestines and then are better able to be assimilated the second time. Thus the rabbits are chewing without taking fresh food into their mouths.[33]

When statements in the Scriptures are understood with their intended meaning, not one of them has been proven erroneous. This is all the more amazing when we consider the many scientific errors that appear in ancient human writings.

Doctrinal and Moral Problems

In most instances questions about doctrinal and ethical statements in the Bible are readily solved when we fully understand what the Bible actually says. In other instances, however, the difficulty arises when a critic of Scripture simply does not agree with the ethics of the Bible. We can label these as problems with inspiration only if we assume that the objector's view is infallible.

The instigation of David's numbering of the people is often cited as a theological contradiction. In 2 Samuel 24:1 we read that God incited David to number Israel and Judah. However, in 1 Chronicles 21:1 Satan is said to have "moved David to number Israel." Some say that this is indicative of two theologies, one in which God controls the world and the other in which Satan is in control. Another critic believes that the chronicler revised the earlier statement in Samuel "apparently on the conviction that his understanding was more accurate. It is obvious that he simply did not believe that God incited David to take a census in order to express his anger against Israel."[34]

The solution is not difficult, however, when we understand something about the relationship between God and Satan. God often allows Satan to perform his evil deeds for some greater purpose. Thus God in this instance is presented as the ultimate cause for Satan's moving David to this act. Parallel situations are found in God's permitting Satan to attack Job (Job 1:12; 2:6) and in His sending an evil spirit to trouble Saul (1 Sam. 16:14). What needs to be remembered is that for the biblical authors nothing is outside the sovereignty of God.

In seeking solutions to problems such as these, it is important that we have a full understanding of the biblical teaching about a given subject.

One verse often brings out one side of the issue, and another looks at it from a different side. While the two sides may seem contradictory, in reality they are parts of the whole truth.

We must also seek to understand words in their own contexts. The alleged difficulty between Paul and James over justification is easily solved when we consider the particular way they used similar words. Paul declared that we are justified by faith without works (Rom. 4:5; Eph. 2:8–9), but James declared that justification comes by faith and works (James 2:24). If we examine the use of the words "faith" and "works," however, we find that James and Paul did not mean exactly the same thing.

James used the word "faith" in two senses. In one sense it meant that kind of mental assent that even the demons possess (2:19). Such faith or belief, he said, is not sufficient to save. It must be a faith instead that is living and gives evidence of life in works. "Works" to him were the outworking of saving faith.

On the other hand, by "faith" Paul meant a genuine belief that issues in action. He spoke of a faith that works through love (Gal. 5:6). When he opposed "works" and "faith," he meant works of a legal nature by which people supposed that they could gain merit before God.

Thus, when we consider the meaning of these words in their contexts, both Paul and James believed the same thing. Each was emphasizing a certain facet of the truth. Paul believed that individuals are saved only by faith, a faith that is alive and working. James also believed that people are saved by faith, a faith that is more than mental assent, one that works.

Some critics say that the Old Testament allows polygamy, while the New Testament doesn't. While the Old Testament does report that some of Israel's leaders had more than one wife, it never teaches that this is God's intent for marriage.[35]

Another problem area pertains to God's commands to the Israelites to destroy their enemies as they conquered the Promised Land (Deut. 20:16–18). And a good number of psalms record prayers that God would destroy their foes (for example, Pss. 55, 59, 79, 109, 137). These passages seem to represent immoral actions and attitudes, and they seem to be in conflict with verses that tell believers to love their enemies (Luke 6:35–36).

Several factors may be noted about these supposed immoral matters. Throughout the Scriptures God is seen not only as a God of infinite love, but also a God of righteous judgment. There is certainly no change between the Old and New Testaments when we consider the reality of the coming judgment foretold clearly in the New Testament (Rev. 19:11–21). In fact, Jesus spoke more about the eternal destruction of those who refuse to come to God than did any of the New Testament writers.

The cries for God's vengeance, which the psalmists raised against God's public enemies and purposes, are evidence of His people sharing His concern for righteousness and truth. They point to the time when sin will be put down and righteousness will triumph.

God's command to slay the Canaanites is more understandable when we recognize the depth of their depravity. God did not move against them until their sin had reached an irreversibly low point (Gen. 15:16; Lev. 18:24–30). Then, because of their addiction to all forms of gross sin which had thoroughly infected their society, God brought judgment on them through His people. William Arndt describes the situation well.

> The Canaanite tribes by their shameless vices had filled the cup of their guilt to overflowing. When the punishment came, it struck all the inhabitants, the women and children included. The fault was not God's; but it lay with those who had trampled underfoot the laws of justice and decency. When men take themselves and their families aboard a ship, sail out upon the ocean for a pleasure trip, and make that ship a place reeking with wickedness and vice, and then all perish in a hurricane which suddenly falls upon them, who is to blame? Will you accuse God for not discriminating between adults and the children? One dreadful aspect of sin is that the woe it produces is like a whirlpool, whose suction draws every object which is nearby to the bottom. That the Canaanitish women were dissolute and instrumental in causing the Israelites to leave the path of truth and purity, that for the children it was better to perish in infancy than to grow up as devotees of idolatry and vice, are points the mere mention of which will suffice here.[36]

When we consider the full scope of God's moral nature as taught in Scripture, these passages no longer pose problems. They deal with the stern reality of judgment; they can be called immoral only if we are prepared to assert our own standard of morality over God's.

THE ABSENCE OF THE INERRANT ORIGINAL TEXT

A seemingly telling blow against the position of inerrant inspiration is the fact that we do not possess the original writings of Scripture. The Hebrew and Greek manuscripts of the Scriptures that we do possess are not perfect copies of the originals, so we do not have an absolutely inerrant text to point to. Some people claim there is no point in arguing for the infallible, inerrant inspiration of the Bible when we simply do not have such a Bible.

While at first this reasoning may seem logical, further thought reveals that it overlooks important facts. First, our belief in inerrant inspiration does not rest on the need to produce the original text of Scripture. Our belief rests instead on the truth that Christ and the biblical writers taught it.

Second, the belief in the inerrancy of the original writings has value for us even though they have perished. Our desk rulers and tape measures are not absolutely accurate; they are close approximations of the master standards maintained by the National Bureau of Standards in Washington, D.C. We may not have been aware that such a standard exists; nevertheless our rulers and tapes have value because they are based on an absolute standard. Similarly our present Bibles—even with minor flaws—have value because there is an absolute standard behind them.

The belief in the inerrancy of the Bible's original manuscripts is a final control in our search for an absolutely reliable guide to truth. If we believe the original Scriptures were inerrant, then we are free to alter Bible translations only in those places where the science of textual studies leads us to believe that such a change brings us closer to the original writings. People who do not believe that the original writings were inerrant feel they can reject anything in the Bible they think is in error, as judged by some outside standard of truth. Believing that the Scriptures' original manuscripts are inerrant inevitably affects our attitude toward the Bible and our use of it.

We must also remember how close our present Bibles are to the original texts. We have spoken of certain minor differences in the ancient copies we possess. But the great number of copies in existence and the general reliability of copyists have made it possible for scholars to ascertain the reading of the original text in virtually every place. One of the greatest authorities on the New Testament manuscripts, Sir Frederic Kenyon of the British Museum, asserted several decades ago, "It cannot be too strongly asserted that in substance the text of the Bible is certain: Especially is this the case with the New Testament. The number of manuscripts of the New Testament, of early translations from it, and of quotations from it in the oldest writers of the Church, is so large that it is practically certain that the true reading of every doubtful passage is preserved in some one or other of these ancient authorities. *This can be said of no other ancient book in the world.*"[37]

More recently Douglas Stuart summarized the situation concerning the original words of Scripture. "It has been argued that 99 percent of the original words in the New Testament are recoverable with a very high degree of certainty. In the case of the Old Testament the figure might be more like 95 percent. When the words that are recoverable with a fairly high degree of certainty are added, we may be confident that we are able to read, reflect upon, and act upon what is practically equivalent to the original itself. There is no area of Christian faith or practice that actually stands or falls on the basis of textual studies."[38]

Some may ask, "Why did not God in His providence preserve the original copies so that His people would have them throughout history?" The answer to this question, of course, is known only to Him. Two thoughts, however, are helpful. If the original copies continued to exist, God's people might have come to honor them as relics and worship them even as they did the bronze serpent that Hezekiah finally destroyed (2 Kings 18:4). Also doubt as to whether a particular copy was actually the original would inevitably arise and could never be resolved, making certainty impossible. A clever person might even have been able to alter the text. Thus possessing original writings could be an unending source of controversy rather than blessing.

FINAL CONSIDERATIONS

In our consideration of the difficulties yet remaining in the Scriptures several thoughts should be kept in mind.

The Number of Problems Is Remarkably Small

When we consider the Scriptures—written a long time ago by more than forty individuals over a period of fifteen hundred years—the possibility for error and discrepancy would seem boundless. Errors in reporting history, in explanation of phenomena, in spiritual doctrines, in exaggeration, and so forth—all could easily be imagined in a work like the Bible. Compared to the multitude or errors that fill the works of the ancient writers the Bible is amazingly free of difficulties. The following comment is well worth consideration. "Moses was instructed in all the wisdom of the Egyptians. What preserved him so that when writing the Pentateuch he did not accept the ancient Egyptian chronology which later Manetho laid down definitely in his writings and which was supposed to start 30,000 years before Christ? What influenced Daniel, who was skilled in Chaldean science, to shut his ears to the monstrous Chaldean fables as to the creation of the world? Paul was acquainted with the best science of his time. Why do we find nothing in his speeches or letters similar to Augustine's scornful rejection of the theory of the antipodes, or to the opinion of Ambrose that the sun draws water up to itself that it may thereby cool and refresh itself from its extraordinary heat?"[39]

Many Difficulties Have Been Eliminated

A second fact to remember is that as our knowledge of the ancient world has increased, the number of biblical problems has decreased. As noted above, many of the problems of the Bible that have been raised against its truthfulness have gone by the wayside as scholarly research in history, archaeology, and linguistics has increased our knowledge of the ancient world. This fact should make anyone hesitant to assert a proven error today unless he is prepared to claim that he has the complete data related to everything that concerns a particular problem and that his interpretation of that data is infallible. We should hold unsolved problems in abeyance, recognizing that when all the data are known, the text here too will be seen to be truthful.

It Is Not Necessary to Be Able to Solve All Biblical Problems

That biblical problems have been and will no doubt continue to be reduced through increased knowledge should make believers content with not being able to solve all problems today. It should also encourage us not to contrive forced solutions in order to rescue the doctrine of inerrancy. Benjamin Warfield's advice is well taken. "Our individual fertility in exegetical expedients, our individual insight into exegetical truth, our individual capacity of understanding are not the measure of truth. If we cannot harmonize without straining, let us leave unharmonized."[40] The doctrine of the inerrancy of the Bible rests not on our ability to demonstrate it, but on its own teaching of its full inspiration, including that of our Lord.[41] Packer's stance with regard to this issue is commendable for all believers. "That the Bible is true in what it says is not a matter of doubt, but what exactly we should be saying about the persons and events referred to in the Bible is not always clear for lack of supplementary information. I do not believe that the honor of God requires me to have an answer, and a complete answer for everything."[42]

CONCLUSION

As we have seen in the past few chapters, the Bible teaches that it is the product of the breath of God (2 Tim. 3:16) and therefore is truthful in its entirety. Such claims, as well as the overwhelming evidence of the supernatural origin of the Scriptures, have led most believers throughout the history of the church to believe in the absolute inerrancy of the original Scriptures. When facing difficulties that they could not explain, their attitude was that of Augustine expressed in a letter to Jerome. "And if in these writings I am perplexed by anything which appears to me opposed to truth, I do not hesitate to suppose that either the MS. [manuscript] is faulty, or the translator has not caught the meaning of what was said, or I myself have failed to understand it."[43]

Augustine's attitude reveals an attitude of trust that should condition our approach to the problems of the Bible. In light of all the evidence we should be willing to trust in the truthfulness of Scripture even though we are unable to explain everything. As William Arndt notes, such trust is appropriate, given our relationship as finite, sinful human beings to our heavenly Father. "What will a pious, obedient, loving child do when it hears the father make a remark which on the face of it appears objectionable? Instead of criticizing him and condemning his utterance as wrong, the child will ask him for an explanation. If we find stumbling blocks in the Holy Scriptures, let us take the attitude of such a loving child."[44] I might add that even if the father for some good reason chooses not to give an explanation at the time, trust still submits.

A straightforward consideration of all that the Bible teaches about itself yields a doctrine of inerrancy. No data disproves this fact.

Twelve

The law of Thy mouth is better to me
Than thousands of gold and silver pieces. . . .
O how I love Thy law!. (Ps. 119:72, 97)

Give ear for a moment that I may tell you how you are to walk in the holy Scriptures. All that we read in the divine books, while glistening and shining without, is yet far sweeter within.[1]

—Jerome, fourth-century church father

Twelve

What Has the Church Believed about the Bible?

Believers today stand in a long tradition of faith. The truth of the gospel on which the church is built is ours today because a train of believers held fast the same gospel described as "the faith which was once for all delivered to the saints" (Jude 3). The question before us in this chapter is what place the Scriptures played in the minds of our forebears as they faithfully maintained the faith. Throughout Bible times God's people, as we have seen in earlier chapters, believed their Scriptures to be the very revelation of God spoken by His Spirit through human authors so that they were in reality the Word of God. Since New Testament times has the church continued to accept the Scriptures the same way?

Many who reject the truthfulness of the Scriptures say that the doctrine of inerrancy as now held by evangelicals was not the historic Christian position.[2] The idea of inerrancy, it is argued, stems from various forces encountered by the church after the Reformation. The conflict with Rome over whether the church or the Bible is the believers' final authority and the coming of the scientific age and the age of rationalism associated with the Enlightenment are said to have led many orthodox theologians to espouse inerrancy.

The modern "intense insistence on the 'inerrancy' of the Bible in scientific and historical detail" is thus said to be related to a "modern style of thinking" and "a long way from the modes of thought of the ancient Hebrews."[3] According to opponents of the Bible's inerrancy, when the church fathers asserted inerrancy, they were talking only about spiritual truths related to salvation and not about details of history, science, and geography. In the words of one proponent of this position, "The fathers did . . . believe that the Bible was an inerrant and . . . infallible repository of revealed religion; but . . . [they] recognized its limitations and time-conditionedness in respect to a continually developing human awareness and factual knowledge."[4] According to this understanding, when God revealed truths about salvation, He accommodated to the human authors' contemporary opinions in other matters. This thesis is often stated as distinguishing between the *form* and *function* of the Scriptures. In its *function* to present the message of salvation, the Bible is infallible, but this purpose is accomplished through the *form* of human writings which are not totally inerrant.

THE EARLY CHURCH

The question of the authority and infallibility of the Scriptures did not receive elaborate systematic treatment in the early church; there was simply no controversy over these issues. As James Bannerman explained more than a century ago, "The belief in the early Church in an infallible Bible was too simple to require to be fenced about with the safeguard of explanations, and too unanimous to need support from argument. There was neither controversy nor theorizing demanded to satisfy the faith of Christians."[5] Church historian Geoffrey Bromiley concurs. "We are struck at once," he says, "by the way in which all writers [in the early church] accepted the inspiration and authority of Holy Scripture as self-evident."[6] Although not fully developed, the writers of this period do provide good evidence of the belief of orthodox Christians regarding the Scriptures.

The Early Church's View of Inspiration

Clearly the early church fathers viewed the whole Bible as inspired by the Holy Spirit. At the end of the first century, Clement of Rome wrote to the Corinthian believers with reference to Paul's first Corinthian letter: "To be sure, under the Spirit's guidance, he wrote to you about himself and Cephas and Apollos." Again he wrote, "You have studied Holy Scripture, which contains truth and is inspired by the Holy Spirit." Introducing portions of Psalms, Clement said, "For this is how Christ addresses us through the Holy Spirit."[7] Early in the second century, Polycarp, bishop of Smyrna, referred to the Scriptures as "the oracles of the Lord."[8]

Second-century apologist Justin Martyr similarly affirmed his belief in the divine inspiration of the Scriptures. "The prophets are inspired by no other than the Divine Word."[9] "Again the same prophet Isaiah, being inspired by the prophetic Spirit, said, 'I have spread out my hands to a disobedient and gainsaying people.' "[10] The prophets who foretold what would take place "spoke by the Divine Spirit."[11]

Irenaeus (around 140–202), who has been called "the greatest of all the Christian writers and scholars of the second century,"[12] strongly affirmed the inspiration and authority of the Bible, which he called "the Lord's Scriptures." "If we cannot discover explanations of all things in Scripture . . . we should leave things of that nature to God who created us, being most properly assured that the Scriptures are indeed perfect, since they were spoken by the Word of God and His Spirit."[13]

This same strong belief in the inspiration of the Scriptures is continued into the third century as seen in the testimony of two great Alexandrian scholars. Clement of Alexandria (around 150–211) declared, "Jeremiah the prophet, gifted in consummate wisdom, or rather the Holy Spirit in Jeremiah, exhibits God."[14] Again, he wrote, "For we have, as the source of teaching, the Lord, both by the prophets, the Gospels, and the blessed apostles."[15] Origen (around 185–254) claimed to speak for the churches of his day when he said, "This Spirit inspired each one of the saints, whether prophets or apostles; and that there was not one Spirit in the men of the old dispensation, and another in those who were inspired at the advent of Christ, is most clearly taught throughout the churches." He also wrote, "The Scriptures themselves are divine, i.e., were inspired by the Spirit of God. . . . The Scriptures were written by the Spirit of God."[16]

According to theologian Gregory of Nyssa (around 335–394), "All things the Divine Scripture says are utterances of the Holy Spirit."[17] The North African bishop Augustine (around 354–430), who is generally recognized as the greatest theologian of the early church, clearly testified to his belief in the divine origin of the Scriptures. Genesis, he said, was authored by God through Moses. "I will have nothing to do with all those who think Moses could have said anything untrue. But in you, Lord, those with whom I wish to be associated . . . are those who feed on your truth. . . . Together with them I would approach the words of your book to seek in them your will through the intention of your servant, by whose pen you imparted them to us."[18] In answering those who criticized Christianity because it did not possess writings from the hand of Jesus, Augustine pointed to Jesus' message through the apostles. "When those disciples have written matters which He declared and spoke to them it ought not by any means be said that He has written nothing Himself: since the truth is, that His members [of His body] have accomplished only what they became acquainted with by the repeated statements of the Head. For all that He was minded to give for our perusal on the subject of His own doings and sayings, He commanded to be written by those disciples, whom He thus used as if they were His own hands."[19]

Similar evidence for a belief in the divine inspiration of the Scriptures could be cited from other leaders of the early church, including Tertullian (around 155–220), Hippolytus (died 236), Cyprian (195–258), and Jerome (around 374–419).[20] As Geoffrey Bromiley states, "That the Fathers accepted the divine inspiration of Holy Scripture, whether as the Old Testament or the New, may be demonstrated with the greatest of ease."[21]

In explicating their concept of inspiration, the early fathers emphasized the divine authorship of Scriptures. Christian apologist Athenagoras, for example, spoke of the Spirit breathing through the human authors even as a flutist uses a flute.[22] The metaphor of musical instruments was used by others as well. Justin Martyr likened the divine Spirit to a "plectrum . . . descending from heaven, and using righteous men as an instrument like a harp or lyre."[23] References were also made to the Scriptures as dictated by the Spirit.[24] Augustine's statement cited above, in which he said Christ used the apostles as "his own hands" could also be interpreted as viewing the human writers as totally passive in the process of inspiration. In the sixth century Gregory the Great summed up this kind of thought by affirming that "the question of human authorship is of little relevance. If we know who is the true author of each work and we understand what He says to us, why should we be curious to learn what pen imprinted the divine words on the page?"[25]

While it is generally agreed that these early church fathers, in their emphasis on the divine origin of Scripture, did not give adequate place to the human authors, it is also clear that they did not exclude genuine human participation. Even those who stressed the divine authorship and thus the authority of the Scriptures with statements like those cited did not mean to imply that the human authors were totally passive.

According to J. N. D. Kelly, an authority on patristic Christian thought, the orthodox tradition of the early church "in general . . . was careful to avoid the implication that [the scriptural writers'] role was purely passive."[26] As evidence he points to the explanation of Hippolytus that "when the Word moved the prophets, the effect was to clarify their vision and instruct their understanding."[27] Origen similarly suggests that "the Spirit's function was to cause [the biblical authors] to apprehend truth more clearly without in any way suspending their free will."[28] Chrysostom (around 347–407) and Cyril of Alexandria made "much of the personal contribution of Moses, St. John and St. Paul in the actual composition of their works," and Jerome (around 374–419) pointed to the differences in style and general cultural background which the different writers exhibited in their writings.[29] Augustine acknowledged that the Gospel writers used their own memories in writing their works—memories, however, that were stimulated and guarded from error by the Spirit.[30] Even Gregory's seeming rejection of any significance for the human author was uttered in relation to the Book of Job, the author of which is unknown and therefore cannot have any specific relevance in the interpretation of the book. In general, however, while acknowledging the contribution of the human authors in the production of the Scriptures, the early fathers did not explore deeply the nature of the Spirit's influence on them. Their emphasis was simply on God as the Author of the Scriptures.

The Question of Inerrancy in the Early Church

Did the early church fathers believe that the Scriptures are true in *all matters*, including history and science? While they did not discuss the subject of inerrancy in detail, it was the natural corollary of their strong conviction that God is the Author of the Scriptures. Although not an advocate of inerrancy, Bruce Vawter declares, "It would be pointless to call into question that biblical inerrancy in a rather absolute form was a common persuasion from the beginning of Christian times, and from Jewish times before that. For both the Fathers and the rabbis generally, the ascription of any error to the Bible was unthinkable; . . . if the word was God's it must be true, regardless of whether it made known a mystery of divine revelation or commented on a datum of natural science, whether it derived from human observation or chronicled an event of history."[31]

Statements in the writings of the early fathers clearly justify Vawter's conclusion. Clement of Rome (around 30–95) wrote in his letter to the Corinthians, "You have studied Scripture which contains the truth and is inspired by the Holy Spirit. You realize that there is nothing wrong or misleading in it."[32] Irenaeus declared that "no person of common sense can permit them [those who object to Luke's Gospel as being authentic] to receive some things recounted by Luke as being true, and to set others aside, as if he had not known the truth."[33] Furthermore, according to Irenaeus, we should be "most properly assured that the Scriptures are indeed perfect, since they were spoken by the Word of God and His Spirit."[34] Justin Martyr boldly asserted in his *Dialogue with Trypho*, "I am entirely convinced that no Scripture contradicts another." If presented with an instance that seems contradictory, he added, "I shall admit rather that I do not understand what is recorded, and shall strive to persuade those who imagine that the Scriptures are contradictory, to be rather of the same opinion as myself."[35]

Origen likewise declared that although there may appear to be conflict in the Scriptures "for those who have not ears to hear," there is in fact "no conflict. . . . [They] are truly at perfect concord."[36] Athanasius (around 293–373) affirmed the inerrancy of every aspect of Scripture when he wrote, "We, however, who extend the accuracy of the Spirit to the merest stroke and tittle, will never admit the impious assertion that even the smallest matters were dealt with haphazard[ly] by those who have recorded them, and have thus been borne in mind down to the present day."[37] Also Chrysostom wrote of the inspiration of all of the details of Scripture. To those who would find in Scripture "a heap of dates or litany of names" and pass them by saying "they are only names, nothing useful in them," Chrysostom responded, "Do not utter such infamy. God speaks, and you have the effrontery to say, Nothing useful in what is said."[38] Again he wrote, "With the Scriptures . . . it is not like this. The gold does not lie before us mixed with earth; instead it is gold and only gold."[39] Chrysostom obviously did not concur with the idea of many today that the inerrancy of the Bible is limited to spiritual truth and not other matters.

Augustine also testified to the truthfulness of all the Scriptures. Referring to the sixty-six canonical books, he said, "Of these alone do I most firmly believe that the authors were completely free from error."[40] Elsewhere he wrote, "Therefore everything written in Scripture must be believed absolutely."[41] Augustine's belief in the inerrancy of the Scriptures extended to biblical statements bearing on science. "Whatever, they [scientists] can readily demonstrate to be true of physical nature," Augustine said, "we must show to be capable of reconciliation with our Scriptures; and whatever they assert in their treatises to be contrary to these Scriptures of ours . . . we must either prove it as well as we can to be entirely false, or at all events, we must without the smallest hesitation believe it to be so."[42]

In a letter to Jerome, Augustine rejected Jerome's contention that a good man (Paul) might deceive out of a sense of duty. "For it seems to me that the most disastrous consequences must follow upon our believing that anything false is found in the sacred books. . . . For if you once admit into such a high sanctuary of authority one false statement, as made in the way of duty, there will not be left a single sentence of these books which, if appearing to any one difficult in practice or hard to believe, may not by the same fatal rule be explained away, as a statement in which, intentionally, and under a sense of duty, the author declared what was not true."[43]

Pointing to this statement, some opponents of biblical inerrancy attempt to portray Augustine's concept of a biblical "error" as the deliberate telling of a lie. Jack Rogers and Donald McKim write, "Error, for Augustine, had to do with the deliberate and deceitful telling that which the author knew to be untrue. It was in that context of ethical seriousness that he declared that the biblical 'authors were completely free from error.' He did not apply the concept of error to problems that arose from the human limitations of knowledge, various perspectives in reporting events, or historical or cultural conditioning of the writers."[44]

However, Augustine's additional correspondence with Jerome shows that he did not intend to limit "error" to deliberate deceit. After declaring, as noted above, that the biblical authors "were completely free from error," Augustine continued,

> As to all other [nonbiblical] writings, in reading them, however great the superiority of the authors to myself in sanctity and learning, I do not accept their teaching as true on the mere ground of the opinion being held by them; but only because they have succeeded in convincing my judgment of its truth either by means of these canonical writings themselves, or by arguments addressed to my reason. I believe, my brother, that this is your own opinion as well as mine. I do not need to say that I do not suppose you to wish your books to be read like those of prophets or of apostles, concerning which it would be wrong to doubt that they are free from error. Far be such arrogance from that humble piety and just estimate of yourself which I know you have.[45]

In suggesting that Jerome would not wish his writings to be considered "free from error" like the Scriptures, it is obvious that Augustine did not mean only "free from deliberate deceit." For in intimating that Jerome's writings contain "errors" he would have been saying that Jerome had included "deliberate deceit," a charge that Augustine would never have made of Jerome. Augustine wrote, "Now if, knowing as I do your life and conversation, I do not believe in regard to you that you have spoken anything with an intention of dissimulation and deceit, how much more reasonable is it for me to believe in regard to the Apostle Paul, that he did not think one thing and affirm another."[46] To affirm that the Scriptures are inerrant only in the sense that they are free from *deliberate* deceit makes them no different than most human writings. For it is safe to say that most human authors do not write with deliberate intent to deceive.

Others suggest that Augustine's statements about God's accommodation to our humanity in the writing of the Scriptures (e.g., like "a mother stooping to her child, so to speak, so as not to leave us behind in our weakness"[47]) point to factual discrepancies or a lack of "harmony in all of its verbal forms." This is particularly said to apply to Augustine's awareness of the different accounts of the Gospel writers, of which he wrote that the Holy Spirit "permitted one to compile his narrative in this way, and another in that."[48] However, no statement by Augustine to the effect than any of the Gospel writers erred can be adduced.[49] In truth Augustine's stated purpose in his *The Harmony of the Gospels* was the refutation of those who sought to discredit Christianity by pointing to discrepancies. "And in order to carry out this design to a successful conclusion, we must prove that the writers in question do not stand in any antagonism to each other. For those adversaries are in the habit of adducing this as the primary allegation in all their vain objections, namely, that the evangelists are not in harmony with each other."[50]

In the words of historian John Woodbridge, Augustine then proceeded "in what becomes almost painful harmonization work [to adduce] explanation after explanation to prove that no 'contradictory accounts' (I, 35, 54) exist in the Evangelists' verbal statements when properly interpreted."[51]

Neither in his recognition of diversity in the Gospel accounts (which he recognized were complementary rather than contradictory), nor in his acknowledgment of phenomenal rather than technical language in the description of nature did Augustine's concept of accommodation mean accommodation to error. Rather, it referred to "the manner or mode of revelation, the gift of the wisdom of infinite God in finite form, not to the quality of the revelation or to the matter revealed."[52] This meaning of accommodation, which was taught also by Origen and Chrysostom as well as others, is seen in their comparison of the written Word with Christ, the living Word. As John Hannah explains, "As the accommodation of the living Word did not involve sinful pollution in any innate sense, so the Spirit's accommodation in the written word must be similarly conceived, as Origen suggested. Certainly, the early church believed in accommodation but not condescension to error in either the written or living Word. The act of condescension was that providence of stooping to be understood by errant humanity, not an incorporation of the errant nature of humanity. As Christ did not take on the sin of humanity in the incarnation, neither did the Spirit succumb to such lowliness in conveying the Scripture."[53]

These and other writings of Augustine provide clear evidence of his firm belief in the absolute inerrancy of the Scriptures.[54] Even Hans Küng, a Roman Catholic scholar, acknowledged that Augustine, "regarded man as merely the instrument of the Holy Spirit; the Spirit alone decided the content and form of the biblical writings, with the result that the whole Bible was free of contradictions, mistakes and errors, or had to be kept free by harmonizing, allegorizing or mysticizing. St. Augustine's influence in regard to inspiration and inerrancy prevailed throughout the Middle Ages and right into the modern age."[55] Augustine's doctrine of the inspiration of the Scriptures, including inerrancy in all matters, is thus the capstone of the common belief of the early church fathers.

THE MEDIEVAL CHURCH

The medieval church was characterized by a paradox of a high view of the inspiration of the Bible and a lessening view of its power in life. Considerable energy was spent defining the authority of the Scriptures in relation to other authorities in the church. Especially in the latter part of the period (eleventh to the fourteenth centuries), the influence of philosophy with its emphasis on reason led to a scholastic approach to the study of Christian doctrine with its sophisticated forms and subtle distinctions. As a result the diminished place of the Bible may be seen in some of Martin Luther's typically unrestrained comments about some of the leading figures of this period. Commenting on Peter Lombard, the noted twelfth-century theologian, Luther wrote that he was "adequate as a theologian; none has been his equal. He read Augustine, Ambrose, Gregory, and also all the councils. He was a great man. If he had by chance come upon the Bible, he would no doubt have been the greatest."[56] To Luther, Thomas Aquinas (1224–1274) was a "chatter-box" because of his consistent references to Aristotle, the Greek philosopher (384–322 B.C.), whom Aquinas referred to as "the Philosopher." Luther's feeling toward the mixture of philosophy and the truth of the Scriptures in Aquinas is evident in his describing Aristotle as " 'that . . . pagan' (in addition to other choice epithets that form a long and impressive catalog)."[57]

Despite the de-emphasis on the Scriptures in the life of the church during this period, the statements by the dominant church authorities demonstrate that a high view of their inspiration continued to be held. The Scriptures were the "words of the Holy Spirit," according to Pope Leo the Great of the fifth century.[58] In the next century Gregory the Great (540–604) wrote of the Bible, "Let it be faithfully believed that the Holy Spirit is the author of the book. He, therefore, wrote these things who dictated the things to be written. . . . The Scriptures are the words of the Holy Spirit."[59]

Anselm of Canterbury (1093–1109) said, "For I am sure that if I say anything that unquestionably contradicts Holy Scripture, it is false, and if I am aware of this I do not want to hold it."[60] Even Thomas Aquinas, hailed in the modern world as "the prince of scholastics," was very much a biblical theologian, writing many commentaries on portions of the Scriptures. His scholastic theological work, *Summa Theologica*, although containing minimal biblical citations, was in the words of one scholar, erected "on the rock of the divine Word." As for his understanding of the inspiration of the Scriptures, Thomas Aquinas affirmed, "All which is spoken of in Holy Scripture is spoken of God."[61] His belief in the absolute authority of Scripture is seen in these words of his: "We must keep to that which has been written in Scripture as to an excellent rule of faith so that we must add nothing to it, detract nothing, and change nothing by interpreting it badly."[62]

John Wycliffe (1320–1384), forerunner of the Reformation, believed strongly in the final authority of the Bible in all matters. According to one historian, Wycliffe "is thoroughly scornful of theologians who slight Holy Scripture. If any such persons find contradictions or errors in the Bible, their own ignorance is at fault rather than the sacred text. . . . Holy Scripture contained not only all Christian doctrine, but all truth generally. It was a 'divine encylopedia,' a *summa* of the wisdom of God."[63]

The dynamic of the Word of God in the churches was certainly dimmed in many places during the Middles Ages. Few people actually read the Scriptures because most people were not able to read or write. Nevertheless the populace and scholars did believe in the complete inerrancy of the Scriptures because of their divine inspiration. As one scholar says of the medieval period, "During all these centuries no one doubted that the Bible in it entirety was God's word, that God was the principal author of the Scriptures, as their human authors had written under the inspiration of God the Holy Spirit, and that, therefore, these books were free from errors and contradictions, even when this did not seem to be the case."[64]

THE REFORMERS

The great cry of the Reformers in regard to the Scriptures was *sola Scriptura*. They affirmed strongly that Scripture alone is our absolute authority. This naturally entailed a new emphasis on the Scriptures. For the Reformers "the Bible was not merely a source-book of Christian teaching to be handled in legalistic rationalism . . . by scholars, ecclesiastics and canonists. It is the book to lead us to Christ."[65] The human aspects of the Bible were also appreciated by the Reformers more than their predecessors, and its meaning was deemed more plain than the complicated variety of senses (for example, the allegorical) seen in the writings of medieval interpreters. Above all, the Reformers in their resistance to church authority emphasized the role of the Holy Spirit in helping believers interpret the Scriptures correctly.[66]

Luther's belief that the inspiration of the Bible involved the very inerrancy of the words seems unambiguous from the following statements: "But everyone, indeed, knows that at times they [the fathers] have erred as men will; therefore I am ready to trust them only when they prove their opinions from Scripture, which has never erred."[67] "The Word of God is perfect: it is precious and pure: it is truth itself. There is no falsehood in it."[68] "Not only the words but expressions used by the Holy Spirit and Scripture are divine."[69] "It is impossible that Scripture should contradict itself; it only appears so to senseless and obstinate hypocrites."[70] "One letter, even a single tittle of Scripture, means more to us than heaven and earth. Therefore we cannot permit even the most minute change."[71] "Consequently, we must remain content with them [words], and cling to them as the perfectly clear, certain, sure word of God which can never deceive us or allow us to err."[72]

John Calvin (1509–1564) also expressed a strong belief in the inspiration and truthfulness of the very words of Scriptures. "Hence the Scriptures obtain full authority among believers only when men regard them as having sprung from heaven, as if there the living words of God were heard."[73]

The apostles were "sure and genuine scribes of the Holy Spirit, and their writings are therefore to be considered oracles of God."[74] Commenting on the apostle's words that "all Scripture is inspired by God" (2 Tim. 3:16), Calvin wrote, "This is the meaning of the first clause, that we owe to Scripture the same reverence as we owe to God, since it has its only source in Him and has nothing of human origin mixed with it."[75] Calvin was not denying the participation of human authorship; he was simply pointing to the ultimate divine origin of the Scriptures.

Regarding the words of the psalmist in Psalm 119:140 ("Thy word is very pure, therefore Thy servant loves it"), Calvin said, "And he affirms that his love to God's word was not a rash, or a blind and inconsiderate affection, but that he loves it, because like gold or silver which has been refined, it was pure and free from all dregs and dross. . . . when it [revealed truth] is compared to gold well refined, . . . it shines pure from all defilement."[76]

Luther and Calvin both acknowledged that God accommodated Himself to humans in communicating His Word. But like the church fathers who spoke of God's "accommodation," Luther and Calvin were simply referring to the humanness of the writings, analogous to the coming of the Son of God and His dwelling among us in human flesh. In contrast to the eloquence of some ancient writings that had received new attention in the Renaissance, Luther wrote that "Holy Scripture possesses no external glory, attracts no attention, lacks all beauty and adornment."[77] But this accommodation or plainness is far from implying that all the words were not equally inspired and accurate, as some wrongly suggest.[78] For Luther added, "You can scarcely imagine that anyone would attach faith to such a *divine* Word, because it is without any glory or charm. Yet faith comes from this *divine* word, through its inner power without any external loveliness."[79] Similarly Luther's well-known comments about whether certain writings should be considered canonical, that is, whether they are part of the holy Scriptures, has no bearing on his belief in the Bible's inerrancy. All writings of the Scriptures are the divinely inspired words of God; the question raised by Luther was simply which books belong in that category.

Because Luther and Calvin stressed the living Christ and His salvation as the theme of the Scriptures and taught that assurance of its truthfulness and authority comes only through the testimony of the Holy Spirit to the heart, many have attempted to argue that the Reformers believed that only the message of the Scriptures, and not the words, are infallible. However, the testimony of both men demonstrates clearly that they held no such separation of the message from the words. Luther, for example, stated, "Believing and reading Scripture means that we hear the Word from Christ's mouth. When that happens to you, you know that this is no mere human word, but truly God's."[80] Similarly Calvin's insistence on the witness of the Spirit to the heart regarding the truth of the Word does not diminish his belief in the inspiration and authority of the form or words in which that truth is communicated. As Woodbridge says, "Calvin joins the authority of Christ, the living Word, with that of the Bible, the written Word; he highlights the role of the Holy Spirit in confirming biblical authority to us. The Bible is also authoritative because God, the source of truth, is its principal author."[81]

The confessions and catechisms of the churches of the early Reformation era show that they too believed in the Bible's inerrancy. Although defense of the reliability of the Bible did not figure prominently in these writings, since this was not in dispute with Rome, such belief is apparent. The Belgic Confession (1561), for example, affirms that "nothing can be alleged" against the Scriptures. They are the "infallible rule" and Christians believe "without doubt, all things contained in them."[82]

THE POST-REFORMATION AND MODERN CHURCH

Belief in the inspiration and inerrancy of the Scriptures held by the Reformers and Roman Catholic leaders continued into the post-Reformation period. New historical conditions, however, began to impact how this doctrine was expressed, especially in Protestantism but also later in Catholicism. These developments included these five:

- The dispute over the issue of authority between Protestants and Catholics, in which Catholics demanded that Protestants show how the Scriptures with their errant copies could function as the final authority without the authority of the Roman Church.

- Rationalism, which declared that truth must be built on the foundation of reason.
- Hostile attacks on the reliability of the Scriptures by rationalist movements, including Socinianism in the seventeenth century and Deism in the late seventeenth and eighteenth centuries.
- New developments in science, which questioned many aspects of biblical history (for example, the date of Creation, the Flood, the descent of all humankind from Noah).
- The increasing willingness of those within the churches to compromise the reliability of the Bible by accepting the views of science and reason.

In the face of these pressures, evangelical orthodox teachers felt increasingly compelled to defend the veracity of the Scriptures, but sometimes they utilized questionable arguments. A few so emphasized the divine authorship of the Scriptures that they promoted a "dictation" theory of inspiration.[83]

With the coming of the full-blown rationalism of the eighteenth-century Enlightenment and increased critical attacks against the reliability of the Scriptures, many theologians were led to compromise solutions, including the view that God, in accommodating Himself to humankind to convey His message of salvation, used time-bound, erroneous human statements. At first they relinquished belief in the Bible's accuracy in historical, geographical, and scientific matters that did not deal with "faith and practice." But eventually even these spiritual and ethical teachings of the Scriptures were questioned.

Despite these attacks the traditional understanding of the inspiration and inerrancy of the Scriptures was maintained throughout the post-Reformation period and subsequent modern times. For example, Samuel Rutherford, one of the framers of the Westminster Confession (1645–1646), wrote, "In writing every jot, tittle or word of Scripture [the biblical writers] were immediately inspired, as touching the matter, word phrases expression, order, method, majesty, stile [*sic*] and all."[84]

Also eighteenth-century evangelical leaders professed the historic belief regarding the Scriptures. John Wesley (1703–1791) declared, "If there be any mistakes in the Bible, there may well be a thousand. If there be one falsehood in that book, it did not come from the God of truth."[85] Jonathan Edwards (1703–1798) recognized by many as America's greatest theologian and respected for his intellect, perplexed the liberal mind by his steadfast trust of the Scriptures. He "accepted totally the tradition established by the Reformers with respect to the primacy and authority of the Bible, and he could approach the biblical writings with . . . conviction of their inerrancy and literal truth."[86]

The New Hampshire Confession of 1833 summarizes the same belief among the Baptists. The well-known nineteenth-century Princetonians, Archibald Alexander, Charles Hodge, A. A. Hodge, and above all, Benjamin B. Warfield (whose ministry extended into the early twentieth century), stood steadfast for biblical inerrancy. Evangelicals today have continued to defend this doctrine. In the late 1970s and 1980s, participants in the International Council on Biblical Inerrancy vigorously championed the inerrancy of the Bible.

CONCLUSION

The question of the nature of the Bible and whether it is true or not rests ultimately on the testimony of Scripture itself. But how the Holy Spirit has led His people to hear and obey that testimony in their confession is also significant. As W. Robert Godfrey has well stated, "Exegesis and theology form the center of the battleline for champions of the inerrancy of the Bible. The strength of that center will ultimately determine the outcome of the struggle to understand the nature of the Scriptures. Yet in this conflict the history of the church's attitudes toward the Bible has become an important flank of the battleline."[87]

The attempt by some to make the inerrancy of the Scriptures a recent doctrine created by fundamentalists in response to the new scientific thought of modern times is contradicted by the teachings of the great leaders of orthodox Christianity throughout history. The fact that the truthfulness of the Scriptures has been the historic conviction of the church is acknowledged by liberal scholars as well. Kirsop Lake, respected Harvard University biblical scholar of the early twentieth century, had little respect for the accuracy of Scriptures. Nevertheless he wrote,

> It is a mistake often made by educated persons who happen to have but little knowledge of historical theology, to suppose that fundamentalism is a new and strange form of thought. It is nothing of the kind; it is the partial and uneducated survival of a theology which was once universally held by all Christians. How many were there, for instance, in Christian churches in the eighteenth century who doubted the infallible inspiration of all Scripture? A few, perhaps, but very few. No, the fundamentalist may be wrong; I think that he is. But it is we who have departed from the tradition, not he, and I am sorry for the fate of anyone who tries to argue with a fundamentalist on the basis of authority. The Bible and the *corpus theologicum* of the Church are on the fundamentalist side.[88]

Our forefathers in the faith bequeathed to us a faithful and often courageous conviction regarding the nature of the Scriptures as the supernaturally inspired Word of God. The record of their attitude and practice in relation to the Scriptures also contains much for modern believers to emulate. They rightly looked at the Scriptures to see Christ, recognizing that He and His salvation are the theme of the Bible. Yet they drove no wedge between the incarnate Word and the written Word. Moreover, nothing in the Scriptures was extraneous; all was useful in accomplishing its saving purpose. As the sixteenth-century Puritan William Whitaker remarked, "Although it may be conceded that all the [biblical] histories are not equally useful and necessary, because many may be saved without the knowledge of many histories; yet in reality they are not only useful, but necessary also. For although they are not all requisite to the being of faith, yet they contribute greatly to its better being."[89] And as Augustine said, "Scripture teaches nothing but charity," and all things taught in the Scriptures "are of value in nourishing and supporting charity and extirpating cupidity."[90]

Our progenitors in the faith also teach us of the absolute need of the Spirit's work in order for the Scriptures to be a life-giving word to us. Doctrine alone, no matter how impeccable, can be stultifying, as the church at times demonstrated. The Word yields its life-giving power only when it is received through the power of the Holy Spirit. Similarly the final assurance of the truthfulness of the Word rests not on human reason but on the testimony of the Holy Spirit in the heart.

Believers today do well to heed what our forebears believed about the Bible's nature as the supernatural inerrant word of God. As the following testimony of Billy Graham illustrates, the strength and effectiveness of the church in this world depends on our attitude to the Bible. "In August of 1949 I was so filled with doubts about everything that when I stood up to preach and made a statement, I would say to myself: 'I wonder if that is the truth. I wonder if I can really say that sincerely.' . . . Then I took the Bible up into the high Sierra Nevada mountains of California. I opened it and got on my knees. 'Father,' I said, 'I cannot understand many things in this book. I cannot come intellectually all the way; but I accept it by faith to be the authoritative, inspired Word of the living God.' A month later in Los Angeles I found that this book had become a sword in my hand. Where human argument had failed, the Word of God did its work."[91]

Thirteen

Those things which have been delivered to us by God in the Sacred Scriptures must be sharply distinguished from those that have been invented by men in the Church, it matters not how eminent they be for saintliness and scholarship.[1]

—Martin Luther

Thirteen

Which Books Belong in the Bible?

How do we know which books belong in the Bible? Do our Bibles include some books that should not be in it? Are some books left out that should have been included?

Protestant Bibles have sixty-six books, whereas Roman Catholic and Eastern Orthodox Bibles have additional books, generally called the Apocrypha. Tobit, one of the books of the Apocrypha, states, "Almsgiving saves from death and purges away every sin" (Tob. 12:9). Another, Ecclesiasticus, also known as Sirach, says, "Yoke and thong will bow the neck, for a wicked slave there are racks and tortures" (Ecclus. 33:26). Are these statements inspired by the Holy Spirit? Do they or do they not belong in the Bible? Are our Bibles lacking something if they do not include the Apocrypha?

How did the people of God come to regard the writings in the Bible as holy Scripture in distinction from the many other writings? What criteria were used in deciding which books to include? Who had the authority to accept certain books and not others? These are the issues of "canonicity" considered in this chapter.

THE IDEA OF A "CANON"

The Meaning of "Canon"

The word "canon" is derived from the Greek word *kanōn*, which originally meant "a straight rod"[2] and then came to mean "a standard or measure." Thus it carried the idea of an authoritative norm. For instance, authoritative standards in ethics, art, or grammar were referred to as canons. Paul used this word in referring to a rule of conduct (Gal. 6:16).

In the early postapostolic church the word "canon" was applied to "the summary of Christian teaching, believed to reproduce what the apostles themselves taught."[3] Called "the rule of faith" or "the rule of truth," this summary was based on the Bible, so that it was "a graph of the interpretation of the Bible by the Church of the second and third centuries."[4]

Because a measuring rod might be marked in units of length like our modern rulers and yardsticks, "canon" also came to have the sense of a series or list. In this sense "canon" came to be applied to the Scriptures as the list of books acknowledged by God's people as belonging to the Bible. The books that were accepted as Scripture were called "canonical," and the collection of such books was "the canon of Scripture." Athanasius, fourth-century bishop of Alexandria, was probably the first one to apply this term to Scripture in a letter that was circulated in A.D. 367. As divine revelation the biblical canon is the ultimate "rule of faith" or the final authority by which all Christian doctrine and practice are to be assessed.

The Concept of Canonization

Some people reject the divine inspiration of Scripture and view the Bible primarily as writings of humans who expressed their faith as witnesses to divine revelation. These same people say that determining which books belong in the Bible was likewise a human endeavor, much like any decision in the church today. Therefore some equally useful works of human religious experience were omitted. However, God, they say, does use the books of the Bible to manifest Himself to us.[5]

Roman Catholics, on the other hand, say that the Roman Church conferred canonical status on the books of Scripture. They argue that the

Roman Church represents the infallible authority of Christ and therefore has the power to determine the extent of the canon.

According to evangelicals God Himself gave authority to the writings by the inspiration of the Holy Spirit, and He also providentially guided His people to recognize these writings as coming from Him and as therefore ultimately authoritative. In this view no human or church council can grant authority to the Scriptures, for they are already authoritative as the inspired Word of God. All we can do is recognize them as such. As J. I. Packer says, "The Church no more gave us the New Testament canon than Sir Isaac Newton gave us the force of gravity. God gave us gravity, by His work of creation, and similarly he gave us the New Testament canon, by inspiring the individual books that make it up."[6]

This view emphasizes that no authority stands above God Himself. How could a church, for example, say that a particular writing is God's Word except on the basis of an authoritative word from God? But of course, such a word from God would have to be acknowledged as such before it could be used as a criterion. So we are left with the conclusion that either God's authoritative revelation, His written Word, is self-authenticating or we have no way of determining His Word from other words.

As the apostle Paul taught, the Holy Spirit reveals spiritual truth and only those who receive His teaching recognize it as such (1 Cor. 2:10–16). Jesus said that only the person who was "willing to do His [the Father's] will . . . shall know of the teaching, whether it is of God, or whether I speak from Myself" (John 7:17). Again he said, "My sheep hear My voice, and I know them, and they follow Me" (10:27). For an infallible judgment on the Word of God, He pointed people to Himself, not to any human authority.

The claim of the Roman Catholic Church to be the infallible determiner of the canon was one of the major disputes in the Reformation. Calvin's comments made in response to that claim are still instructive for us today.

> A most pernicious error widely prevails that Scripture has only so much weight as is conceded to it by the consent of the church. As if the eternal and inviolable truth of God depended upon the decision of men! For they

> mock the Holy Spirit when they ask: Who can assure us that Scripture has come down whole and intact even to our very day? Who can persuade us to receive one book in reverence but to exclude another, unless the church prescribe a sure rule for all these matters? What reverence is due Scripture and what books ought to be reckoned within it can depend, they say, upon the determination of the church. . . .
>
> But such wranglers are neatly refuted by just one word of the apostle. He testifies that the church is "built upon the foundation of the prophets and apostles" (Eph. 2:20). If the teaching of the prophets and apostles is the foundation, this must have had authority before the church began to exist. . . . If the Christian church was from the beginning founded upon the writings of the prophets and the preaching of the apostles, wherever this doctrine is found, the acceptance of it must certainly have preceded the church. It is utterly vain, then, to pretend that the power of judging Scripture so lies with the church that its certainty depends upon churchly assent. Thus, while the church receives and gives its seal of approval to the Scriptures to be the truth of its own God, as a pious duty it unhesitatingly venerates Scripture. As to their question—How can we be assured that this has sprung from God unless we have recourse to the decree of the church?—it is as if someone asked: Whence will we learn to distinguish light from darkness, white from black, sweet from bitter? Indeed, Scripture exhibits fully as clear evidence of its own truth as white and black things do of their own color, or sweet and bitter things do of their own taste. . . .
>
> And the certainty it deserves with us, it attains by the testimony of the Spirit. Therefore illumined by his power, we believe neither by our own nor by any one else's judgment that Scripture is from God; but above human judgment we affirm with utter certainty . . . that it has flowed to us from the very mouth of God by the ministry of men.[7]

The actual historical process of the collection of the canonical books bears this out, as Packer explains in relation to the New Testament canon. "Had one suggested to Christians of the second, third, or fourth century that by this means [the process of recognizing the canonical books] the Church was creating a canon for itself, choosing out some good-quality Christian literature to authorize as a standard of faith for the future, they would have shaken their heads and marveled that anyone could dream up an idea so perverse and far from the truth. The belief that apostolic writings as such were inspired, and therefore intrinsically authoritative, was the presupposition of their whole inquiry."[8]

In summary, in developing the canon the people of God recognized the Word of God that He gave to serve as a norm for their faith and life. The nineteenth-century Swiss Reformed pastor, Louis Gaussen, who is well known for his defense of a high view of the inspiration of the Scriptures, illustrates the development of the canon by the picture of a woman walking through a garden with its owner. As they stroll along the paths, he presents her with one flower after another until he has gathered a whole bouquet for her. The bouquet exists and is admired from the moment she receives the first flowers. In the same way, the canon existed among God's people from the moment the first inspired writings were given by God. God gave His people the books that He wanted to include in the canon of Scripture.[9]

THE OLD TESTAMENT CANON

When Malachi, the last canonical book of the Old Testament, was written (probably around 432 B.C.), classical prophecy in the postexilic period ceased. We don't know how soon after Malachi the Old Testament canon was recognized as closed, but it was well before the New Testament era.[10]

Some writers, however, say the development of the Old Testament canon occurred much later. The Pentateuch, for example, is said to be a composite of various traditions written much later than Moses. The Book of Daniel, according to this view, was written by an unknown author in the time of the Maccabees around 165 B.C. This view thus posits three stages in the formation of the canon: The Pentateuch was closed around 400 B.C., the Prophets about 200 B.C., and the Writings toward the end of the first century A.D.

However, the historical evidence for the canonical process supports the traditional understanding. Moreover, it is increasingly recognized that the discussion of the canon at the Jamnia Council in A.D. 90 "did nothing more than review arguments for two of the books in the Writings

(Ecclesiastes and Song of Songs)—much as Luther would later review the arguments for James."[11] The issue was not whether certain books should be added to the canon, but whether certain books should be retained. The council members had no serious discussion about receiving new books or excluding any book previously recognized. One scholar concludes that Jamnia "had no perceptible effect on Jewish discussions about the Canon."[12]

The Historical Formation of the Old Testament Canon

The Scriptures do not give us a full historical account of the acceptance of each book in the Old Testament and their collection into a canon. This is not surprising since the writings were accepted by God's people as they were received. No leading person or council was necessary to make them canonical. As Dunbar states, "There is no historical evidence for the biblical books 'acquiring' such a position [i.e., scriptural status]. The earliest references for the biblical books (or portions of them) treat them as authoritative."[13] We do, however, find examples of the reception of canonical writings that illustrate something of the gradual development of the canon.

The formation of the canon began with the writings of Moses, as evidenced in Exodus 24:3–4: "Then Moses came and recounted to the people all the words of the LORD and all the ordinances; and all the people answered with one voice, and said, 'All the words which the LORD has spoken we will do!' And Moses wrote down all the words of the LORD." We are then told that "when Moses finished writing the words of this law in a book until they were complete, [he] commanded the Levites who carried the ark of the covenant of the LORD, saying, 'Take this book of the law and place it beside the ark of the covenant of the LORD your God, that it may remain there as a witness against you'" (Deut. 31:24–26).

The writing of Moses was considered the rule of faith and practice for God's people Israel. It was to be read to them at stated times so that they would "be careful to observe all the words of this law" (31:10–12). Joshua was told, "Meditate on it day and night, so that you may be careful to do according to all that is written in it" (Josh. 1:8; see 11:15). The king of Israel was to have a personal copy of the Law so that "he shall read it all the days of his life, that he may learn to fear the LORD his God, by carefully observing all the words of this law and these statutes" (Deut. 17:18–19). Throughout Israel's history, the destiny of the kings and the nation was determined by their attitude toward the revelation of God's will written in the book of the Law (for example, 1 Kings 2:3; 3:14; 2 Kings 17:7–13; 21:7–9; 23:2–3; 2 Chron. 33:8; Dan. 9:11).

Moses predicted that future prophets would arise after him to speak God's Word among the people (Deut. 18:15–22). That the people in the Old Testament recognized such a chain of prophetic writers is seen in the gradual acceptance of further sacred writings. Joshua's words were written "in the book of the law of God" (Josh. 24:26). Samuel also "told the people the ordinances of the kingdom, and wrote them in the book and placed it before the LORD," the latter action indicating their authority for God's people. The writers of the books of Kings and Chronicles were aware of the many prophetic writings covering the entire history of Israel from David to the Exile (1 Chron. 29:29; 2 Chron. 9:29). Prophet after prophet brought God's word to Israel, and much of what they wrote under the inspiration of the Holy Spirit was added to the canonical writings. Isaiah referred to his own words as the authoritative "testimony" and "law" of divine revelation (Isa. 8:16).[14] Jeremiah likewise directed that his words be written (Jer. 36). Daniel, a young contemporary of Jeremiah, not only recognized Jeremiah's words as the "word of the Lord," but also found his words "in the books" that contained "the prophets" and "the law of Moses" (Dan. 9:2, 6, 11). This reference to "the books" is often viewed as the first reference to a canonical collection of the sacred writings.

Evidence of a growing canon is also seen in some writers' use of earlier writings. The books of Moses are mentioned throughout the Old Testament (Josh. 1:7; 1 Kings 2:3; Mal. 4:4). Israel's history from Genesis through Kings is reviewed in Chronicles (1 Chron. 1:1–2:15). Solomon's proverbs and songs are mentioned in 1 Kings 4:32, and Daniel referred to Jeremiah (Dan. 9:2). More than once, prophets warned the people by referring to their forefathers, who did not listen to the words of former prophets (Hos. 6:5; Zech. 1:4–5; 7:12).

When the period of Old Testament prophetic ministry came to an end, canonical writings ceased. According to Jewish tradition the Holy Spirit, who inspired the canonical writings, ceased that ministry at the time of the postexilic prophets. "Since the last prophets Haggai, Zechariah and Malachi died, the Holy Spirit has ceased in Israel" (*T. Sota*, 13, 2).[15] First Maccabees 9:23, 27 implies that by 100 B.C. there had already been a considerable lapse of time since the days of the prophets: "After the death of Judas [Maccabeus] . . . there was great distress in Israel such as had not been since the time that prophets had ceased to appear among them." Similarly Jewish historian Josephus wrote in the first century A.D., "From the death of Moses until Artaxerxes [464–424 B.C., the time of the postexilic prophets] . . . [and] to our own time the complete history has been written but has not been deemed worthy of equal credit with the earlier records, because of the failure of the exact succession of the prophets."[16] This belief that a long period of time, often referred to as "the silent years," elapsed between the cessation of Old Testament prophecy and its inauguration again in the New Testament, along with the anticipation of the coming of a Faithful Prophet, was common during the intertestamental times and the early church fathers.[17]

The Criteria for the Canonicity of the Old Testament

The question as to why certain books were accepted as canonical and others were not has received different answers, depending largely on what one believes about the nature of the Scriptures. As mentioned earlier, some say that the formation of the canon was a human endeavor, based on the idea that the Scriptures are merely human expressions of the writers' faith. Expressing this opinion, one scholar says, "Out of the vast body of national Hebrew literature the books of the OT were selected because of their literary beauty or their nationalistic appeal, because they contributed to keep alive the nation and the worship of Jehovah."[18] He adds that this process was somewhat haphazard. "It is only an accident in transmission that only this canonical literature . . . has come down to us. This is only a small portion of the Hebrew literature mentioned in the Bible: the history of the kings of Israel, the history of the kings of Judah (I Kings 14:19, 29, etc.), and poetic anthologies (Josh. 10:13; II Sam. 1:18; Num. 21:14). Many other compositions have been lost without being mentioned, as happened in all ancient literatures."[19]

As we have already seen, however, the biblical writings were accepted as authoritative by the people of God on the belief that the writings were inspired by Him and are His words. Those who concur with this view generally note four factors that were followed in determining which books belong in the Old Testament.[20]

Prophetic authorship. Many of the Old Testament writings expressly claim prophetic authorship. Many of the later writers were identified as prophets (for example, Hag. 1:3; Zech. 1:1). Although not every book is said to have been written by a prophet, later prophets referred to God addressing His people through "former prophets" (Zech. 1:4; 7:12). This could possibly suggest that all the writings that had been recognized earlier were seen as coming through prophecy.

More importantly, in several places the New Testament referred to part or all of the Old Testament writings as prophetic. The writer of Hebrews declared, "God . . . spoke long ago to the fathers in the prophets in many portions and in many ways" (Heb. 1:1). Peter referred to "the word of the prophets" (2 Pet. 1:19, NIV), a reference to prophets of the Old Testament. When Jesus was arrested, He said, "But all this has taken place that the Scriptures of the prophets may be fulfilled" (Matt. 26:56). After His resurrection He chided His disciples for not believing "all that the prophets have spoken" (Luke 24:25). Peter's reference to the "prophecy of Scripture" as "men moved by the Holy Spirit spoke from God" (2 Pet. 1:20–21), suggests that all inspired Scripture (2 Tim. 3:16) may also be termed prophetic.

The testimony of the Holy Spirit. In addition to the inherent nature of a canonical writing as the inspired Word of God, there must also be the recognition of that writing as such by the people of God. In other words, the formation of the canon involved both divine revelation and human recognition. How did the people recognize that a person was a true prophet of God so that his writing was seen as the authoritative Word of God? Although some, like Moses, were given power to work supernatural acts that pointed to divine authority, the ultimate answer is that the ministry of the Holy Spirit testified to the truth of His own revelation in the hearts of those who were open to receive it. As noted earlier, Jesus said of His own teaching, "If any man is willing to do His will, he shall know of the teaching, whether it is of God, or whether I speak from Myself" (John 7:17).

Providential care. Another factor in the development of the canon is God's providence. The preservation of the biblical writings throughout the centuries in the midst of a nation that was often disobedient to those writings and suffered God's judgment of exile as well as persecution by their enemies is testimony of God's faithful care. Beyond this is the preservation of certain prophetic words from among other inspired words that were spoken and possibly even written. Just as we do not have all the words that Jesus spoke, so the prophets undoubtedly spoke inspired messages that were not written or, if written, were not included among the canonical writings. But God in His providence preserved exactly what He considered useful for His people, to which nothing need be added.

Validation by Christ. The final validation of the canonicity of the Old Testament writings is the testimony of Christ. As noted in chapter 8, Jesus repeatedly testified to the authority of "the Scripture" (for example, John 10:35) and quoted them in His teaching (Matt. 21:42; 26:54; John 5:39). In speaking of the "Scriptures" or "the Law and the Prophets" or "the Law," Jesus was undoubtedly referring to the well-known collection of sacred writings accepted as canonical among the Jews of His day. The New Testament apostles, whom Jesus commissioned to bring further authoritative revelation, also accepted the "Scriptures" as the canonical Word of God.

The Extent of the Old Testament Canon

The Jewish testimony. In the Hebrew Bible the Old Testament has twenty-four books arranged in three divisions: (1) the Torah (Law), consisting of the five books of Moses (Genesis, Exodus, Leviticus, Numbers, Deuteronomy); (2) the Prophets, which is further divided into the four "Former Prophets" (Joshua, Judges, Samuel, Kings) and the four "Latter Prophets" (Isaiah, Jeremiah, Ezekiel, and the book of the Twelve Prophets, that is, the Minor Prophets, so named because of their shorter length); and (3) the Writings (Psalms, Proverbs, Job, Song of Songs, Ruth, Lamentations, Ecclesiastes, Esther, Daniel, and Ezra-Nehemiah [which was viewed as one book]).

Writing in the first century A.D., Josephus referred to the three divisions of inspired books that totaled twenty-two. These are the same as the twenty-four, with Judges and Ruth being counted as one book and Jeremiah and Lamentations being counted as one.

One of the earliest references in Jewish tradition to the list of twenty-four books in a threefold division is in *Baba Bathra* 14b–15a, a passage in the Talmud dating from A.D. 70–200. This listing of books in each of the three divisions is followed in later Jewish manuscripts and the present Hebrew Bible, although the order of books in the Prophets and Writings has varied somewhat. This variation in order occurred because the books were written on separate scrolls and not bound together. The order of the first five books, however, was fixed, because of their chronological sequence.

Exactly when this threefold division came to be the standard is not known. Although the New Testament refers, as we have seen, to all the Old Testament as written by "prophets," it also frequently refers to a twofold division, "the Law or the Prophets" (Matt. 5:17; 7:12; Rom. 3:21) or "Moses and the prophets" (Luke 16:29). Jesus' reference to "the Law of Moses and the Prophets and the Psalms" in Luke 24:44, however, may indicate something of the three divisions, with Psalms as the most prominent work in "the Writings." Ecclesiasticus, a second-century B.C. apocryphal work, refers in the preface to "the Law and the Prophets and the other books of our ancestors," probably a reference to the three categories.

Evidence from Jewish tradition thus points to a canon of twenty-four Old Testament books, which is identical to the Protestant canon of thirty-nine books. In our thirty-nine books the Book of the "Twelve Prophets" become the twelve Minor Prophets and the four books of Samuel, Kings, Chronicles, and Ezra-Nehemiah become eight books.

The Christian testimony. The New Testament gives validation to this same Old Testament canon. In their repeated use of the term "Scripture"—which often refers to a definite passage but is also used for the Old Testament as a whole (John 2:22; Acts 18:24; 2 Tim. 3:16; 2 Pet. 1:20)—or "the Scriptures" (Acts 17:2, 11; Rom. 1:2; 15:4), the writers of the early church, which had its beginning among the Jews, were clearly referring to the sacred writings recognized by their people.

The New Testament includes approximately 250 quotations and 900 or more allusions to the Old Testament.[21] Scholars differ on these estimates, depending on whether certain statements are direct citations or paraphrases. In those references every portion of the Old Testament is represented. Roger Nicole suggests that the New Testament has 278 "specific quotations [from] and direct allusions" to the Old Testament. Of that number, he says 94 are from the Law, 99 from the Prophets, and 85 from the Writings.[22] Only Judges, Ruth, Song of Solomon, Ecclesiastes, Esther, Ezra-Nehemiah, Chronicles, Obadiah, Nahum, and Zephaniah are not quoted in the New Testament. The three prophets (Obadiah, Nahum, and Zephaniah), of course, were part of one book in the Jewish canon, the Twelve Prophets. That some books are not explicitly cited does not mean they were not considered part of the canon. In fact, when we consider the extensive lists of passages reminiscent of the Old Testament (allusions), as suggested by some scholars, all thirty-nine Old Testament books are represented.[23]

In some instances a quotation is difficult to trace to a specific Old Testament passage. For example, although introduced as "Scripture," Jesus' statement, "From his innermost being shall flow rivers of living water" (John 7:38), cannot be found explicitly in the Old Testament. However, the metaphor of water for spiritual blessing promised through the indwelling Spirit is found in several passages, including Isaiah 44:3. Some citations may therefore be combinations of the teachings of several Old Testament passages.

Some have argued that the New Testament writers also cited pseudepigraphal and apocryphal writings as authoritative. For example, Jude 14–15 refers to Enoch's prophecy, which is often taken as a citation from the pseudepigraphal work of 1 Enoch 1:9. However, both Jude and the writer of 1 Enoch could have been referring to an oral tradition. Yet, even if Jude did cite from 1 Enoch, this does not suggest that that book is canonical. Three times the apostle Paul quoted secular authors—Epimenides in Acts 17:28 and Titus 1:12, and Menander in 1 Corinthians 15:33—but that does not mean the writings of those men were viewed as part of Scripture.

Following the New Testament era, the early church "confined themselves in the main to the books of the traditional Jewish canon, as we see from the list of Melito of Sardis (A.D. 160), and those of Origen, Athanasius, Cyril of Jerusalem, and others."[24] However, as discussed in the following section, a number of leaders also appealed to noncanonical Jewish writings, at times citing them as "Scripture." The Reformers, following Athanasius (around A.D. 293–373) and others, strongly reaffirmed the books of the traditional Jewish canon as the only canonical writings of the Old Testament.[25]

The question of the Pseudepigrapha and the Apocrypha. "Pseudepigrapha," which means "false inscriptions," is the name given to a large group of Jewish writings produced between 200 B.C. and A.D. 200. Some of these claim to have been written by Adam, Enoch, Moses, and Ezra. These books, many of which include legendary histories, apocalyptic dreams, and visions, were written to sustain the faith of the Jews during times of unusual suffering. However, the false claims of these books to divine authority, along with the fanciful nature of some of the stories and some outright false doctrinal teachings, kept the Jews from accepting these writings as part of the biblical canon.

Our concern is primarily with the books of the Apocrypha, which both the Roman Catholic Church and the Eastern Orthodox Church say are canonical. Although the term "apocrypha" comes from a Greek word meaning "hidden," it came to be applied to those books that Protestants consider noncanonical.[26] These books, also called deutero-canonical ("second canon"), were afforded full canonical status by the Roman Catholic Church at the Council of Trent on April 8, 1548, with the pronouncement of anathema (excommunication) on anyone who rejects them.

Some church fathers of the early church did accept the Apocrypha as part of Scripture, and others used them for devotional or preaching purposes without viewing them as canonical. They were included in the Septuagint, the Greek translation of the Old Testament, produced between 150 and 250 years before Christ. It is not certain, however, that the Apocrypha was part of the first-century A.D. edition of the Septuagint. It is significant that between the first and fourth centuries the format of books changed from scrolls to bound books. With scrolls, these additional books, which the Jews considered useful but not canonical, were separate from the others. However, their inclusion in the bound Greek version no doubt contributed to their use in the early church, especially as many in the church outside of Palestine would not have been acquainted with the Hebrew canon. In general, however, the fact that some of the early church fathers (for example, Clement of Rome, Clement of Alexandria, and Jerome) cited the Apocrypha frequently provides little support that these books were regarded as Scripture.[27]

The church's use of the apocryphal books did increase somewhat after this early period, but the lists of canonical books, with some variation, still point to the books of the traditional Jewish canon. With Augustine the apocryphal books gained a degree of acceptance in the church, although it is not clear that he viewed them as equal in authority with the other canonical books. They remained in a sort of secondary canonical status until, as noted, the Roman Catholic Church officially pronounced them canonical at the time of the Reformation.

Written between 200 B.C. and A.D. 100, the writings of the Apocrypha reflect the religious, political, and social conditions of the years between the Old and New Testaments. However, there are several reasons for rejecting them as canonical.

First, no Jewish list of Old Testament books contains these apocryphal books. *Second*, while Christ and the New Testament writers quoted liberally from the Old Testament, they never cited the Apocrypha as authoritative Scripture, even though they were aware of these books.

Third, in the first four centuries all the lists of the canonical books, with a few minor exceptions, exclude these books. *Fourth*, the contents of the books speak against their canonicity. Erroneous doctrines are taught, such as the citation from Tobit 12:8–9, noted at the beginning of this chapter, which teaches that almsgiving makes atonement for sin (also Ecclus. [Sirach] 3:30). Prayers and offerings for the dead are taught, which supposedly support the doctrine of purgatory (2 Macc. 12:41–45). Ecclesiasticus 33:25–27 justifies cruelty to slaves, and scorn for womanhood is seen in Ecclesiasticus 22:3 ("the birth of a daughter is a loss") and 42:14 ("Better is the wickedness of a man than a woman who does good"). In addition, historical errors, folklore, and myth are found in a number of the books of the Apocrypha. *Fifth*, they make no claim to inspiration; in fact, they even refer to the absence of prophets in Israel (1 Macc. 9:27).

THE NEW TESTAMENT CANON

The New Testament, like the Old, nowhere includes a list of the books that are to be included in it. Our determination of the New Testament canon must therefore come from theological factors found in both the Old and New Testament Scriptures as well as the testimony of believers in the history of the church. This process took several centuries.

The Historical Formation of the New Testament Canon

The acceptance of the Old Testament canonical Scriptures set the stage for the development of the New Testament canon. No doubt the New Testament believers soon received the teachings of Jesus as having equal (or greater) authority than those of the prophets of the Old Testament (John 1:17; Heb. 1:2; 2:3). The words and works of Jesus thus formed the first elements of a new "canon" for His disciples. Its development was also authorized by Jesus Himself when He appointed the apostles as His authoritative witnesses (Mark 3:14; Acts 10:39–42). As authoritative representatives of Christ, the apostles were the pillars and foundation of the church (Matt. 16:18; Eph. 2:20; Rev. 21:14). The teachings of the apostles were thus considered authoritative, as seen in Paul's command to the Thessalonian believers to "hold to the traditions which you were taught, whether by word of mouth or by letter from us" (2 Thess. 2:15; see also 1 Cor. 14:37).

The apostles' oral communications naturally had a certain historical priority, but, as H. N. Ridderbos notes, the written documents became the definitive form of the apostolic tradition. "With the passing of time and the church spreading over the whole world, the apostles could only keep written contact with the churches. And with the death of the apostles, oral tradition diminished in certainty and became less trustworthy, so that the written fixation of the apostolic tradition naturally acquired more significance."[28]

When some of the New Testament writers asked that their letters be circulated and read in the churches, they were putting their writings on a par with the Old Testament Scriptures, which were commonly read in the churches. Undoubtedly copies were made during this process so that different locations could have the same books. Peter's reference to Paul's letters along with the "rest of the Scriptures" (2 Pet. 3:16) puts Paul's writings on an equal basis with the Old Testament and may suggest that Peter had joined them to that collection.

The postapostolic church fathers had their hands full with the practical and moral issues of an expanding church and therefore had little time for reflection on the canon. Thus they did not make any explicit statements about it. Their ultimate authority was Christ and God's revelation of Him proclaimed both by the Old Testament prophets and the New Testament apostles. At first the church fathers' references to "Scripture" referred to the Old Testament, although they considered the apostolic writings of equal authority. By the middle of the second century Polycarp, Barnabas, and *2 Clement* cited the New Testament. It was also the custom then, according to Justin Martyr (around 100–165), for Christians when they met on Sundays to listen to the reading of the apostolic "memoirs" (referring to the Gospels) or the writings of the prophets (the Old Testament). Thus the New Testament writings were beginning to take their place as canonical writings alongside the Old Testament canon.[29]

In the second century several outside movements, especially Gnosticism and Marcionism, challenged the limits of the New Testament canon. Gnosticism's attempt to get many Gnostic writings accepted as apostolic and the efforts of Marcion to limit the canon to ten Pauline letters and an edited version of Luke obviously pushed the church to reflect more consciously on the limits and extent of true apostolic writings.[30]

According to Eusebius (around 260–339) the church discussed three categories of writings: "recognized," "disputed," and "heretical."[31] Among the books eventually accepted as the New Testament, seven were in dispute for a time, either because of some teaching in them or because they were not yet widely known in both the East and the West. These included Hebrews, James, 2 Peter, 2 John, 3 John, Jude, and Revelation. In the case of Hebrews, apostolic authorship was uncertain. According to early testimony, however, when the facts about these books were known, all were received as canonical. The first witness to our canon of twenty-seven New Testament books is in a letter by Athanasius (dated A.D. 367). The same canonical list was set forth at the Third Council of Carthage in 397 and again in another council at Carthage in 419. Dunbar concludes that "it is appropriate . . . to speak of the [New Testament] canon as having achieved its present form throughout most of the church during the fifth century."[32]

The Criteria for the Canonicity of the New Testament

Because the apostles were recognized as authoritative representatives of Christ, the chief criterion for recognizing a New Testament book as canonical was whether it was written by an apostle or an associate of an apostle whose teachings were consistent with those of an apostle. The oral and written witness of the apostles to the words and works of Christ was the "foundation" of the new church and its ultimate rule of faith and practice. Thus, for example, Justin Martyr spoke of the Gospel of Mark as "Peter's Memoirs." This apostolic criterion is clearly seen in Tertullian's statement against the Marcionites. "I lay it down to begin with that the documents of the gospel have the apostles for their authors, and that this task of promulgating the gospel was imposed upon them by our Lord himself. If they also have for their authors apostolic men, yet these stand not alone, but as companions of apostles or followers of apostles."[33] Apostolicity as the essential criterion is also demonstrated by the fact that many noncanonical Gnostic writings were falsely credited to different apostles in an attempt to validate those writings as authoritative.

In the instances where clear apostolicity was not known (as, for example, the Book of Hebrews) the writing was evaluated by whether it conformed to the "rule of faith" or matched the acknowledged orthodoxy of the apostolic tradition. Also the fact that a writing was viewed as authoritative and enjoyed widespread and continuous usage by the churches played a part in determining its canonicity.

CONCLUSION

The establishing of the canon of the Old and New Testament Scriptures was the work of God in first revealing Himself and then enabling His people, by means of attesting signs and the witness of the Spirit in their hearts, to recognize His revelatory Word.

This special revelation of God in both Testaments is intrinsically connected to His plan of salvation centered in Christ. Prophets inspired by the Holy Spirit (1 Pet. 1:11) prepared the way for the coming of the Messiah and salvation through Him. Apostles, authorized by Christ and inspired by that same Spirit, proclaimed and wrote of Jesus of Nazareth and His works as the fulfillment of that prophetic promise. The inspired record of God's historical acts of salvation, which culminated in Christ's work on the cross, thus define the extent of the canon.

Fourteen

My conscience is captive to the Word of God; to go against conscience is neither right nor safe; here I stand, there is nothing else I can do: God help me; amen.[1]

—Martin Luther

I want to know one thing—the way to heaven: how to land safe on that happy shore. God Himself has condescended to teach the way. He hath written it down in a book. O give me that book! At any price, give me the book of God! I have it: here is knowledge enough for me. Let me be a man of one book.[2]

—John Wesley

Fourteen

Is the Bible Important Today?

LIBERAL THEOLOGIAN Don Cupitt asserts that "modern people want to live their own lives, which means making their own rules, steering a course through life of one's own choice."[3] Authority in our day is a negative, repressive concept. One of the telling truths of history, however, is that as finite human beings, we will inevitably serve some authority. Either we will live under the authority of God our Creator, or we will live under some other god, who finally turns out to be ourselves. As Seneca (around 4 B.C.–A.D. 65), the Roman statesman and philosopher, indicated, if we are our own authority we enslave ourselves to ourselves, which is the worst bondage of all.[4]

True freedom, according to Scripture and common sense, comes only as we submit to the authority of our Creator, who loves His creatures and has revealed to them how to have the fullness of life for which He created us. No one was more free than Jesus, who knew His Father's will and always did it. "I did not speak of My own initiative, but the Father Himself who sent Me has given Me commandment, what to say, and what to speak. And I know that His commandment is eternal life" (John 12:49–50; see also 5:30; 8:28–29; 14:31). Jesus promised to give that same freedom and life to those who would submit to Him and His teaching. "If therefore the Son shall make you free, you shall be free indeed" (8:36). That freedom would be realized through submission to His Word: "If you abide in My word . . . you shall know the truth, and the truth shall make you free" (8:31–32).

That freedom, which is so desired today, the freedom that leads to fullness of life, is thus found only in our submitting to God's authority in Christ, which is conveyed to us in His Word. Since the Scriptures are the Word of God, it is vitally important that we submit to their authority.

Our spiritual enemy, Satan, does everything he can through various means to hinder us from being totally obedient to God and His Word. His success in doing this is seen in the fact that the Bible, though a best-selling book, is seldom read or studied and is even belittled.

What does it take to make the Scriptures authoritative in our lives? We must do three things: elevate the Bible as our ultimate authority, understand its message so that it can function as our authority, and allow the Scriptures to control our lives.

ELEVATING THE SCRIPTURE AS OUR ULTIMATE AUTHORITY—SOLA SCRIPTURA

It is one thing to acknowledge that the Bible is the revealed Word of God, which He gave for our salvation and guidance in life. It is another matter, however, to ascertain how God's authority through His Word actually encounters our lives. To put it another way, how can we know the authoritative will of God? How a person responds to this question determines whether he or she has made the Scriptures his or her ultimate authority.

Through the centuries people have answered this question in one of three ways: God's will is determined either by human spiritual experience or by the authoritative teaching of the church or by the Scriptures themselves as taught by the Holy Spirit. Some people may accept more than one of these as the voice of God, but inevitably only one can be considered supreme and therefore final.

Human Spiritual Experience

In this approach God's authoritative will is found in the subjective opinions of the individual. The Scriptures as well as the testimony of God's people may be useful in the process, but one's own personal experiences finally determine God's will.

In this view the Scriptures are authoritative to the extent that they are in harmony with reason. This may mean surrendering scriptural teaching and data to the latest conclusions of the historical-critical approach to the Bible. Or it may mean accommodating the Scriptures to the dominant ideas of modern culture.

This option in relation to the Bible's authority is often held by those who reject the full inspiration of the Scriptures and its inerrancy. They feel that some authority outside the Scriptures must tell them where the Bible speaks God's truth and where it is only the voice of a fallible human. Human knowledge and reason serve as the final court of appeal.

This view is held even by some who profess to believe in the highest view of divine inspiration. For example, some teach that homosexuality, when practiced in committed relationships, is in accord with Scripture. Also in the case of some who say that the roles of men and women are fully interchangeable in the home and in the church, human experience carries a strong if not determinative authoritative role. The following was written by a professed evangelical (at the time) to the editor of a popular Christian magazine for collegians. "At the historical moment when secular society is just beginning to wake up concerning centuries of injustice to women, it is unwise and unjust for evangelical publications to stress biblical passages concerning ancient inequalities between the sexes. By continuing on such a course, evangelicals will only add fuel to the widespread secular concept that the Christian church is an outmoded institution dedicated to the maintenance of the status quo, no matter how unjust and inhuman that status quo may be."[5]

More recently an elder of an evangelical church acknowledged to a colleague of mine that he would be ashamed to read Paul's teaching concerning husbands and wives in Ephesians 5:21–33 to those whom he invited to church.

For some people rational thought becomes the ultimate religious authority even over the Scriptures. For others that authority is religious feelings or mystical experiences. The prominence of this kind of thinking is evident in the recent work *Fire from Heaven*, written by liberal theologian Harvey

Cox. Viewing the religious clash of the past three centuries between scientific modernity and traditional religion, Cox says the next struggle will be between fundamentalism, by which he means those who put a premium on cognitive truth, and experientialism, a sort of cafeteria-style spirituality wherein only those truths are accepted that "click" with their everyday experience.[6]

But on what basis can we conclude that a certain human experience (rational or emotional) is an authoritative expression of God's voice? And whose experience is to be taken as normative? Rather than judging the Scriptures, our human experience is to be judged and transformed by them. The Bible must be received as the objective Word of God, standing above us so that all human experience is submitted to it.

The Teaching Authority of the Church

A second approach to the authority of the Scriptures says that the Bible's authority is conveyed to us through the authority of the church. The *Catechism of the Catholic Church* (1994), initiated by Pope John Paul II and produced under his direction, states that the divine revelation of the gospel is transmitted in two forms: sacred Scripture and tradition.[7] While these have traditionally been viewed as two separate sources of revelation, there is a tendency in recent Roman Catholic thought to view them as a unit. Citing a document from the Second Vatican Ecumenical Council, the *Catechism* states, "Sacred Tradition and Sacred Scripture make up a single sacred deposit of the Word of God."[8] Everything in church tradition is allegedly found in the Scriptures either explicitly or implicitly.[9]

In this view the teaching office of the church, called the church's Magisterium, has the task, as the successor of the apostles, of giving an authentic interpretation of the Word of God (that is, Scripture and tradition), which, when set forth as dogma, is considered infallible truth.[10] This infallible truth then becomes part of the tradition or divine truth. The Roman Church, in her assumed role as infallible interpreter of tradition and Scripture, thus mediates the authority of the divine revelation of God's Word to His people. As the *Catechism* explains, "Sacred Tradition, Sacred Scripture, and the Magisterium of the Church as so connected and associated that one of them cannot stand without the others. . . . The Church, in her doctrine, life, and worship, perpetuates and transmits to every generation all that she herself is, all that she believes."[11] Roman Catholic writer Mark Shea explains this understanding of the relationship of the Bible to the church and tradition.

> The Catholic faith can agree that Scripture is sufficient. But . . . it also warns that there is a distinction between *material* and *formal* sufficiency. What's the difference? Simply put, it is the difference between having a big enough pile of bricks to build a house and having a house made of bricks. Material sufficiency means that all the bricks necessary to build doctrine is [*sic*] there in Scripture. However, it also teaches that since the meaning of Scripture is not always clear and that sometimes a doctrine is implied rather than explicit, other things besides Scripture have been handed to us from the apostles: things like Sacred Tradition (which is the mortar that holds the bricks together in the right order and position) and the Magisterium or teaching authority of the Church (which is the trowel in the hand of the Master Builder). Taken together, these three things—Sacred Scripture, Sacred Tradition, and the Magisterium—are formally sufficient for knowing the revealed truth of God.[12]

Roman Catholicism is not alone in asserting the infallibility of tradition alongside the Scriptures. Timothy Ware, in a popular work on the Orthodox Church, says plainly, "The doctrinal definitions of an Ecumenical Council are infallible. Thus the eyes of the Orthodox Church, the statement of faith put out by the seven councils, possess, along with the Bible, an abiding and irrevocable authority."[13] Thus certain teachings of the church are placed alongside Scripture as having equal ultimate authority.

Some Protestants today are encouraging Christians to grant a more respectful place for tradition. They rightfully point out that the historic orthodox teachings on the central tenets of the Christian faith can help guard the church against the dangers of accommodating to the prevalent cultural norms. They also hope that this emphasis will bring about greater unity in a fractured church in the battle against secularism. However, sometimes their emphasis on appreciating tradition comes dangerously close to blurring the status of the Scriptures alone as our ultimate authority. An example of this is seen in the recent work *Retrieving the Tradition and Renewing Evangelicalism*, by Daniel H. Williams, an ordained Baptist minister who also teaches patristics and historical theology at Loyola University of Chicago. He frequently links the Scriptures and the early church fathers together as the normative authority for believers. He refers to "the one apostolic and patristic foundation."[14] Again he says, "Like Scripture, the consensual Tradition of the church has its source in the triune God himself, coming to us from the Father, through the Son in the Spirit. Scripture and Tradition are not two different sources of authority and truth."[15] The statement that "the early Tradition of the church provides the grounds for ascertaining its foundation"[16] sounds close to the Roman Catholic view that the church is needed to mediate the authority of the Scriptures to Christians.

The Scriptures Alone

A third view is that the Holy Spirit presents His authority to His people through the Scriptures alone. This classic Protestant doctrine known as *sola Scriptura* ("Scripture alone") is well stated in the French Confession of Faith in 1559. "We believe that the Word contained in these books has proceeded from God, and receives its authority from him alone, and not from men. And in as much as it is the rule of all truth, containing all that is necessary for the service of God and for our salvation, it is not lawful for men, nor even for angels to add to it, or to take away from it, or to change it. Whence it follows that no authority, whether of antiquity, or custom, or numbers, or human wisdom, or judgments, or proclamations, or edicts, or decrees, or councils, or visions, or miracles, should be opposed to these Holy Scriptures, but on the contrary, all things should be examined, regulated, and reformed according to them."[17]

The term *sola Scriptura* also refers to the sufficiency of Scripture, that is, the fact that the Bible contains all truth that is necessary for salvation and the spiritual life. To a people of unbelief who were looking to mediums for direction, Isaiah declared, "Should not a people inquire of their God? . . . To the law and to the testimony! If they do not speak according to this word, they have no light of dawn" (Isa. 8:19–20, NIV). These words of Isaiah were a favorite saying of John Wesley as he "sought to implement his dictum that every teaching must be tested by Scripture."[18]

Similarly Jesus continually pointed only to the Scriptures as God's final authority. In response to the rich man's request that someone from the dead be resurrected to warn his brothers of the judgment of hades, Jesus pointed only to the authority and sufficiency of the Scriptures: "If they do not listen to Moses and the Prophets, neither will they be persuaded if someone rises from the dead" (Luke 16:31). His response to His questioners on one occasion is illustrative of His continual use of the Scriptures alone as the ultimate arbitrator of truth in their conflicts: "You are mistaken, not understanding the Scriptures" (Matt. 22:29). He said of the Scriptures, "It is these that bear witness of Me" (John 5:39).

Most telling are the times when Jesus rejected the traditions that had been built up around the Scriptures by Jewish religious authorities. Questioned as to why His followers "transgress the tradition of the elders," Jesus replied, "And why do you yourselves transgress the commandment of God for the sake of your tradition? . . . You invalidated the word of God for the sake of your tradition" (Matt. 15:2–3, 6). Then, citing the words of Isaiah, Jesus rebuked these authorities for "teaching as doctrines the precepts of men" (15:7–9; see also Mark 7:5–13). Several times in the Sermon on the Mount Jesus said, "You have heard . . . but I say to you. . . ." He was no doubt correcting traditions that had grown up around the Scriptures. For example, "You have heard that it was said, 'You shall love your neighbor and hate your enemy.' But I say to you, love your enemies, and pray for those who persecute you" (Matt. 5:43–44).

Also the apostles appealed only to the Scriptures as their final court of appeal. Paul commended the believers at Berea because they were "examining the Scriptures daily, to see whether these things [his teachings] were so" (Acts 17:11). The apostle desired that the Corinthians "not go beyond what is written" (1 Cor. 4:6, NIV), that is, to live only by the Scriptures.[19] The Scriptures alone are sufficient for believers. As Paul wrote to his son in the faith, "The sacred writings . . . are able to give you the wisdom that leads to salvation through faith which is in Christ Jesus." The inspired Scriptures are "profitable for teaching, for reproof, for correction, for training in righteousness; that the man of God may be adequate [capable, proficient, able to meet life's demands], equipped [completely outfitted] for every good work" (2 Tim. 3:15–17). Chrysostom, the great fourth-century preacher and church father, paraphrased these words of the apostle in this way: "Thou hast Scripture for a master instead of me; thence thou canst learn whatever thou wouldst know."[20]

It would seem reasonable that if there is an authoritative nonwritten apostolic tradition, which is a revelatory word of God in addition to the written Scriptures in the church, we could expect a similar authoritative nonwritten tradition in relation to the Old Testament prophets. However, the New Testament shows no evidence of such an authoritative nonwritten prophetic tradition equal to the Scriptures. In fact, as we have seen, it points up the danger of placing extrabiblical tradition on a par with the written Word.

True, the people of God were to submit to the authoritative teachings of the apostles (and of the Old Testament prophets), whether written or spoken. Thus Paul exhorted the believers at Thessalonica to "stand firm and hold to the traditions which you were taught, whether by word of mouth or by letter from us" (2 Thess. 2:15; see also 3:6; 1 Cor. 11:2). Timothy was to pass on to others the things he had "heard" from the apostle Paul, not just what he had read in Paul's letters (2 Tim. 2:2). True prophetic or apostolic teaching is authoritative, whether spoken or written, for it is communicating God's will. But after the apostolic era the only teaching that can be authenticated as genuinely apostolic is what we have in written form. There is no biblical evidence for a succession of apostles, who give an infallible interpretation of the words of Scripture and add to this written tradition through their own development of infallible dogmas. Those who are given the responsibility of passing on the apostolic tradition to succeeding generations are never called "apostles." Rather they, as teachers and preachers, are to proclaim faithfully the "apostolic" faith which "was once for all delivered to the saints" (Jude 3). The apostolic word thus continues in the church through the authoritative Scriptures and not in an authoritative teaching office of the church. As Oscar Cullmann says, "The apostle cannot, therefore, have any successor who could replace him as bearer of revelation for future generations, but must continue *himself* to fulfill his function in the Church of today: *in* the Church, not *by* the Church, but *by his word* . . . (John 17.20), in other words, by his *writings*."[21]

This truth is born out in the recognition by the church of a canon of Scripture (see chapter 13). In identifying a closed canon of the Bible, the church distinguished between canonical revelation and all subsequent tradition. It was saying in essence that subsequent tradition must be submitted to the control of the Scriptures.

This is, in fact, the testimony of some of the great leaders of the church. To be sure, the early fathers at times spoke of the "rule of faith" as the tradition taught by the church, because there was yet "no clear distinction between the apostolic tradition and the writing of the apostles." By the middle of the second century, however, it was apparent that the apostles' oral teaching, which had been heard by the first-generation church and was passed on to others, was becoming polluted with unreliable legend. The Scriptures, then, which recorded the teachings of the apostles, along with the Old Testament, gradually became the only decisive authority.[22]

The following statements serve as examples of the historical witness to the belief in the doctrine of *sola Scriptura*. Fourth-century theologian Athanasius, wrote, "For indeed the holy and God-breathed Scriptures are self-sufficient for the preaching of the truth."[23] Cyril (around 315–387), bishop of the church in Jerusalem, declared, "In regard to the divine and holy mysteries of the faith, not the least part may be handed on without the Holy Scriptures. . . . Even to me, who tell you these things, do not give ready belief, unless you receive from the Holy Scriptures the proof of the things which I announce. The salvation in which we believe is not proved from clever reasoning, but from the Holy Scriptures."[24] Augustine, perhaps the most influential theologian from Paul until Calvin, respected by both Roman Catholics and Protestants, wrote, "There is a distinct boundary line separating all productions subsequent to apostolic times from the authoritative canonical books of the Old and New Testaments. . . . In the innumerable books that have been written latterly we may sometimes find the same truth as in Scripture, but there is not the same authority, Scripture has a sacredness peculiar to itself."[25] Even the great thirteenth-century Roman Catholic theologian, Thomas Aquinas, clearly believed in *sola Scriptura*. He declared that "we believe the successors of the apostles and prophets only in so far as they tell us those things which the apostles and prophets have left in their writings."[26]

We have seen that the term *sola Scriptura* means that the Bible is the final and ultimate authority for believers, and that the Scriptures are sufficient for salvation and Christian living. A third sense of *sola Scriptura* is the clarity of the Bible (sometimes called its perspicuity). This means that the average believer can understand the Scriptures and lead a life of obedience to God. People do not need some interpreter to tell them what is true.

An interesting example of this truth is the people at Berea. After Paul and Silas proclaimed the gospel there, those new believers "were more noble-minded than those in Thessalonica, for they received the word with great eagerness, examining the Scriptures daily, to see whether these things were so" (Acts 17:11). The Bereans could evaluate whether the message of the apostles was in accord with the Scriptures, and they could understand the apostles' proclamation of that gospel to them. There is no reason to believe that the letters of the apostles are not similarly understandable. Most of the New Testament epistles were addressed not to church leaders, but to the entire congregations, apparently with the thought that they could be understood by all (for example, "to all the saints in Christ who are at Philippi," Phil. 1:1; see also Gal. 1:2; 1 Cor. 1:2). As Paul's comment to the Colossian believers indicates, his letters were read to the recipient church and then were passed on to be read in other churches: "And when this letter is read among you, have it also read in the church of the Laodiceans; and you, for your part read my letter that is coming from Laodicea" (Col. 4:16). The apostle's belief that his writings could be understood by the churches is expressly stated in these words to the Corinthians: "For we write nothing else to you than what you read and understand and I hope you will understand until the end" (2 Cor. 1:13).

Similarly the Old Testament emphasizes the responsibility of believers to read and understand their Scriptures. People had to be able to understand the Word of God when Moses commanded them, "You shall teach them diligently to your sons and shall talk of them when you sit in your house and when you walk by the way and when you lie down and when you rise up" (Deut. 6:7). Surely every believer is to "delight . . . in the law of the LORD" and to "meditate on it day and night" (Ps. 1:2, NIV).

This evidence for the clarity of Scripture, of course, does not deny the value of teachers among God's people to help people gain greater understanding of God's Word. But there is no hint in Scripture that any individual is dependent on an authoritative teacher in order to understand the fundamental truths of the Scriptures sufficiently for salvation and Christian living. There is no intimation that any person will be able to say to the Lord at the final judgment, "I didn't obey Your Word because You made me dependent on a teacher and he taught me falsely." In fact, strong evidence for the clarity of the Word of God is seen in Paul's rebuke of the Galatian believers for listening to false teachers and in his command for them to reject "any man" (including himself) who "is preaching to you a gospel contrary to that which you received" (Gal. 1:9).

Conclusion

The belief that the Scriptures alone are the final authority for the believer is crucial to Christianity. For only as the authority of the Bible stands supreme over the authority of the individual and even the church can we truly be addressed by the Word of God and not our own word. Only when the difference between the work of the Holy Spirit in the inspiration of the Holy Scriptures is recognized as different from His work in the teaching ministry of the church can the church hear a word from God rather than its own voice.[27] John Calvin wrote that we must distinguish between the apostles and their successors. The apostles, he said, "were sure and genuine scribes of the Holy Spirit, and their writings are therefore to be considered oracles of God; but the sole office of others is to teach what is provided and sealed in the Holy Scriptures."[28]

The recognition of the Scriptures' final authority does not negate the value of the teaching of the church and the decrees of historic councils. The church is called to be "the pillar and support of the truth" (1 Tim. 3:15), to teach and uphold God's truth, but at the same time the church remains under it. The church's teaching must always be judged by the truth of Scripture, for history clearly reveals that such teaching has not always been in accord with Scripture. Even the writings of the earliest postapostolic fathers, who because of their proximity to the apostles are often held up as giving us normative Christianity, must be recognized as different from the Scriptures.[29]

Only if the Scriptures are viewed as the infallible Word of God and made the final authority over our thoughts, feelings, and actions can we truly live by the Word of God. Only through an objective Word, which addresses our needs, can our Lord exercise His lordship over us.

UNDERSTANDING THE MESSAGE OF THE SCRIPTURES

The Scriptures can have their rightful place in our lives only if we understand their message. Thus we find the psalmist praying again and again, "Teach me, O Lord, the way of Thy statutes. . . . Give me understanding, that I may observe Thy law" (Ps. 119:33–34; see also 119:12, 26–27, 64, 66, 73, 108, 124–125, 135, 144, 171). It is finally God "who teaches man knowledge" (94:10). But along with asking for the Lord's instruction, the psalmist was also actively engaged with the Word, meditating on it (119:15, 48, 78, 99) and diligently considering it (119:95). Coming to a true understanding of the Scriptures, through which God communicates His life-giving truth, involves both God's activity and our own.

The Teaching Ministry of the Spirit of God

The need of God's teaching ministry. God and His truth can be revealed only by God. For it transcends human thought, involving "things which eye has not seen and ear has not heard, and which have not entered the heart of man" (1 Cor. 2:9). Through revelation and inspiration God communicates His truth to us objectively, bringing it into the realm of human history. But He must also address that word to our hearts, for personal communication with another person is ultimately spirit with spirit, in this case God's Spirit with our spirit. Created in the image of God, we were designed for fellowship with God. The presence of sin in our lives simply makes it all the more imperative that we tune our hearts to hear

God's Spirit. (For the effects of sin on our spiritual understanding see 2 Cor. 4:3–4; Eph. 4:18; and Heb. 5:11.)

The ministry of the Spirit is clearly expressed by the apostle Paul in 1 Corinthians 2:11–13. "For who among men knows the thoughts of a man, except the spirit of the man, which is in him? Even so the thoughts of God no one knows except the Spirit of God. Now we have received . . . the Spirit who is from God, that we might know the things freely given to us by God, which things we also speak . . . in words . . . taught by the Spirit." The apostle proclaimed the message in words taught by the Spirit, and it was only by the same Spirit that his hearers could come to "know the things freely given to us by God."

The nature of the Spirit's ministry of teaching. When we speak of the teaching or illuminating ministry of the Holy Spirit, we are entering an important truth and yet one that remains somewhat mysterious. To some extent the activities of God in our innermost being will always remain beyond our understanding. For we do not even fully understand the depths of our own hearts, including our motives, where our thoughts come from, and so forth. Nevertheless the Scriptures do give us some fundamental truths about the Spirit's teaching and His illuminating the Word to our hearts.

This work of the Spirit begins at conversion. Those who are "taught of God" and have "learned from the Father" come to Christ for salvation (John 6:45). The Holy Spirit brings conviction about the truth of God's Word (16:8–11) and witnesses to Christ in the world (15:26). His work continues in believers as the Holy Spirit ("the anointing") abides in them and "teaches you about all things" (1 John 2:27).

But what exactly does the Spirit do in His teaching ministry? First, He gives us understanding of the Word of God. This does not mean that an unbeliever without the Spirit cannot comprehend what the Scripture says. Scholarly studies by unbelievers into the Bible's historical backgrounds and its languages have thrown helpful light on the meaning of Scripture. The ministry of the Spirit, however, is not so much to give intellectual understanding but to give true understanding to the heart, which enables believers to respond to the truth. The person without the ministry of the Spirit can understand the words on the pages of the Bible, but he cannot grasp their true meaning for himself, and he does not appropriate them to himself. As Paul wrote, "The word of the cross is to those who are perishing foolishness" (1 Cor. 1:18). In the words of Jesus, citing the prophet Isaiah, they "keep on hearing, but will not understand . . . keep on seeing, but will not perceive. . . . For the heart of this people has become dull" (Matt. 13:14–15).

It is like the words of a loving parent who forbids his youngster to play with a gun or to eat too many sweets. The words are perfectly clear and understandable to the child. The problem is that the child does not really perceive them or see their truthfulness, and so he rejects them. In later years, however, the child, now as an adult, sees the truthfulness and the significance of his parents' words and probably gives the same instruction to his own children.

The illuminating work of the Spirit, therefore, does not take the place of study. Nor does it mean that "you have no need for anyone to teach you" (1 John 2:27). The same Spirit has gifted some for a teaching ministry in the church (Rom. 12:7; 1 Cor. 12:29; Eph. 4:11). These teachers can help others understand God's Word, but they are not necessary *mediators* of that truth to us, nor can they really teach it to our hearts.

A second aspect of the Spirit's illuminating ministry of the Scriptures is seen in the psalmist's prayer, "Open my eyes, that I may behold wonderful things from Thy law" (Ps. 119:18). The Scriptures are like a boundless mine out of which one may continually discover new treasures. These treasures, however, are garnered only by the eyes that have been opened by God through the Spirit. Under the Spirit's tutelage we can read the Scriptures again and again, receiving new insights and applications to our lives.[30]

Interpreting the Scriptures

Along with the Spirit's ministry of teaching and illuminating God's Word to us, the Scriptures encourage us to apply ourselves to reading, studying, and listening to the teaching of the Bible. Our knowledge of the Word of God, which is instrumental in our salvation from beginning to end, thus partakes of the same relationship of human and divine activity as seen in the apostle's words, "[You] work out your salvation with fear and trembling; for it is *God* who is at work in you, both to will and to work for His good pleasure" (Phil. 2:12–13, italics added).

Despite the often-heard claim that the Bible is difficult to understand, the necessity of the Scriptures in the life of all believers for spiritual health and growth suggests that every believer can understand its basic teachings. God's life-giving truths in His Word are like the treasures of wisdom, of which Solomon said, "If you seek for her as silver, and search for her as for hidden treasures; then you will discern the fear of the LORD, and discover the knowledge of God" (Prov. 2:4–5). The knowledge of God's Word is available to all who will put forth the effort to search and mine for it. Without attempting to go fully into a discussion of biblical interpretation, the following general principles are helpful to keep in mind in pursuing the all-important task of coming to an understanding of the life-giving truths of the Scriptures.

Natural interpretation. God inspired the human authors of the Scriptures to write in ordinary human language, not in some cryptic language for which we need a key to unlock the meaning. As in all human language, we grasp the message of the Bible by paying close attention to the meanings of the words and their relationships in sentences. As in ordinary language, the Bible uses words in a variety of figurative ways such as similes, metaphors, hyperboles, and parables. In seeking to differentiate the literal sense from the figurative, we must use all the teaching of Scripture as well as our knowledge of the world about us with care so that we do not exclude the supernatural in our understanding of reality. When Scripture, for example, refers to God riding on a cherub (2 Sam. 22:11), we must not hastily conclude that the cherub is figurative simply because we have had no experience of one.

The writers also wrote each book in a certain historical and cultural setting, intending for their readers to understand what they wrote. Thus as much as possible, we must put ourselves in the shoes of the writers and initial readers of the Bible books. At times it may be useful to look for help on the historical background of a text, but for the most part the meaning of the text can be ferreted out by careful study and comparison with other portions of the Scriptures.

Situational interpretation. The Bible is a record of God's involvement with His people in history, spanning many centuries. As His plan of redemption unfolds, there is development involving change. For example, the Mosaic Law with its many legal regulations came to an end with Christ (Gal. 3:24–25). Thus in approaching any passage it is important to ask, For whom was this passage written? All of Scripture is meaningful and profitable for us today in understanding God and His relationship to us. But as in the detailed commandments of the Mosaic Law, every statement is not applicable to us today in exactly the same way it was to the people to whom it was addressed before the finished work of Christ.

We must also ask whether a certain instruction was intended as universal (for everyone at all times) or whether it is a particular, limited-to-that-time expression of a universal principle. For example, are we to obey the apostle's injunction to "greet all brethren with a holy kiss" (1 Thess. 5:26)? Knowledge of various customs of biblical times and how they relate to spiritual truths will generally help us sort out cultural expressions from the permanent truths God is communicating.

Holistic interpretation. Thomas Watson, the Puritan divine, pointed to perhaps the most important principle for gaining an understanding of Scripture when he said, "The Scripture is to be its own interpreter, or rather the Spirit speaking in it. Nothing can cut the diamond but the diamond; nothing can interpret Scripture but Scripture."[31]

Although written by various human authors over centuries, the Bible is a unified harmonious whole, because it was at the same time authored by the one Spirit of truth. Thus the various portions of Scripture do not exist in isolation; they are part of the whole revelation of God. So each portion should be interpreted in relation to the whole Bible. Jesus' prohibition against judging another person (Matt. 7:1), for example, must be understood in relation to His teaching on church discipline (18:15–17). The unity of the Scriptures also means that a knowledge of earlier writings often provides help in understanding later writings. And many earlier statements are developed more fully as God's historical plan of salvation unfolded.

Christological interpretation. A true understanding of the Scriptures also requires that we constantly keep the words of our Lord in mind, namely, the fact that, as Jesus said, "the Scriptures . . . bear witness of Me" (John 5:39). A true interpretation of a passage will therefore be in harmony with God's revelation in Christ and will tell us something about Him and His work. For "all the treasures of wisdom and knowledge" are hidden in Christ (Col. 2:2–3).

Mutual interpretation. Because we are all fallible and carry with us our cultural background with its limited and sometimes perverted perspectives, the mutual help of other believers is valuable in understanding the Scriptures. Thus the apostle declared, "Let the word of Christ dwell in you richly as you teach and admonish one another with all wisdom" (Col. 3:16). This includes listening to gifted teachers in our churches as well as learning from the gifted teachers God has given the church throughout the centuries. The best understanding of the Scriptures is more likely to come from biblical students sharpening each other than from "Lone-Ranger" interpreters.

Obviously anything more than a superficial understanding of Scripture requires time and effort in study. But if we had a letter from someone we loved, even if it were written in another language, we would make every effort to understand its content. The nature of the Bible as the Word of God and its life-giving truths for our lives surely make it worth our effort.[32]

USING THE SCRIPTURES AS OUR AUTHORITY

What one believes inevitably demonstrates itself in life, "for out of [the heart] are the issues [the starting point and course] of life" (Prov. 4:23, KJV). Recognizing the divine treasure that our Lord has given us in His Word, we should manifest the truths of Scripture both in the community of God's people and in our own personal lives.

The Word of God in the Church

Julius Wellhausen was a German biblical critic who almost a century ago undermined the concept of the inspiration of Scripture through his view of the Pentateuch as a composite of late traditions. Yet he clearly recognized the significance of a high view of the authority of the Scriptures in the ministry of the church. So he resigned from his position on the Theological

Faculty in Griefswald, Germany, giving the following explanation in his letter of resignation: "I became a theologian because I was interested in the scientific treatment of the Bible; it has only gradually dawned upon me that a professor of theology likewise has the practical task of preparing students for service in the Evangelical Church, and that I was not fulfilling this practical task, but rather, in spite of all reserve on my part, was incapacitating my hearers for their office."[33]

If we believe that the Scriptures are the inerrant revelation of the saving truth of God to humankind, we must give them a central place in the community of God's people. And this is exactly what we find in the Scriptures. As Israel's worship began with hearing God ("Hear, O Israel!" Deut. 6:4), so church worship begins with listening to the voice of God through His Word. Thus the early believers were "continually devoting themselves to the apostles' teaching" (Acts 2:42). So important is the Word that the growth of the church is essentially synonymous with growth in the Word: "And the word of God kept on spreading; and the number of the disciples continued to increase greatly in Jerusalem" (6:7; see also 12:24; 19:20). C. E. B. Cranfield does not overstate the case when he concludes that "this hearing of the Word of God, hearing what the Lord of the church wants to say to his church in its actual situation, is the primary task of the church."[34]

Believers in the early church heard the Word of God as it was read publicly and was preached. Paul charged Timothy, a young pastor, to "give attention to the public reading of Scripture, to exhortation and teaching" (1 Tim. 4:13). As noted earlier, the apostle expected his letters to be read publicly in the church assemblies (Col. 4:16; 1 Thess. 5:27). Also the Book of Revelation was read publicly, for it refers to "those who hear" it (Rev. 1:3). The public reading of the Scriptures acknowledges their importance while at the same time making an impact as one listens audibly and attentively to the words, which are in fact the words of God.

The preaching and teaching of the Word is also significant in biblical church life. The task of the preacher is not only to proclaim the Word, but also to help the people respond to it by applying it to their various needs. If the Bible is to function as the authoritative Word of God in preaching, it cannot be used merely as a resource for the preacher to say what he thinks the people need to hear or what they want to hear. Instead it means listening to the Bible for what God knows the people need. Someone has well said that the duty of the preacher is to expound the Scriptures in such a way that in reality the Lord of the church is holding a conversation with His people. While particular methods of preaching or style of delivery may be open for evaluation, the belief in the Scriptures as the means by which God speaks His saving Word to the world and to His people makes the proclaiming and hearing of the Bible of supreme importance to the church.

The Word of God in Personal Life

Spiritual growth and health can be present as we personally feed on God's Word regularly, in addition to hearing it proclaimed in church. For many believers this is a difficult task. Our time is filled with other activities. But what is more important than nourishing our lives on the life-transforming words of God? Some try to spend time in the Scriptures regularly, but they often lose motivation because, they say, "It doesn't work." Donald Miller wrote, "If God speaks through the Bible, we should listen for His voice *there.* We can only hear where He has chosen to speak. I may have preferred Him to speak elsewhere, but if the Bible is where He has spoken that is where I must listen. We should not, therefore, despair of hearing the voice of God through the Scriptures until we have exposed ourselves to them directly and faithfully in order that they may do their work in our lives. But how few [people] do any regular or systematic reading or study of the Bible."[35]

From personal experience I have come to realize what the Bible has always taught, namely, that God's blessing is promised not so much for the reading or studying of the Scriptures, but for *meditating* on them. The blessed man, according to Psalm 1:1–2, is one who "meditates day and night" on God's Word (see also Josh. 1:6–8). Meditating on the Word means mulling and praying over its truths and its meaning for our lives until it touches our heart, the "wellspring" of our life (Prov. 4:23, NIV).

The power of meditation is seen in psychiatrist Paul Meier's attempt to find a correlation between a person's psychological state and his or her spiritual life. He asked each seminary student in a class he taught to complete a standard psychological test and a spiritual-life questionnaire. At first he acknowledged surprise and disappointment. The students who had been Christians for many years were only slightly healthier and happier than those who had been believers for a shorter time. The difference was not statistically significant. His disappointment, however, turned to joy when he found the crucial factor that made the difference. That difference was meditating daily or almost daily on the Scriptures. While Meier acknowledges that the renewal of the mind through the Bible can come from a variety of sources, especially through Christian friends, he concludes, "Daily meditation on Scripture, with personal application, is the most effective means of obtaining personal joy, peace, and emotional maturity.... On average, it takes about three years of daily Scripture meditation to bring about enough change in a person's thought patterns and behavior to produce statistically superior mental health and happiness."[37]

Martin Luther described the power of meditation on God's Word to bring about transformation of life. "Since these promises of God are holy, true, righteous, free, and peaceful words, full of goodness, the soul which clings to them with a firm faith will be so closely united with them and altogether absorbed by them that it not only will share in all their power but will be saturated and intoxicated by them. If a touch of Christ healed, how much more will this most tender spiritual touch, this absorbing Word of God, communicate to the soul all things that belong to the Word."[38]

CONCLUSION

To ask the question, Is the Bible important? is somewhat like asking, Is food important? Simply stated, we can no more experience spiritual life without the Word of God than we can experience physical life without food. The Scriptures tell about Christ, and the Holy Spirit opens our eyes to behold the wonders of our Savior. The Bible is our light (Ps. 119:105), our food (1 Pet. 2:2; Heb. 5:11–14), our medicine (Pss. 19:7; 119:93), our sword for spiritual battle (Eph. 6:17), and the implanted seed which is able to save (James 1:21; 1 Pet. 1:23). In short it is everything we need, as John Newton, converted slave trader, wrote in this poem.

Precious Bible? What a treasure
Does the Word of God afford!
All I want for life or pleasure,
Food and medicine, shield and sword;
Let the world account me poor—
Christ and this, I need no more.[38]

Endnotes

INTRODUCTION

1. Immanuel Kant, quoted in Gwynn McLendon Day, *The Wonder of the Word* (Westwood, N.J.: Revell, 1957), 105.
2. King George V, quoted in ibid., 100.
3. Coronation Souvenir, 2 June 1953, Grosvenor House, London, 21, quoted in ibid., 96.
4. Patrick Henry, quoted in ibid., 102.
5. Feodor M. Dostoyevsky, quoted in ibid., 108.
6. Billy Graham, *Peace with God* (Garden City, N.Y.: Doubleday, 1953).

CHAPTER 1—WHY IS THE BIBLE CALLED THE BOOK OF LIFE?

1. J. B. Phillips, *Letters to Young Churches: A Translation of the New Testament Epistles* (New York: Macmillan, 1955), xii.
2. F. W. Farrar, *The Bible: Its Meaning and Supremacy* (London: Longmans, Green and Co., 1897), 251.
3. Augustine, *Confessions* (reprint, Oxford: Oxford University Press, 1992), 152–53.
4. Martin Luther, in *Luther's Works* (Minneapolis: Mühlenberg, 1960), 34:336–37.

5. D. L. Moody, quoted in Day, *The Wonder of the Word*, 43.
6. Andrew T. Lincoln, *Ephesians*, Word Biblical Commentary (Dallas: Word, 1990), 288.
7. Ibid., 290.
8. Peter Craigie, *Psalms 1–50*, Word Biblical Commentary (Waco, Tex.: Word, 1983), 183–84.
9. Derek Kidner, *Psalms 73–150* (Downers Grove, Ill.: InterVarsity, 1975), 416.
10. Ibid., 421–22.

CHAPTER 2—WHAT IS DIVINE REVELATION?

1. Immanuel Kant, quoted in Peter J. Kreeft, *Heaven: The Hearts Deepest Longing* (San Francisco: Ignatius, 1989), 11.
2. Immanuel Kant, *Critique of Pure Reason,* trans. J. M. D. Meiklejohn (New York: Willey, 1943), 13.
3. *Phaedo*, 85 D, in *Dialogues of Plato*, ed. Eric H. Warmington and Philip Rouse, trans. W. H. D. Rouse (New York: American Library of World Literature, 1956), quoted in Merrill C. Tenney, "The Meaning of the Word," in *The Bible—The Living Word of Revelation*, ed. Merrill C. Tenney (Grand Rapids: Zondervan, 1968), 13.
4. Immanuel Kant, "What Is Enlightenment?" in *The Philosophy of Emmanuel Kant's Moral and Political Writings*, ed. Carl. J. Friedrich (New York: Random House, 1949), 132.

CHAPTER 3—WHAT IS GENERAL REVELATION?

1. Hymn, "The Spacious Firmament on High," by Joseph Addison (1672–1719).
2. Henry Wadsworth Longfellow, *Hyperion* (1839), 3.5.
3. Richard Wurmbrand, *Tortured for Christ* (London: Hodder and Stoughton, 1967), 23 (italics his).
4. Kenneth Kantzer, "The Communication of Revelation," in *The Bible—The Living Word of Revelation*, 64.

CHAPTER 4—WHAT IS SPECIAL REVELATION?

1. J. I. Packer, *God Has Spoken* (London: Hodder and Stoughton, 1965), 34.
2. Gordon J. Wenham, *Genesis 1–15*, Word Biblical Commentary (Waco, Tex.: Word, 1987), 76.
3. John Calvin, *Institutes of the Christian Religion*, ed. John T. McNeill, trans. Ford Lewis Battle (Philadelphia: Westminster, 1960), 1.6.1.
4. Bernard Ramm, *Special Revelation and the Word of God* (Grand Rapids: Eerdmans, 1971), 78 (italics his).
5. Benjamin B. Warfield, *The Inspiration and Authority of the Bible* (Philadelphia: Presbyterian and Reformed, 1948), 76.

CHAPTER 5—ARE THE BIBLE'S TEACHINGS UNIQUE?

1. Robert L. Dabney, "The Bible: Its Own Witness," in *Discussions: Evangelical and Theological* (1890; reprint, London: Banner of Truth, 1967), 131.
2. Farrar, *The Bible: Its Meaning and Supremacy*, 243.
3. J. G. Whittier, *Miriam*, quoted in ibid., 245.
4. Colin Chapman, *Christianity on Trial* (Wheaton, Ill.: Tyndale, 1975), 201 (italics his).
5. Radhakrishnan, *Hindu View*, 20, quoted in ibid., 168.
6. Christmas Humphreys, *Buddhism* (Harmondsworth, U.K.: Penguin, 1958), 79–80.
7. John Mibiti, *African Religions and Philosophy* (London: Heinemann, 1969), 35.
8. Reynold A. Nicholson, *The Mystics of Islam* (London: Routledge and Kegan Paul, 1966), 22–23.
9. Herman Bavinck, *The Doctrine of God* (Grand Rapids: Eerdmans, 1951), 333.
10. Helmut Thielicke, *The Evangelical Faith* (Grand Rapids: Eerdmans, 1977), 2:158–60.
11. W. G. T. Shedd, *Dogmatic Theology* (1888; reprint, Grand Rapids: Zondervan, 1953), 1:250.
12. J. N. D. Anderson, *Christianity and Comparative Religion* (Downers Grove, Ill.: InterVarsity, 1970), 51.

13. H. D. Lewis and R. L. Slater, *World Religions* (London: C. A. Watts, 1966), 174.
14. W. H. Griffith Thomas, *Christianity Is Christ* (London: Longmans, Green and Co., 1919; reprint, New Canaan, Conn.: Keats, 1981), 7.
15. Ibid., 34.
16. *An Appeal to Unitarians,* quoted in ibid., 26.
17. John R. W. Stott, *Basic Christianity* (Downers Grove, Ill.: InterVarsity, 1995), 43–44.
18. John Hick, "Jesus and the World Religions," in *The Myth of God Incarnate*, ed. John Hick (London: SCM, 1977), 168–70.
19. Jean-Jacques Rousseau, quoted in Thomas, *Christianity Is Christ*, 70.
20. Dabney, *Discussions: Evangelical and Theological,* 125.
21. Ibid., 126.
22. H. G. Wells, *The Outline of History* (Garden City, N.Y.: Garden City Books, 1956), 1:425–26.
23. Dabney, *Discussions: Evangelical and Theological,* 121.
24. Ibid., 122.
25. K. Klostermaier, *Hindu and Christian in Yrindaban* (London: SCM, 1969), 20–21.
26. Lewis and Slater, *World Religions,* 78.
27. Leon Morris, *The Cross of Jesus* (Grand Rapids: Eerdmans, 1988), 9–10.
28. Dabney, *Discussions: Evangelical and Theological,* 122–23.
29. Ajith Fernando, *The Supremacy of Christ* (Wheaton, Ill.: Crossway, 1995), 149.
30. Joseph Jacobs, "Jesus of Nazareth—In History," in *The Jewish Encyclopedia*, ed. Isidore Singer (London: Funk and Wagnalls, 1906), 7:166.
31. J. Gresham Machen, *Christianity and Liberalism* (New York: Macmillan, 1923), 70.

CHAPTER 6—HOW ELSE IS THE BIBLE UNIQUE?

1. Sir Walter Scott, "The Monastery," quoted in Farrar, *The Bible: Its Meaning and Supremacy*, 259.

2. René Pache, *The Inspiration and Authority of Scripture* (Chicago: Moody, 1969), 282.
3. For more details on Ezekiel's prophecy of Tyre, see Josh McDowell, *Evidence That Demands a Verdict* (San Bernardino, Calif.: Campus Crusade for Christ, 1972), 285–91.
4. Day, *The Wonder of the Word*, 63–64.
5. H. P. Liddon, quoted in Floyd Hamilton, *The Basis of the Christian Faith*, rev. ed. (New York: Harper and Row, 1964), 160.
6. McDowell, *Evidence That Demands a Verdict*, 19–20.
7. Bernard Ramm, *Protestant Christian Evidences* (Chicago: Moody, 1957), 230–31.
8. John W. Lea, *The Greatest Book in the World* (Philadelphia: J. W. Lea, 1929), 15.
9. *The Enduring Word* (New York: American Bible Society), quoted in Day, *The Wonder of the Word*, 18.
10. Farrar, *The Bible: Its Meaning and Supremacy*, 197.
11. Day, *The Wonder of the Word*, 26.
12. Ramm, *Protestant Christian Evidences*, 233.
13. Ibid., 232.
14. Cleland B. McAfee, *The Greatest English Classic* (New York: Harper, 1912), 134.
15. Ralph Waldo Emerson, quoted in Farrar, *The Bible: Its Meaning and Supremacy*, 253.
16. T. Tiplady, *The Influence of the Bible*, quoted in Ramm, *Protestant Christian Evidences*, 233.
17. Monier-Williams, quoted in Sidney Collett, *All about the Bible* (New York: Revell, n. d.), 315.
18. Ibid.
19. Lewis Sperry Chafer, *Systematic Theology* (Dallas: Dallas Seminary Press, 1948), 1:22 (italics his).

CHAPTER 7—IS THE BIBLE THE INSPIRED "WORD OF GOD"?

1. Warfield, *The Inspiration and Authority of the Bible*, 41–42.

2. John M. Frame, *Perspectives on the Word of God* (Phillipsburg, N.J.: Presbyterian and Reformed, 1990), 15. The basic definition and categories follow Frame's discussion on pages 9–15.
3. Siegfried Wagner, "*ʾāmar,*" in *Theological Dictionary of the Old Testament*, ed. G. Johannes Botterweck and Helmer Ringgren (Grand Rapids: Eerdmans, 1974), 1:329–30.
4. Ibid., 1:335.
5. R. Laird Harris, "*ʾāmar,*" in *Theological Wordbook of the Old Testament*, ed. R. Laird Harris, Gleason L. Archer, Jr., and Bruce K. Waltke (Chicago: Moody, 1980), 1:55.
6. J. N. Sanders, "Word, The," in *Interpreter's Dictionary of the Bible*, ed. George Arthur Buttrick (Nashville: Abingdon, 1962), 4:868.
7. O. Grether, *Name und Wort Gottes im AT* (Berlin: 1934), 62, 66, 76, quoted in W. H. Schmidt, "*dābar,*" in *Theological Dictionary of the Old Testament,* 3 (1978): 111.
8. See also 2 Chronicles 9:29; 12:15; 13:22; 20:34; 26:22; 32:32.
9. O. Procksch, "*legō,*" in *Theological Dictionary of the New Testament*, ed. Gerhard Kittel and Gerhard Friedrich, trans. and ed. Geoffrey R. Bromiley (Grand Rapids: Eerdmans, 1967), 4:96.
10. Ibid.
11. Ibid., 126.
12. Ibid.
13. *Random House Webster's College Dictionary* (New York: Random House, 1996), 697.
14. George W. Knight III, *The Pastoral Epistles: A Commentary on the Greek Text* (Grand Rapids: Eerdmans, 1992), 446. For a thorough discussion of the meaning of "All Scripture is inspired by God," see Warfield, *The Inspiration and Authority of the Bible*, 245–96.
15. Peter T. O'Brien, *Colossians and Philemon*, Word Biblical Commentary (Waco, Tex.: Word, 1982), 257.
16. George Eldon Ladd, *A Commentary on the Revelation of John* (Grand Rapids: Eerdmans, 1972), 23.
17. William Chillingworth, *The Religion of Protestants* (London: H. G. Bohn, 1854), quoted in Farrar, *The Bible: Its Meaning and Supremacy*, 20.

18. John Barton, *People of the Book? The Authority of the Bible in Christianity* (Louisville: Westminster/John Knox, 1988), 25.
19. Donald G. Bloesch, "The Primacy of Scripture," in *The Authoritative Word: Essays on the Nature of Scripture*, ed. Donald K. McKim (Grand Rapids: Eerdmans, 1983), 132.
20. Alister E. McGrath, *A Passion for the Truth: The Intellectual Coherence of Evangelicalism* (Downers Grove, Ill.: InterVarsity, 1996), 54.
21. Walter J. Ong, *The Presence of the Word* (Minneapolis: University of Minnesota Press, 1981), 167.

    Our means of communicating with another, according to the Old Testament, are seen in our "face," with the most important being our eyes, mouth, and ears. Both hearing and speaking are the most essential for communicating. But what truly sets humans apart from lower creatures is the ability to speak. "The animal also has an ear as such, as well as an eye. It is in Man's speech that his ear evinces itself as being a truly human ear and his eye as being a human eye. . . . The capacity for language provides the essential condition for the humanity of man" (Hans Walter Wolff, *Anthropology of the Old Testament* [Philadelphia: Fortress, 1974], 74, 78). As someone has rightly noted, lovers are apt to "hear" through their eyes, but the surer way is to "see" through their ears. As someone said, "Speak, that I may see you."

    Our nature as human beings is therefore linguistic. We are designed to share ourselves with others in loving verbal communication. Our words are not simple things that we choose to use. They are the expression of our nature. We are created as social beings. As God said, "It is not good for the man to be alone" (Gen. 2:18). Our words are not separate from us, instead they are the "actualization" of our created nature in communication with others.
22. Trent C. Butler, *Joshua*, Word Biblical Commentary (Waco, Tex.: Word, 1983), 276.

CHAPTER 8—HOW DID CHRIST VIEW THE SCRIPTURES?

1. Bishop H. C. G. Moule, quoted in John Battersby Harford and

Frederick Charles MacDonald, *The Life of Bishop Moule* (London: Hodder and Stoughton, 1922), 138.

2. Graham Scroggie, *A Guide to the Gospels* (London: Pickering and Inglis, 1943), 193.
3. John W. Wenham, "Christ's View of Scripture," in *Inerrancy*, ed. Norman Geisler (Grand Rapids: Zondervan, 1980), 22.
4. T. T. Perowne, *Obadiah and Jonah* (Cambridge: University Press, 1898), 51.
5. Further evidence that Jesus saw the entire Old Testament as Scripture is in Matthew 23:35. Pronouncing a coming judgment on His generation because of their unbelief, He declared that the guilt would fall on them "from the blood of righteous Abel to the blood of Zechariah . . . whom you murdered between the temple and the altar." The murder of Abel is recorded in Genesis, the first book of the canon, and that of Zechariah in 2 Chronicles (24:21), which in Jesus' day was the last book of the Old Testament. Jesus was thus referring to all of the Scriptures of His day, much as we would say "from Genesis to Revelation."
6. Charles Haddon Spurgeon, quoted in John R. W. Stott, *The Preacher's Portrait* (London: Tyndale, 1961), 27 (italics his).
7. Adolph Schlatter, *Das Evangelium nach Matthäus*, 61, quoted in Frederick Dale Bruner, *Matthew: A Commentary* (Dallas: Word, 1987), 1:167.
8. Gerhardus Vos, *The Teaching of Jesus concerning the Kingdom of God and the Church* (New York: American Tract Society, 1903), 12.
9. For a discussion of Jesus' use of Old Testament predictions see R. T. France, *Jesus and the Old Testament* (London: Tyndale, 1971), 83–163.
10. On Jesus' extensive use of questions see Roy B. Zuck, *Teaching as Jesus Taught* (Grand Rapids: Baker, 1995), 235–76.
11. On Jesus' responses to the many questions addressed to Him see ibid., 277–304.
12. Matthew 7:12; 11:13; 22:40; Luke 16:16; John 1:45; Acts 13:15; 28:23; and Romans 3:21 use the term "the Law and the prophets" to refer to the entire Old Testament. John 10:34; 12:34; 15:25; and 1

Corinthians 14:21 use the word "Law" in reference to the Old Testament.

13. D. A. Carson, *The Gospel according to John* (Grand Rapids: Eerdmans, 1991), 505.
14. Gottlob Schrenk, "*graphō*," in *Theological Dictionary of the New Testament*, 1 (1964): 755.

CHAPTER 9—IS THE BIBLE A HUMAN BOOK?

1. Benjamin B. Warfield, *Selected Shorter Writings of Benjamin B. Warfield*, ed. John E. Meeter (Nutley, N.J.: Presbyterian and Reformed, 1973), 2:548.
2. J. I. Packer, "The Necessity of the Revealed Word," in *The Bible: The Living Word of Revelation*, 32.
3. Karl Barth, *Church Dogmatics* (Edinburgh: Clark, 1936), 1.1.127.
4. Hans Küng, *On Being a Christian* (Garden City, N.Y.: Doubleday, 1976), 463.
5. Walter Rauschenbusch, *A Theology for the Social Gospel* (New York: Macmillan, 1917), 192.
6. Dewey Beegle, *Scripture, Tradition, and Infallibility* (Grand Rapids: Eerdmans, 1973), 306, 308–9.
7. William J. Abraham, *The Divine Inspiration of the Holy Scriptures* (Oxford: Oxford University Press, 1981), 68.
8. Ibid., 63–75.
9. Barth, *Church Dogmatics*, 1.2.533.
10. Theodore Engelder, *Scripture Cannot Be Broken: Six Objections to Verbal Inspiration Examined in the Light of Scripture* (St. Louis: Concordia, 1944), 129.
11. I. Howard Marshall holds this view, as his remarks show: "The purpose of God in the composition of the Scripture was to guide people to salvation and the associated way of life. . . . We may surely conclude that God made the Bible all that it needs to be in order to achieve this purpose. . . . Inspiration [thus] means that God made the Bible what he wanted it to be for his purposes" (*Biblical Inspiration* [Grand Rapids: Eerdmans, 1982], 53, 70).

12. Herman Ridderbos, *Studies in Scripture and Its Authority* (St. Catherines, Ont.: Paideia, 1978), 24.
13. Warfield, *The Inspiration and Authority of the Bible*, 173.
14. Augustine, *Harmony of the Gospels* 1.35.54, quoted in Bruce Demarest and Gordon Lewis, *Integrative Theology* (Grand Rapids: Zondervan, 1987), 1:136.
15. John Calvin, *Commentary on the Book of Psalms* (reprint, Grand Rapids: Baker, 1979), 3:205.
16. Calvin, *Institutes of the Christian Religion*, 4.8.8–9.
17. James I. Packer, *Fundamentalism and the Word of God* (Grand Rapids: Eerdmans, 1958), 79 (italics his).
18. J. N. D. Kelley, *The Epistles of Peter and of Jude* (London: Adam and Charles Black, 1969), 321.
19. Eugene Peterson, *The Message* (Colorado Springs: NavPress, 19995), 585.
20. Warfield, *The Inspiration and Authority of the Bible*, 83.
21. Gustav Oehler, *Theology of the Old Testament* (Grand Rapids: Zondervan, 1983), 482.
22. Demarest and Lewis, *Integrative Theology*, 1:162.
23. Ibid.
24. Warfield, *The Inspiration and Authority of the Bible*, 83.
25. Ibid., 95.
26. Augustine, *The City of God*, 11.6, in *A Select Library of the Nicene and Post-Nicene Fathers of the Christian Church*, ed. Philip Schaff (1886; reprint, Grand Rapids: Eerdmans, 1979), 2:208.
27. Richard Gaffin, Jr., in *Redemptive History and Biblical Interpretation: The Shorter Writings of Geerhardus Vos* (Phillipsburg, N. J.: Presbyterian and Reformed, 1980), xvii.
28. Warfield, *The Inspiration and Authority of the Bible*, 162–63.

CHAPTER 10—IS THE BIBLE RELIABLE?

1. Augustine, *The Letters of St. Augustine* 82.3.
2. Marshall, *Biblical Interpretation*, 53 (italics his).
3. Clark Pinnock, "The Inerrancy Debate among the Evangelicals," in

Theology, News and Notes (Pasadena, Calif.: Fuller Theological Seminary, special issue, 1976), 11, (italics his).

4. Donald G. Bloesch, "The Primacy of Scripture," in *The Authoritative Word*, 135.
5. Alfred Jepsen, "*'emet*," in *Theological Dictionary of the Old Testament*, 1 (1974): 312.
6. Roger Nicole, "The Biblical Concept of Truth," in *Scripture and Truth*, ed. D. A. Carson and John D. Woodbridge (Grand Rapids: Eerdmans, 1983), 291. See also Anthony C. Thiselton, "Truth," in *New International Dictionary of New Testament Theology*, ed. Colin Brown (Grand Rapids: Eerdmans, 1978), 3:881–82.
7. According to Nicole, *alētheia* was used in six of the seven occurrence of *ʾemet* in the Hebrew Scriptures ("The Biblical Concept of Truth," 292).
8. For more verses illustrating the various uses of the Greek term for "truth" (*alētheia*) and related words see Walter Bauer, William F. Arndt, and F. Wilbur Gingrich, *A Greek-English Lexicon of the New Testament and Other Early Christian Literature,* 2d ed., rev. F. Wilbur Gingrich and Frederick W. Danker (Chicago: University of Chicago Press, 1979), 35–37.
9. Kidner, *Psalms 73–150*, 429.
10. Thiselton, "Truth," 892.
11. Ibid.
12. Wayne A. Grudem, "Scripture's Self-Attestation and the Problem of Formulating a Doctrine of Scripture," in *Scripture and Truth*, 30.
13. Craigie, *Psalms 1–50*, 167.
14. David S. Dockery, *Christian Scripture: An Evangelical's Perspective on Inspiration, Authority, and Interpretation* (Nashville: Broadman & Holman, 1995), 64.
15. Kevin J. Vanhoozer, "The Semantics of Biblical Literature: Truth and Scripture's Diverse Literary Forms," in *Hermeneutics, Authority, and Canon,* ed. D. A. Carson and John D. Woodbridge (Grand Rapids: Zondervan, 1986), 96–103.
16. Although the concept of inerrancy is normally related to the issue of truth as conformity to reality, there is a sense in which it relates to the

full biblical sense of truth as an attribute of God and the manifestation of Himself in all of creation, including His norms (laws), values, and orders, both physical and spiritual. God's created reality and thus His truth is more than cognitive information. The expressive language conveying emotion is also part of God's Word, designed, as Vanhoozer notes, "to communicate something of the nature of human response when confronted with the majesty and character of God" (ibid., 94). The belief that the Holy Spirit was leading the human writer in this expression thus leads us to conclude that these human emotional responses are included as "normative responses in which the reader is invited to share and participate. . . . [Thus] not only our minds, but also our emotional responses are brought under scriptural authority" (ibid.). "Scripture successfully and truly speaks about many things in many ways, all of which 'correspond' to reality" (ibid., 103).

As God's reality, truth is multifaceted. As Thiselton notes, "The truth of a poem is something different than the truth of a report. In one sense, to speak of factual truth, historical truth, existential truth or personal truth, poetic truth, and moral truth, is to speak of different things. Yet in another sense, there is a closer relation between these different uses of the word 'truth' than mere family resemblances. Many Christians would wish to claim that whilst the Bible contains more than one kind of truth, nevertheless there is a comprehensiveness about the truth of God which embraces all this particular variety. . . . On the one hand, truth is multiform, and criteria for different kinds of truth may vary. On the other hand, the truth of God lays claim to a universality which somehow undergirds and holds together particular expressions and experiences of truth in thought and life" ("Truth," 894).

Truth is both information and experience, as seen in the emotion of love. Love is more than what can be cognitively defined. To know it truthfully one must experience it. The same can be said of tasting food or, for that matter, life itself. The complexity of truth in Scripture may be likened to the knowledge of the heart, in which meaning is joined inseparably with affect and volition or act. When Jesus said, "You shall know the truth, and the truth shall make you free" (John

8:32), He was not talking about truth merely in the cognitive sense, but in the full sense of meaning-affect-act. Freedom from sin comes only from knowing or receiving truth that impacts us cognitively, affectively, and behaviorally. Thus while cognitive meaning is essential to biblical truth, that truth also includes power, beauty, and other dimensions of reality that are part of the richness of life. These added dimensions of God's truth are seen in the comment of C. S. Lewis: "The most valuable thing the Psalms do for me is to express the same delight in God which made David dance" (*Reflections on the Psalms* [New York: Harcourt, Brace, and Co., 1958], 45). God's communication to us is intended to convey information, but also to draw us to Himself. Thus the Scriptures convey inerrantly the fact of the complexity of God's reality.

17. Roger Nicole, "The Nature of Inerrancy," in *Inerrancy and Common Sense*, ed. Roger R. Nicole and J. Ramsey Michaels (Grand Rapids: Baker, 1980), 82.
18. J. I. Packer, "Encountering Present-Day Views of Scripture," in *The Foundation of Biblical Authority*, ed. James Montgomery Boice (Grand Rapids: Zondervan, 1978), 77.
19. Ibid.
20. C. F. H. Henry, "Bible, Inspiration of," in *Evangelical Dictionary of Theology*, ed. Walter A. Elwell (Grand Rapids: Baker, 1984), 148.
21. William Newton Clark, *The Use of the Scriptures in Theology* (New York: Charles Scribner's Sons, 1905).
22. Harry Emerson Fosdick, *The Modern Use of the Bible* (New York: Macmillan, 1924).
23. "The Chicago Statement on Inerrancy," in *Inerrancy*, 502.
24. Ibid.
25. Nicole, "The Nature of Inerrancy," 94.

CHAPTER 11—DOES THE BIBLE CONTRADICT ITSELF?

1. Justin Martyr, *Dialogue with Trypho* 65.
2. J. C. Ryle, quoted in Frank E. Gaebelein, *The Meaning of Inspiration* (Downers Grove, Ill.: InterVarsity, 1950), 25.

3. Richard N. Soulen, *Handbook of Biblical Criticism* (Atlanta: John Knox, 1981), 87–88.
4. Ibid.
5. Richard Purtill, *Thinking about Religion* (Englewood Cliffs, N. J.: Prentice-Hall, 1978), 84–85.
6. Howard Vos, *Can I Trust My Bible?* (Chicago: Moody, 1968), 176.
7. Unidentified author, quoted in Farrar, *The Bible: Its Meaning and Supremacy*, 189.
8. Paul J. Achtemeier, *The Inspiration of Scripture* (Philadelphia: Westminster, 1980), 80–81.
9. John Barton, *What Is the Bible?* (London: SPCK, 1991), 71.
10. Packer, "Encountering Present-Day Views of Scripture," 61 (italics his).
11. Carson, *The Gospel according to John,* 312–13 (italics his).
12. A. Pholuck, quoted in Day, *The Wonder of the Word*, 188.
13. Gleason L. Archer, Jr., *Encyclopedia of Bible Difficulties* (Grand Rapids: Zondervan, 1982). Other helpful works include John W. Haley, *Alleged Discrepancies of the Bible* (1874; reprint, Nashville: Goodpasture, 1951); W. Arndt, *Does the Bible Contradict Itself?* (St. Louis: Concordia, 1955); W. Arndt, *Bible Difficulties* (St. Louis: Concordia, 1962); and L. Gaussen, *The Inspiration of the Holy Scriptures* (Chicago: Moody, n.d.).
14. William F. Albright, *The Biblical Period from Abraham to Ezra* (New York: Harper & Row, 1963), 1–2.
15. Millar Burrows, *What Mean These Stones?* (New Haven, Conn.: American Schools of Oriental Research, 1941), 292.
16. Nelson Glueck, *Rivers in the Desert: A History of Negev* (New York: Farrar, Straus, and Cudahay, 1959), 31.
17. Gleason L. Archer, "Alleged Errors and Discrepancies in the Original Manuscripts of the Bile," in *Inerrancy*, 62–63.
18. Day, *The Wonder of the Word*, 186–87.
19. Leon Morris, *The Gospel according to John* (Grand Rapids, Eerdmans, 1971), 134–35.
20. D. A. Carson, "Matthew," in *The Expositor's Bible Commentary* (Grand Rapids: Zondervan, 1984), 8:357–58.
21. F. F. Bruce, "Calendar," in *The New Bible Dictionary*, ed. J. D. Dou-

glas (Grand Rapids: Eerdmans, 1962), 178. See also D. F. Morgan, "Calendar," in *International Standard Bible Encyclopedia*, ed. Geoffrey W. Bromiley (Grand Rapids: Eerdmans, 1979), 1:578.

22. K. A. Kitchen and T. C. Mitchell, "Chronology of the Old Testament," in *New Bible Dictionary*, 213.
23. Ibid., 216. The same could be said about other areas such as the weight of the shekel (the basic measure of weight in the Old Testament), which varied at different times and in different areas.
24. John N. Oswalt, "Chronology of the Old Testament," in *International Standard Bible Encyclopedia*, 1:673 (italics his).
25. Craig L. Blomberg, "The Legitimacy and Limits of Harmonization," in *Hermeneutics, Authority, and Canon*, 157 (italics his).
26. Oswalt, "Chronology of the Old Testament," 673.
27. S. Wagner, "*dārash*," in *Theological Dictionary of the Old Testament*, 3 (1978): 300.
28. For a good discussion of various copyists' errors see Archer, *Encyclopedia of Bible Difficulties*, 32–42.
29. R. A. H. Gunner, "Number," in *The New Bible Dictionary*, 895; and B. C. Birch, "Number," in *International Standard Bible Encyclopedia*, 3 (1986): 556.
30. Douglas Stuart, "Inerrancy and Textual Criticism," in *Inerrancy and Common Sense*, 113.
31. Ibid., 113–15.
32. See, for example, Michael Denton, *Evolution: A Theory in Crisis* (Bethesda, Md.: Adler & Adler, 1986); Michael Denton, *Nature's Destiny: How the Laws of Biology Reveal Purpose in the Universe* (New York: Free, 1996); Michael J. Behe, *Darwin's Black Box: The Biochemical Challenge to Evolution* (New York: Free, 1996); and Phillip Johnson, *Darwin on Trial* (Downers Grove, Ill.: InterVarsity, 1991).
33. Gordon J. Wenham, *The Book of Leviticus* (Grand Rapids: Eerdmans, 1979), 171–72.
34. Dewey M. Beegle, *Scripture, Tradition, and Infallibility* (Grand Rapids: Eerdmans, 1973), 194–95.
35. In ethics we must consider the fact of the progress of revelation and of God's demands for humankind. As we move from the Old

Testament to the New, God's demands are higher. This does not mean that God changed His perfect standards. It simply means that He applies them graciously according to the human situation. A father is more apt to treat less severely certain actions by a child who is five than he is the same act by a young person who is eighteen. This does not mean that the act is right in one instance and wrong in the other. It simply indicates that the standard is applied according to the stage of maturity. In the course of biblical history God has done the same thing with humanity.

36. Arndt, *Bible Difficulties*, 53–54.
37. Frederic G. Kenyon, *Our Bible and the Ancient Manuscripts* (New York: Harper, 1941), 23 (italics his).
38. Stuart, "Inerrancy and Textual Criticism," 115–16.
39. Saphir, quoted in Eric Sauer, *From Eternity to Eternity*, trans. G. H. Lang (Grand Rapids: Eerdmans, 1954), 106.
40. Warfield, *The Inspiration and Authority of the Bible*, 219.
41. James I. Packer, "Problem Areas related to Biblical Inerrancy," in *The Proceedings of the Conference on Biblical Inerrancy 1987* (Nashville: Broadman, 1987), 207.
42. Ibid.
43. Augustine, *The Letters of St. Augustine* 82–83.
44. Arndt, *Bible Difficulties*, 16.

CHAPTER 12—WHAT HAS THE CHURCH BELIEVED ABOUT THE BIBLE?

1. Jerome, *The Letters of Jerome* 58.9.
2. For a discussion of the alleged newness of the doctrine of inerrancy and its refutation see John D. Woodbridge, "Some Misconceptions of the Impact of the 'Enlightenment' on Scripture," in *Hermeneutics, Authority, and Canon*, 241–70.
3. George M. Marsden, "Preachers of Paradox: The Religious New Right in Historical Perspective," in *Religion and America: Spirituality in a Secular Age*, ed. Mary Douglas and Steven M. Tipton (Boston: Beacon, 1983), 163.

4. Bruce Vawter, "Creationism: Creative Misuse of the Bible, in *Is God a Creationist?* ed. Roland M. Frye (New York: Scribner's, 1983), 76.
5. James Bannerman, *Inspiration: The Infallible Truth and Divine Authority of Holy Scripture* (Edinburgh: Clark, 1865), 2:123.
6. Geoffrey W. Bromiley, "The Church Doctrine of Inspiration," in *Revelation and the Bible*, 207.
7. Clement, *Clement's First Letter* 47, 45, 22, in *Early Church Fathers*, ed. Cyril C. Richardson (New York: Simon & Schuster, 1996), 65, 64, 54.
8. Polycarp, *Epistle to the Philippians* 7, quoted in J. Barton Payne, "The Biblical Interpretation of Irenaeus," in *Inspiration and Interpretation*, ed. John F. Walvoord (Grand Rapids: Eerdmans, 1957), 15.
9. Justin Martyr, *The First Apology* 33, quoted in John D. Hannah, "The Doctrine of Scripture in the Early Church," in *Inerrancy and the Church*, ed. John D. Hannah (Chicago: Moody, 1984), 7.
10. Ibid., 34, quoted in Hannah, "The Doctrine of Scripture in the Early Church," 7.
11. Justin Martyr, *Dialogue with Trypho* 7, quoted in Hannah, "The Doctrine of Scripture in the Early Church," 7.
12. Charles Augustus Briggs, *History of the Study of Theology* (New York: Scribners, 1916), 1:78, quoted in Payne, "The Biblical Interpretation of Irenaeus," 13.
13. Irenaeus, *Against Heresies* 2.28, 2, quoted in Payne, "The Biblical Interpretation of Irenaeus," 18.
14. Clement of Alexandria, *Exhortation to the Heathen* 8, quoted in Hannah, "The Doctrine of Scripture in the Early Church," 8.
15. Clement of Alexandria, *The Stromata* 7.16, quoted in Hannah, "The Doctrine of Scripture in the Early Church," 8.
16. Origen, *De Principiis* Preface 4; 4.1; Preface 8, quoted in Hannah, "The Doctrine of Scripture in the Early Church," 8–9.
17. Gregory of Nyssa, *Against Eunomius* 7.1, quoted in Hannah, "The Doctrine of Scripture in the Early Church," 10.
18. Augustine, *Confessions*, trans. Henry Chadwick (Oxford: Oxford University Press, 1991), 12.23.32.
19. Augustine, *The Harmony of the Gospels* 1.35.54, in *A Select Library of the Nicene and Post-Nicene Fathers of the Christian Church*, 6:65–236.

20. For a more complete study of the beliefs of the early church fathers, see Hannah, "The Doctrine of Scripture in the Early Church"; Wayne R. Spear, "Augustine's Doctrine of Biblical Infallibility," in *Inerrancy and the Church*, 3–65; and John D. Woodbridge, *Biblical Authority* (Grand Rapids: Zondervan, 1982), 31–48.
21. Geoffrey W. Bromiley, "The Church Fathers and Holy Scriptures," in *Scripture and Truth*, 204.
22. Athenagoras, *A Plea for the Christians* 7.9.
23. Justin Martyr, *Hortatory Address to the Greeks* 8, quoted in Hannah, "The Doctrine of Scripture in the Early Church," 14.
24. Irenaeus, *Heresies* 2.28.2, quoted in Woodbridge, *Biblical Authority*, 165, n.10; and Caius, *Fragments*, 3, quoted in Hannah, "The Doctrine of Scripture in the Early Church," 15.
25. Bromiley, "The Church Fathers and Holy Scriptures," 205.
26. J. N. D. Kelly, *Early Christian Doctrines*, 5th ed. (New York: Harper & Row, 1978), 63.
27. Hippolytus, *Treatise on Christ and Antichrist* 2.
28. Origen, *Against Celsus* 7.4.
29. Chrysostom, *Homilies on Genesis* 7.4; 12.1; 20.4; Cyril of Alexandria, *Commentary on John* 1.10; 1.18; *Fragments of Saint Paul's Epistle to the Romans* 7.25; 8.3; and Jerome, *In Isaiah* Prologue.
30. Augustine, *Sermons* 246, 1; and Augustine, *The Harmony of the Gospels* 3.30.
31. Bruce Vawter, *Biblical Inspiration* (Philadelphia: Westminster, 1972), 132–33.
32. Clement, *Clement's First Letter* 45, quoted in *Early Christian Fathers*, 64.
33. Irenaeus, *Against Heresies* 3.14. 3–4, quoted in Payne, "The Biblical Interpretation of Irenaeus," 20.
34. Irenaeus, *Against Heresies* 2.28.2, quoted in Woodbridge, *Biblical Authority*, 165.
35. Justin Martyr, quoted in Woodbridge, *Biblical Authority*, 33.
36. Origen, *Commentary on Matthew* 2, quoted in Hannah, "The Doctrine of Scripture in the Early Church," 26.
37. Athanasius, *Orations* 11.105, quoted in Hannah, "The Doctrine of Scripture in the Early Church," 26–27.

38. "St. John Chrysostom's Teaching on Inspiration in 'Six Homilies on Isaiah,'" *Bigilae Christianae* 22 (April 1968): 29–30.
39. Ibid., 28.
40. Augustine, *The Letters of St. Augustine* 82.3.
41. Augustine, *The City of God* 21.6.1.
42. Augustine, *Genesis according to the Literal Sense* 2.9.20.
43. Augustine, *The Letters of St. Augustine* 28.3.
44. Jack B. Rogers and Donald K. McKim, *The Authority and Interpretation of the Bible: An Historical Approach* (San Francisco: Harper & Row, 1979), 31.
45. Augustine, *The Letters of St. Augustine* 82.3.
46. Ibid., 82.4.
47. Augustine, *Genesis according to the Literal Sense*, quoted in Rogers and McKim, *The Authority and Interpretation of the Bible*, 27.
48. Augustine, *The Harmony of the Gospels* 2.21.52.
49. Although Rogers and McKim assert that Augustine did not believe in the "formal harmony" of all of the "verbal forms, in which God's message was expressed," they do not include any statement in which Augustine asserted mistakes or errors to any scriptural writers. See their discussion of Augustine's accommodation in *The Authority and Interpretation of the Bible*, 27–30.
50. Augustine, *The Harmony of the Gospels* 1.7.10, quoted in Woodbridge, *Biblical Authority*, 40–41.
51. Woodbridge, *Biblical Authority*, 41.
52. "Accomodatio," in Richard A. Muller, *Dictionary of Latin and Greek Theological Terms* (Grand Rapids: Baker, 1985), 19.
53. Hannah, "The Doctrine of Scripture in the Early Church," 33–34.
54. For a good discussion of Augustine's position on inerrancy, especially in relation to attempts to say he held to a limited inerrancy, see Woodbridge, *Biblical Authority*, 37–46, and the many scholarly treatments of Augustine's concept of the inspiration of the Scriptures mentioned in this work.
55. Hans Küng, *Infallible? An Enquiry* (London: Collins, 1972), 173–74.
56. Martin Luther, quoted in John F. Johnson, "Biblical Authority and Scholastic Theology," in *Inerrancy and the Church*, 68.

57. Martin Luther, *Table Talk* (Philadelphia: Fortress, 1967), 26.
58. John H. Gerstner, "The Church's Doctrine of Biblical Inspiration," in *The Foundation of Biblical Authority*, 32.
59. Gregory the Great, *Preface to Moralia in Job* 1.1, 2, quoted in Gerstner, "The Church's Doctrine of Biblical Inspiration," 32.
60. Anselm, quoted in *Scholastic Miscellany: Anselm to Ockham*, ed. Eugene Fairweather (New York: Macmillan, 1970), 132.
61. Thomas Aquinas, *Summa Theologiae* I-I, q. 1, a.7, quoted in Johnson, "Biblical Authority and Scholastic Theology," 90.
62. Thomas Aquinas, *Concerning the Divine Names* II, lecture 1, quoted in Johnson, "Biblical Authority and Scholastic Theology," 96.
63. William Mallard, "John Wycliffe and the Tradition of Biblical Authority," *Church History* 30 (March 1961): 51–52 (italics his).
64. Herman Sasse, "The Rise of the Dogma of Holy Scriptures in the Middle Ages," *Reformed Theological Review* 18 (June 1959): 45.
65. Geoffrey W. Bromiley, "The Church Doctrine of Inspiration," in *Revelation and the Bible*, 211.
66. Ibid.
67. *Luther's Works*, ed. Jaroslav J. Pelikan and Helmut T. Lehmann (Philadelphia: Fortress, 1958), 32:11.
68. Ibid., 23:236.
69. *D. Martin Luthers Werke, Kirtische Gesamtausgabe*, ed. J. F. K. Knaake et al. (Weimar, Ger.: Bohlau, 1883), 40.3.254.
70. Martin Luther, quoted in Robert D. Preus, "The View of the Bible Held by the Church: The Early Church through Luther," in *Inerrancy*, 380.
71. *D. Martin Luthers, Werke*, 40, 2.52.19–20.
72. *Luther's Works*, 37.308.
73. Calvin, *Institutes of the Christian Religion*, 1.7.1.
74. Ibid., 4.7.9.
75. John Calvin, *New Testament Commentaries*, ed. D. W. Torrance and T. F. Torrance (Grand Rapids: Eerdmans, 1964), 10:330.
76. Calvin, *Commentary on the Book of Psalms*, 5:20.
77. *D. Martin Luthers Werke*, 48.31.
78. According to Rogers and McKim, for example, "The wonder was

that God had chosen to use weak and imperfect human speech adequately to communicate his divine message. Luther thought in biblical and human images. He was far from attributing scientific and technical accuracy to the Bible" (ibid., 79).

79. Ibid. (italics added).
80. *D. Martin Luthers Werke,* 33.144.
81. Woodbridge, *Biblical Authority*, 57.
82. Belgic Confession, Article 4, 7.5, quoted in Godfrey, "Biblical Authority in the Sixteenth and Seventeenth Centuries: A Question of Transition," in *Scripture and Truth,* 230.
83. In the increasing cultural climate of rationalism orthodox evangelicals increasingly tended to make greater use of reason to defend the veracity of the Scriptures. While this was to some extent beneficial in providing increased evidence from the Bible's truthfulness, it also tended to make that truthfulness depend on the results of human reason rather than on the witness of the Scriptures themselves and the testimony of the Spirit, as commonly taught by the first Reformers.
84. Samuel Rutherford, quoted in Woodbridge, *Biblical Authority*, 111; see also pages 102–55 for a discussion of the view of the framers of the Westminster Confession.
85. John Wesley, *Journal*, Wednesday, July, 1776, quoted in Richard Lovelace, "Inerrancy: Some Historical Perspectives," in *Inerrancy and Common Sense*, 25.
86. John E. Smith, *Review of Metaphysics* 30 (December 1976): 306.
87. Godfrey, "Biblical Authority in the Sixteenth and Seventeenth Centuries," 243.
88. Kirsop Lake, *The Religion of Yesterday and Tomorrow* (Boston: Houghton, 1926), 61.
89. William Whitaker, *Disputation on Holy Scripture*, 660–61, quoted in Woodbridge, *Biblical Authority*, 75.
90. Augustine, *On Christian Doctrine* 3.10, quoted in Woodbridge, *Biblical Authority*, 45.
91. Billy Graham, "In Training for Christ," *Decision 3* (February 1962): 15.

CHAPTER 13—WHICH BOOKS BELONG IN THE BIBLE?

1. Martin Luther, in *Luther's Works*, 2:261.
2. The Greek word *kanōn* was probably borrowed from the Hebrew word *qānâ*, which originally meant a reed or rod.
3. F. F. Bruce, *The Canon of Scripture* (Downers Grove, Ill.: InterVarsity, 1988), 18.
4. R. P. C. Hanson, *Tradition in the Early Church* (London: SCM, 1962), 127.
5. William J. Abraham, "Revelation Reaffirmed," in *Divine Revelation*, ed. Paul Avis (Grand Rapids: Eerdmans, 1997), 210; see also James Barr, *The Bible in the Modern World* (New York: Harper & Row, 1973), 118–19.
6. Packer, *God Has Spoken*, 81.
7. Calvin, *Institutes of the Christian Religion*, 1.7. 1, 2, 5.
8. Packer, *God Has Spoken*, 81.
9. Louis Gaussen, *The Canon of the Holy Scriptures*, 26; referred to in René Pache, *The Inspiration and Authority of Scripture* (Chicago: Moody, 1969), 162.
10. David G. Dunbar, "The Biblical Canon," in *Hermeneutics, Authority, and Canon*, 315.
11. D. A. Carson, "Approaching the Bible," in *New Bible Commentary, Twenty-first Century Edition*, ed. D. A. Carson, R. T. France, J. A. Motyer, and G. J. Wenham (Downers Grove, Ill.: InterVarsity, 1994), 6.
12. J. P. Lewis, "What Do We Mean by Jabneh?" *Journal of Bible and Religion* 32 (1964): 132.
13. Dunbar, "The Biblical Canon," 314.
14. John N. Oswalt, *The Book of Isaiah, Chapters 1–39* , New International Commentary on the Old Testament (Grand Rapids: Eerdmans, 1986), 235–36.
15. Quoted in Erik Sjoberg, "*pneuma*," in *Theological Dictionary of the New Testament*, 6 (1968): 385, n. 294; see also Rudolph Meyer, "*prophētēs*," in *Theological Dictionary of the New Testament*, 6 (1968): 816–17.
16. Josephus, *Against Apion* 1.37.

17. Wenham, *Christ and the Bible*, 132. Some maintain that manifestations of prophecy continued among the Palestinian Jews during this period, but even they distinguish this "prophecy" from the classical canonical "prophets" (David F. Aune, *Prophecy in Early Christianity and in the Ancient Mediterranean World* [Grand Rapids: Eerdmans, 1983], 103–53, 197, 368, n. 2).
18. Robert H. Pfeiffer, "Canon of the OT," in *Interpreter's Dictionary of the Bible*, 1:500.
19. Ibid.
20. R. Laird Harris, "Canon of the Old Testament," in *Zondervan Pictorial Encyclopedia of the Bible*, ed. Merrill C. Tenney (Grand Rapids: Zondervan, 1975), 1:730–31.
21. Curt Kuhl, *The Old Testament: Its Origins and Composition* (Richmond, Va.: John Knox, 1961), 3. Roger Nicole notes that scholars vary in their estimates of the number of New Testament allusions to the Old Testament all the way from 613 to 4,105 ("New Testament Use of the Old Testament," in *Revelation and the Bible*, 138).
22. Nicole, "New Testament Use of the Old Testament," 138.
23. Ibid.
24. N. H. Ridderbos, "Canon of the Old Testament," in *New Bible Dictionary*, 192.
25. For a history of the Old Testament canon in the early church to the present, see F. F. Bruce, *The Canon of Scripture* (Downers Grove, Ill.: InterVarsity, 1988), 68–114.
26. The books that are generally considered the Apocrypha are 1 and 2 Esdras, Tobit, Judit, The Rest of Esther, The Wisdom of Solomon, Ecclesiasticus, Baruch, A Letter of Jeremiah (which some attach to Baruch), The Song of the Three Holy Children, Susanna, Bel and the Dragon, The Prayer of Manasses (or Manasseh), and 1 and 2 Maccabees.
27. For a brief summary of the opinions of the primary church leaders and canonical lists to the time of Augustine, see Harris, "Canon of the Old Testament," 727–29.
28. Merrill F. Unger, *Introductory Guide to the Old Testament* (Grand Rapids: Zondervan, 1951), 111.

29. H. N. Ridderbos, *The Authority of the New Testament Scriptures* (Philadelphia: Presbyterian and Reformed, 1963), 24.
30. For a survey of this period, see Dunbar, "The Biblical Canon," 323–28; and Donald Guthrie, "Canon of the New Testament," in *Zondervan Pictorial Encyclopedia of the Bible*, 1:734–36.
31. Montanism also stimulated interest in the question of which books were canonical. Montanus claimed inspiration for himself, and so, since he favored certain books such as John's Gospel and the Book of Revelation, some of his opponents rejected the authenticity of these books.
32. Eusebius, *Ecclesiastical History* 3.25.
33. Dunbar, "The Biblical Canon," 317.
34. Tertullian, *Against Marcion* 4.2.1.

CHAPTER 14 — IS THE BIBLE IMPORTANT TODAY?

1. Roland H. Bainton, *Here I Stand: A Life of Martin Luther* (Nashville: Abingdon, 1950), 185.
2. John Wesley, quoted in Farrar, *The Bible: Its Meaning and Supremacy*, 258.
3. Don Cupitt, *Taking Leave of God* (London: SCM, 1980), 9.
4. Seneca, *Moral Essays On the Happy Life*, v.
5. Virginia Mollenkott, letter to *His* magazine, 33 (June 1973): 23.
6. Harvey Cox, *Fire from Heaven: The Rise of Pentecostal Spirituality and the Reshaping of Religion in the Twenty-first Century* (Reading, Mass.: Addison-Wesley, 1994), 229–308.
7. *Catechism of the Catholic Church* (Mahwah, N.J.: Paulist, 1994), par. 81.
8. Ibid., par. 97.
9. At times it is difficult to see even an implicit link between Roman Catholic tradition and the teaching of the Scriptures, such as the Catholic dogmas on the immaculate conception of Mary (born without original sin), her sinlessness, and her "assumption" into heaven (being taken bodily into heaven at the moment of death).
10. This authoritative teaching voice of the church is also based on the belief that the church is the continuation of the incarnation of Christ in the world.

11. Ibid., par. 95.
12. Mark P. Shea, "What Is the Relationship between Scripture and Tradition," in *Not by Scripture Alone*, ed. Robert A. Sungenis (Santa Barbara, Calif.: Queenship, 1997), 181 (italics his).
13. Timothy Ware, *The Orthodox Church* (London: Penguin, 1993), 202.
14. Daniel H. Williams, *Retrieving the Tradition and Renewing Evangelicalism* (Grand Rapids: Eerdmans, 1999), 36.
15. Ibid., 215–16.
16. Ibid., 205.
17. *French Confession of Faith*, quoted in John H. Armstrong, "The Authority of Scripture," in *Sola Scriptura*, ed. Don Kistler (Morgan, Pa.: Soli Deo Gloria, 1995), 121–22.
18. Oswalt, *The Book of Isaiah, Chapters 1–39*, 238.
19. C. K. Barrett, *The First Epistle to the Corinthians*, Harper's New Testament Commentaries (New York: Harper & Row, 1968), 106.
20. Chrysostom, quoted in William Whitaker, *A Disputation on Holy Scripture against the Papist* (Cambridge: Cambridge University Press, 1849; reprint, New York: Johnson, 1968), 637.
21. Oscar Cullmann, *The Early Church*, ed. A. J. B. Higgins (London: SCM, 1966), 80 (italics his).
22. A. N. S. Lane, "Scripture, Tradition and Church: An Historical Survey," *Vox Evangelica* 9 (1975): 38–40.
23. Robert Thomson, ed., *Athanasium: Contra Gentes and De Incarnatione* (Oxford: Clarendon, 1971), 2, quoted in James White, "*Sola Scriptura* and the Early Church," in *Sola Scriptura*, 49.
24. Cyril of Jerusalem, *Catechetical Letters* 4.17, quoted in White, "*Sola Scriptura* and the Early Church," 27.
25. Augustine, *Reply to Faustus* 11.5, quoted in Norman L. Geisler and Ralph E. MacKenzie, *Roman Catholics and Evangelicals: Agreements and Differences* (Grand Rapids: Baker, 1995), 200.
26. Thomas Aquinas, *De veritate* 14.10–11, quoted in Geisler and MacKenzie, *Roman Catholics and Evangelicals: Agreements and Differences*, 201.
27. If, as some believe, there is a succession of apostles that continues throughout church history with the same gift of infallibility of

teaching as the original apostles who wrote the Scriptures, church teaching itself then becomes the revelatory Word of God. The church no longer stands under the Word, but instead it speaks the Word itself. The following comments by Rudolph J. Ehrlich on the position of the Roman Catholic Church in this regard help to clarify this situation. "The magisterial interpretation of the Word of God, prevented from erring by the assistance of the Holy Spirit, makes the question who has authority over whom [the Church or the Word of God] futile because in the Roman system this problem does not really arise. Much more important is the question whether the quasi-identification of Tradition (and so of Scripture which belongs to it and contains it in a special way) with the total being, teaching and action of the Church does not mean that ultimately it is not Tradition (in any sense of the term) or Scripture that is the source of revelation but the Church itself. In any case, how can Scripture stand *vis-à-vis* the Church as its superior and judge it, when its total being, teaching and action are equated with Tradition to which Scripture belongs?" (*Rome: Opponent or Partner?* [Philadelphia: Westminster, 1965], 284).

The uniqueness of Scripture is also lost when the Spirit's work of the inspiration of the Scriptures is seen as essentially no different from His continued ministry of illumination. While there are certainly other factors (such as the need for a more united Christianity in the battle against secularism) that are behind the new emphasis on church tradition and its authority, the weakening of a high view of inspiration and inerrancy may also be a motivating factor. If the Scriptures are not the inerrant Word of God, but rather the words of faithful men giving witness to the revelation of God (rather than being that revelation itself), then it is difficult for the Bible to hold a place of absolute authority among God's people.

28. Calvin, *Institutes of the Christian Religion*, 4.8.9.
29. Paul W. Barnett writes about the difference between apostles and the earliest postapostolic fathers on salvation. "Although these writers [the postapostolic fathers] are in close historical continuity with the New Testament, we now step into a different world. . . . The

future salvation brought into the present by the death and resurrection of Jesus Christ . . . are muted or absent in the postapostolic literature" ("Salvation," in *Dictionary of the Later New Testament and Its Development*, ed. Ralph P. Martin and Peter H. Davids [Downers Grove, Ill.: InterVarsity, 1997], 1074–75). Similarly at the conclusion of his scholarly study on the Lord's Supper, I. Howard Marshall points to many distinctions between the biblical teaching and several church practices. He writes, "The New Testament does not indicate that the bread and the cup were 'consecrated' in any way for the sacrament. Neither the practice of offering the elements to God nor that of offering a prayer of epiclesis ['invocation upon'] for the Spirit to bless the elements [changing them into the body and blood of Christ] has any foundation in Scripture" (*Last Supper and Lord's Supper* [Grand Rapids: Eerdmans, 1980], 156.)

30. For more on the Holy Spirit's role in interpretation and illumination see Roy B. Zuck, *Spirit-Filled Teaching,* Swindoll Leadership Library (1963; rev. ed., Nashville: Word, 1998), 31–47, 101–8.
31. Thomas Watson, *A Body of Divinity: Contained in Sermons upon the Westminster Assembly's Catechism* (1890; reprint, London: Banner of Truth, 1958), 22.
32. For more on the principles and practices of interpreting the Bible see Roy B. Zuck, *Basic Bible Interpretation* (Wheaton, Ill.: Victor, 1991); and Bernard Ramm, *Protestant Biblical Interpretation*, 3d ed. (Grand Rapids: Baker, 1970).
33. Julius Wellhausen, quoted in Alfred Jepsen, "The Scientific Study of the Old Testament," in *Essays on Old Testament Hermeneutics*, ed. Claus Westermann (Richmond, Va.: John Knox, 1963), 247.
34. C. E. B. Cranfield, "Divine and Human Action," *Interpretation* 12 (October 1958): 392.
35. Donald G. Miller, "The Bible," in *The Authoritative Word: Essays on the Nature of Scripture*, ed. Donald K. McKim (Grand Rapids: Eerdmans, 1983), 110 (italics his).
36. Paul Meier, "Spiritual and Mental Health in the Balance," in *Renewing Your Mind in a Secular World*, ed. John D. Woodbridge (Chicago: Moody, 1985), 26–28.

37. Martin Luther, "The Freedom of a Christian," in *Luther's Works*, 31:349.
38. John Newton, quoted in J. I. Packer, *Truth and Power: The Place of Scripture in the Christian Life* (Downers Grove, Ill.: InterVarsity, 1996), 175.

Bibliography

Archer, Gleason L. *Encyclopedia of Biblical Difficulties*. Grand Rapids: Zondervan Publishing House, 1982.

Boice, James Montgomery, ed. *The Foundation of Biblical Authority*. Grand Rapids: Zondervan Publishing House, 1978.

Bruce, F. F. *The Canon of Scripture*. Downers Grove, Ill.: InterVarsity Press, 1988.

Carson, D. A., and John D. Woodbridge, eds. *Hermeneutics, Authority and Canon*. Grand Rapids: Zondervan Publishing House, 1986.

Dockery, David S. *Christian Scripture: An Evangelical Perspective on Inspiration, Authority, and Interpretation*. Nashville: Broadman & Holman Publishers, 1994.

Gaussen, L. *The Inspiration of the Holy Scriptures*. Chicago: Moody Press, 1949.

Geisler, Norman L., ed. *Inerrancy*. Grand Rapids: Zondervan Publishing House, 1979.

________, and William E. Nix. *From God to Us: How We Got Our Bible*. Chicago: Moody Press, 1974.

Hannah, John D., ed. *Inerrancy and the Church*. Chicago: Moody Press, 1984.

Henry, Carl F. H., ed. *Revelation and the Bible*. Grand Rapids: Baker Book House, 1958.

Kistler, Don, ed. *Sola Scriptura*. Morgan, Pa.: Soli Deo Gloria Publications, 1995.

Pache, René. *The Inspiration and Authority of Scripture*. Translated by H. I. Needham. Chicago: Moody Press, 1969.

Packer, J. I. *"Fundamentalism" and the Word of God*. Grand Rapids: Wm. B. Eerdmans Publishing Co., 1958.

_______. *God Has Spoken*. Downers Grove, Ill.: InterVarsity Press, 1979.

_______. *Truth and Power: The Place of Scripture in the Christian Life*. Downers Grove, Ill.: InterVarsity Press, 1996.

Pinnock, Clark H. *Biblical Revelation*. Chicago: Moody Press, 1971.

Radmacher, Earl D., and Robert D. Preus, eds. *Hermeneutics, Inerrancy and the Bible*. Grand Rapids: Zondervan Publishing House, 1984.

Russell, Walt. *Playing with Fire: How the Bible Ignites Change in Your Soul*. Colorado Springs: NavPress, 2000.

Tenney, Merrill C., ed. *The Bible: The Living Word of Revelation*. Grand Rapids: Zondervan Publishing House, 1968.

Turretin, Francis. *The Doctrine of Scripture*. Edited and translated by John W. Beardslee III. Grand Rapids: Baker Book House, 1981.

Walvoord, John F., ed. *Inspiration and Interpretation*. Grand Rapids: Wm. B. Eerdmans Publishing Co., 1957.

Warfield, Benjamin B. *The Inspiration and Authority of the Bible*. Philadelphia: Presbyterian and Reformed Publishing Co., 1948.

Wenham, John W. *Christ and the Bible*. London: Tyndale Press, 1972.

Vanhoozer, Kevin J. *Is There a Meaning in This Text?* Grand Rapids: Zondervan Publishing House, 1998.

Zuck, Roy B. *Basic Bible Interpretation*. Wheaton, Ill.: Victor Books, 1991.

Scripture Index

Subject Index

The Swindoll Leadership Library

ANGELS, SATAN AND DEMONS—*Dr. Robert Lightner*
Dr. Robert Lightner answers questions about the supernatural world as expressed in Scripture.

BIBLICAL COUNSELING FOR TODAY—*Dr. Jeffrey Watson*
This handbook explores counseling from a biblical perspective—how to use Scripture to help others work through issues, choose healthy goals, and work toward those goals for a healthier, more spiritually grounded life.

THE CHURCH—*Dr. Ed Hayes*
In this indispensible guide, Dr. Ed Hayes explores the labyrinths of the church, delving into her history, doctrines, rituals, and resources to find out what it means to be the Body of Christ on earth.

COACHING MINISTRY TEAMS—*Dr. Kenn Gangel*
Kenn Gangel looks at effective discipleship by examining, among other topics, leading by example, empowering the team, and strategic planning.

COLOR OUTSIDE THE LINES—*Dr. Howard G. Hendricks*
Dr. Howard Hendricks vividly charges us to learn the art of living creatively, reflecting the image of the Creator rather than the culture.

EFFECTIVE CHURCH GROWTH STRATEGIES—*Dr. Joseph Wall and Dr. Gene Getz*
Wall and Getz examine the groundwork essential for church growth, qualities of biblically healthy churches, methods for planting a new church, and steps for numerical and spiritual growth.

EFFECTIVE PASTORING—*Dr. Bill Lawrence*
Lawrence discusses often overlooked issues, writing transparently about the struggles of the pastor, the purpose and practice of servant leadership, and the roles and relationships crucial to pastoring.

EMPOWERED LEADERS—*Dr. Hans Finzel*
Dr. Hans Finzel takes readers on a journey into the lives of the Bible's great leaders, unearthing powerful principles for effective leadership in any situation.

END TIMES—*Dr. Kenn Gangel*
By examining all of the prophetic passages in the Bible, Walvoord clearly explains the mystery behind confusing verses and conflicting viewpoints.

EVANGELISM AND MISSIONS—*Ron Blue*
Working on the premise that evangelism is the main mission of God's people, author Ron Blue challenges Christians to honor the Great Commission at home and around the world.

THE FORGOTTEN BLESSING—*Dr. Henry Holloman*
The Forgotten Blessing clarifies the doctrine of sanctification, showing us what it means to be set apart, and how the process of sanctification can forever change our relationship with God.

GOD—*Dr. J. Carl Laney*
Dr. J. Carl Laney presents a practical path to life-changing encounters with the goodness, greatness, and glory of our Creator.

THE HOLY SPIRIT—*Dr. Robert Gromacki*
Dr. Robert Gromacki examines the personality, deity, symbols, ministry, and gifts of the Holy Spirit.

HUMANITY AND SIN—*Dr. Robert A. Pyne*
Dr. Robert A. Pyne takes a close look at humankind and the consequences of sin through the pages of Scripture and the lens of modern culture.

IMMANUEL—*Dr. John A. Witmer*
Dr. John A. Witmer shows us a full picture of Christ in four distinct phases: the Son of God before He became man, the divine suffering man on Earth, the glorified and ascended Christ, and the reigning King today.

A LIFE OF PRAYER—*Dr. Paul Cedar*
Dr. Paul Cedar explores prayer through three primary concepts, showing us how to consider, cultivate, and continue a lifestyle of prayer.

MINISTERING TO TODAY'S ADULTS —*Dr. Kenn Gangel*
In an easy-to-grasp, easy-to-apply style, Gangel offers proven systematic strategies for building dynamic adult ministries.

MORAL DILEMMAS —*J. Kerby Anderson*
In this comprehensive, cutting-edge book, J. Kerby Anderson challenges us to thoughtfully analyze the dividing issues facing our age, while equipping believers to maneuver through the ethical and moral land mines of our times.

THE NEW TESTAMENT EXPLORER —*Mark Bailey and Tom Constable*
Mark Bailey and Tom Constable guide the reader paragraph by paragraph through the New Testament, providing an up-close-and-to-the-point examination of the leaders behind the page and the theological implications of the truths revealed.

The Old Testament Explorer —*Dr. Charles Dyer and Dr. Gene Merrill*

With *The Old Testament Explorer,* Charles Dyer and Gene Merrill guide you step-by-step through the depths of each Old Testament book and provide a variety of tools for understanding God's message.

Salvation—*Earl D. Radmacher*

From defining the essentials of salvation to explaining the result of Christ's sacrifice, this book walks readers through the spiritual meaning, motives, application, and eternal result of God's work of salvation in our lives.

Spirit-Filled Teaching—*Dr. Roy B. Zuck*

Acclaimed teacher Roy Zuck reveals how educators can tap into the power of divine energy to fulfill their calling and use their gifts at a deeper level.

Tale of the Tardy Oxcart and 1501 Other Stories—*Dr. Charles R. Swindoll*

In this rich volume, you'll have access to a 30-year collection of Swindoll's favorite anecdotes, illustrations, poems, and quotations—both his own and those from other great teachers like C.S. Lewis, Billy Graham, and Martin Luther.

The Theological Wordbook—*Campbell, Johnson, Walvoord, Witmer*

This reference guide gives definitions, scriptural references, engaging explanations—all in one easy-to-find, applicable resource—for both the lay person and serious Bible student.

The Wonder of Worship—*Ronald B. Allen*

This three-part study examines the issues surrounding the corporate worship of God, including biblical models and the current revolution in evangelical worship.

Women and the Church—*Dr. Lucy Mabery-Foster*

Women and the Church provides an overview of the historical, biblical, and cultural perspectives on the unique roles and gifts women bring to the church, while exploring what it takes to minister to women today.